MORNINGS
with JESUS
2019

DAILY ENCOURAGEMENT *for your* SOUL

 DEVOTIONS

SUSANNA FOTH AUGHTMON
ELIZABETH BERNE DEGEAR
GWEN FORD FAULKENBERRY
GRACE FOX
HEIDI GAUL
JEANETTE HANSCOME
SHARON HINCK
REBECCA BARLOW JORDAN
CAROL MACKEY
DIANNE NEAL MATTHEWS
CYNTHIA RUCHTI
ISABELLA YOSUICO

 **Guideposts**
New York

 ZONDERVAN®

ZONDERVAN

Mornings with Jesus 2019
Copyright © 2018 by Guideposts. All rights reserved.

Requests for information should be addressed to:
Zondervan, *3900 Sparks Dr. SE, Grand Rapids, MI 49546*

ISBN 978-0-310-35476-5 (softcover)

ISBN 978-0-310-35477-2 (ebook)

Acknowledgments: Every attempt has been made to credit the sources of copyrighted material used in this book. If any such acknowledgment has been inadvertently omitted or miscredited, receipt of such information would be appreciated.

Scripture quotations marked (AMP) are taken from the Amplified® Bible. Copyright © 1954, 1958, 1962, 1964, 1965, 1987 by The Lockman Foundation. Used by permission. (www.Lockman.org)

Scripture quotations marked (ERV) are taken from Easy-to-Read Version Bible. Copyright © 2006 by Bible League International.

Scripture quotations marked (ESV) are taken from the ESV® Bible (The Holy Bible, English Standard Version). Copyright © 2001 by Crossway, a publishing ministry of Good News Publishers. Used by permission. All rights reserved.

Scripture quotations marked (GNT) are taken from Good News Translation in Today's English Version—Second Edition. Copyright © 1992 by American Bible Society. Used by permission.

Scripture quotations marked (GW) are taken from *God's Word®*. Copyright © 1995 by God's Word to the Nations. Used by permission of Baker Publishing Group. All rights reserved.

Scripture quotations marked (HCSB) are taken from the Holman Christian Standard Bible. Copyright © 1999, 2000, 2002, 2003, 2009 by Holman Bible Publishers, Nashville, Tennessee. All rights reserved.

Scripture quotations marked (ICB) are taken from International Children's Bible®. Copyright © 1986, 1988, 1999 by Thomas Nelson. Used by permission. All rights reserved.

Scripture quotations marked (ISV) are taken from the *Holy Bible, International Standard Version*. Copyright © 1995-2014 by ISV Foundation. All rights reserved internationally. Used by permission of Davidson Press, LL.

Scripture quotations marked (KJV) are taken from The King James Version. Public domain.

Scripture quotations marked (MSG) are taken from *The Message*. Copyright © by Eugene H. Peterson. 1993, 1994, 1995, 1996, 2000, 2001, 2002. Used by permission of NavPress. All rights reserved. Represented by Tyndale House Publishers, Inc.

Scripture quotations marked (NAS) are taken from the New American Standard Bible®. All rights reserved. Copyright © 1960, 1962, 1963, 1968, 1971, 1972, 1973, 1975, 1977, 1995 by the Lockman Foundation. Used by permission. (www.Lockman.org)

Scripture quotations marked (NCV) are taken from the New Century Version. © 2005 by Thomas Nelson, Inc. Used by permission. All rights reserved.

Scripture quotations marked (NIV) are taken from two editions: The Holy Bible, New International Version®, NIV®. Copyright © 1973, 1978, 1984, 2011 by Biblica, Inc®. The Holy Bible, New International Version®, NIV®. Copyright © 1973, 1978, 1984 by Biblica, Inc®. Used by permission of Zondervan. All rights reserved worldwide. www.Zondervan. com. The "NIV" and "New International Version" are trademarks registered in the United States Patent and Trademark Office by Biblica, Inc®.

Scripture quotations marked (NKJV) are taken from New King James Version. © 1982 by Thomas Nelson, Inc. Used by permission. All rights reserved.

Scripture quotations marked (NLT) are taken from the Holy Bible, New Living Translation. © 1996, 2004, 2007, 2013, 2015 by Tyndale House Foundation. Used by permission of Tyndale House Publishers, Inc., Carol Stream, Illinois 60188. All rights reserved.

Scripture quotations marked (NRSV) are taken from the New Revised Standard Version Bible. Copyright © 1989 by the National Council of the Churches in the United States of America. Used by permission. All rights reserved.

Scripture quotations marked (RSV) are taken from the Revised Standard Version of the Bible. Copyright © 1946, 1952, 1971 by the National Council of the Churches of Christ in the United States of America. Used by permission. All rights reserved.

Scripture quotations marked (TLB) are taken from The Living Bible. Copyright © 1971 by Tyndale House Publishers Inc., Carol Stream, Illinois 60188. All rights reserved.

Cover and interior design by Müllerhaus
Cover photo by Shutterstock
Indexed by Indexing Research
Typeset by Aptara

First printing July 2018 / Printed in the United States of America

Dear Friend,

Welcome to *Mornings with Jesus 2019*! Whether you are a new reader or are already familiar with this devotional, know that each reading offers comfort, encouragement, and the joy that can only come from spending time with Him.

Our hope is that you experience renewed faith each morning through the enlightening Scripture verse, intimate narrative, and motivating "Faith Step" included in each daily devotion. *Mornings with Jesus 2019* is written with care by twelve women of faith. They share stories about their lives and how Jesus's presence in moments of crisis and quiet helps them know they are loved. These friendly, and often familiar, voices affirm this truth: Jesus's love is all around us.

New voices for 2019 include Jeanette Hanscome, who talks about dealing with a vision impairment and being guided by His love, and Elizabeth (Lizzie) Berne DeGear, whose love for Jesus leads her ministry in the church every day. And then there are favorites like full-time missionary Grace Fox and farmer's daughter Dianne Neal Matthews. They are among the women who share how their relationship with Jesus has blossomed into something worth celebrating. We know you will relate to their stories of courage after loss, grace in moments of surrender, and wisdom when it's most needed, as they share how they journey through life with the love of Jesus in their hearts.

John 1:17 says, "God's unfailing love and faithfulness came through Jesus Christ" (NLT). *Mornings with Jesus 2019* is a loving reminder that you are always in His care.

This year, we've included an inspiring series of Easter reflections written by Lizzie Berne DeGear and an insightful Advent series by Sharon Hinck. Both offer hope specially influenced by the season.

Mornings with Jesus 2019 helps you begin each day with Him. Though we endure personal challenges, the love of Jesus provides the strength we need to overcome anything. He offers us the greatest love of all and wants us to share every aspect of our lives with Him.

It is our hope that *Mornings with Jesus 2019* will encourage you to walk through your life with Him by your side. May you always carry the love of Jesus in your heart.

Faithfully yours,
Editors of Guideposts

P.S. We love hearing from you! Let us know what *Mornings with Jesus 2019* means to you by emailing BookEditors@guideposts.org or writing to Guideposts Books & Inspirational Media, 110 William Street, New York, New York 10038. You can also keep up with your *Mornings with Jesus* friends on Facebook.com/MorningswithJesus.

Especially for You!

Enjoy the daily encouragement of *Mornings with Jesus 2019* wherever you are! Receive each day's devotion on your computer, tablet, or smartphone. Visit MorningswithJesus.org/MWJ2019 and enter this code: peace2019. Sign up for the online newsletter *Mornings with Jesus* through MorningswithJesus. org. Each week, you'll receive an inspiring devotion or personal thoughts from one of the writers about her own devotional time and prayer life, how focusing on Jesus influenced her relationship with Him, and more!

TUESDAY, JANUARY 1

I, yes, I alone am he who blots away your sins for my own sake and will never think of them again. Isaiah 43:25 (TLB)

ONE OF MY FAVORITE VERSES to meditate on for New Year's Day is Isaiah 43:19: "For I am about to do something new. See, I have already begun! Do you not see it?" (NLT). These words fill me with excitement the same way hanging a new calendar on the wall does. A new year stretches ahead with new experiences and adventures, new friends to make, and fresh opportunities to serve Christ and grow to be more like Him. But cleaning out my pantry last week helped me understand that before we can embrace the new, we may need to get rid of some of the old.

To make room for the beautiful ceramic baking dishes I'd bought, I threw out old plastic storage containers that had cracked or missing lids. I tossed canned and boxed foods that had passed their expiration dates. I pared down our collection of travel mugs and tumblers to the ones we actually use. Next week, I plan to look over the bookcases in our house and pull out a few volumes to give away, making space for the reference books I just ordered.

Before we make plans for the new year ahead, we would do well to engage in some serious self-evaluation to see what we need to get rid of. Habits that compromise our walk with Christ. Doubts that keep us from using our gifts to fully serve Him. And especially guilt and regret over past failures and sins. Just a few verses after God promises to do new things, we see His promise not only to forgive our sins when we repent, but to never think about them again. And neither should we. —DIANNE NEAL MATTHEWS

FAITH STEP: *Ask Jesus to show you what you need to throw out so you can fully receive the new things He has planned for you this year.*

WEDNESDAY, JANUARY 2

And now, just as you accepted Christ Jesus as your Lord, you must continue to follow him. Let your roots grow down into him, and let your lives be built on him. Then your faith will grow strong in the truth you were taught, and you will overflow with thankfulness. Colossians 2:6–7 (NLT)

A RECORD SNOWFALL BEGAN A few hours after my husband, Gene, left town to attend a three-day conference. At first, I figured shoveling could wait until he returned. But I changed my mind after sixteen inches fell in less than twenty-four hours and the weatherman predicted more.

My plans to spend the weekend preparing for upcoming speaking engagements fell apart, and my thoughts slipped into a grumbly mood as I began shoveling. *Why did this happen when I need to work? Why when Gene's away? What if I have a heart attack and no one sees me lying in a heap on the driveway?*

Suddenly a thought came to mind: *I washed your sin-stained heart whiter than the pristine snow you're shoveling.*

That thought stopped me mid-shovel. I gazed at the scene around me with a fresh perspective. "Thank You, Jesus," I said aloud. "Thank You for that reminder." And then the most amazing thing happened—my grumbly mood melted away, replaced with other reasons to give thanks: "Thank You for a healthy body that's able to work. Thank You for the mild temperature and no wind. Thank You for shelter from the storm and hot chocolate and a winter jacket."

The warmth of Jesus's presence and pleasure enveloped me as I focused my thoughts on Him and the gifts He'd given me, and I smiled. "Thank You, too, for the storm. I can't think of a better way to spend the weekend than enjoying it with You." —GRACE FOX

FAITH STEP: *Today's key verse reminds us that a relationship with Jesus gives us plenty for which to give thanks. What's one thing for which you're grateful today?*

THURSDAY, JANUARY 3

Consider the ravens: They do not sow or reap, they have no storeroom or barn; yet God feeds them. And how much more valuable you are than birds! Luke 12:24 (NIV)

HAVE YOU EVER FELT LIKE you're being watched? I have. It can be scary. But it can also be a good thing, depending on who is watching.

One morning, I was unaware I was being watched. As I stared at our bills, my lids brimmed with tears. Since my husband David's retirement, we've struggled to make ends meet. We've managed up to this point, but that particular month, I worried we wouldn't. Unexpected expenses left us with more month than money, and I'd run out of ideas. No clever solutions burbled to the surface of my mind. Broken, I bowed my head to pray. I needed Jesus's attention. I begged Him for wisdom, perseverance—and tangible help.

Glancing outside, I noticed the mail had been delivered. Probably more bills. As I retrieved it, I scanned the envelopes. One return address caused my heart to jump. *Do I owe even more than I've already paid?* Biting my lip, I opened that piece first. The enclosed letter said a miscalculation left us due a refund of several hundred dollars. We'd been saved! Again!

When the shock had worn off, other instances of Jesus rescuing me came to mind. Over the years, one problem after another had been solved by unexpected blessings. Each Godsend delivered us in an unconventional manner, leaving us better off than before. But the biggest benefit? Knowing that when things seem impossible, Jesus steps in and takes over. He's been watching all along. —HEIDI GAUL

FAITH STEP: *On paper, draw three columns titled Unexpected, Unconventional, and Impossible (For Me). Under each, write different ways Jesus has rescued you. Next time problems seem too large to solve, read the list and trust in His watchful eye.*

FRIDAY, JANUARY 4

Then they said to him, "What must we do, to be doing the works of God?"
Jesus answered them, "This is the work of God, that you believe
in him whom he has sent." John 6:28–29 (ESV)

A GOOD WORK ETHIC IS ingrained in my genes. On my father's side, generations survived wars in Europe and rebuilt their homes time and again. They dug in to each task as if their lives depended on it. On my mother's side, farmers in Pennsylvania Dutch country always finished the work before playing. Since there was always more work, time for leisure was rare.

With this background, it's no wonder that I'm sometimes accomplishment-driven. That's not all bad. A passion for work motivates me to provide service to others and to Jesus. However, it can also push me into pride, self-reliance, and tunnel vision that misses the needs of others. That's why Jesus's words in John 6 are challenging for me. I wake each morning thinking, *What work can I do today?* It's not a bad impulse. However, Jesus reminds me that it's not about me and certainly not about what I accomplish. Life is about Him. His task for me is both simple and dizzyingly difficult: believe in Him.

When a long-term illness interrupted my productive life, this truth became a huge comfort. We all face seasons like this. Physical limitations, or work layoffs, or a move, or other changes in circumstance keep us from doing the work we long to do. There may even be times we feel like we are causing work for others and not carrying our load. Yet Jesus invites us to draw our gaze away from our question of "What must we do?" and trust that He has already accomplished the work that matters. —SHARON HINCK

FAITH STEP: *Look for any tasks you are "doing" that keep you from "being" with Jesus, and ask Him to help you focus on trusting Him.*

SATURDAY, JANUARY 5

There are "friends" who destroy each other, but a real friend sticks closer than a brother. Proverbs 18:24 (NLT)

I HAVE THREE COLLEGE FRIENDS that I group-text every morning. We tell each other the crazy things our kids do. We laugh. We share what struggles we are facing. We pray for each other's families. And we send inspirational Scripture.

This last year has been a rough year for me. It's been a season where life has been difficult and Jesus seemed far away. But my friends have been reminding me of the great love that Jesus has for me—in spite of crazy circumstances and the uncertainty I am feeling. These friends tell me the truth.

The other morning, I had an epiphany while I was doing my devotions. I realized that while I may feel far from Jesus, He is near. He has always been. My feelings can change moment by moment. But Jesus is steadfast. And He has used my friends to show me this. They speak His words into my life. They listen to me. They encourage me to keep going. They celebrate with me. They cry with me. Whatever season I am going through, good, bad, or ugly, they stick with me. They are true friends. And they always point me back to the truest friend of all. The One who never leaves me or forsakes me. The One who brings light into my darkness. The One who offered His life for mine. And yours. We may not always feel that Jesus is close to us. But He is. His love surrounds us and draws us near. He hems us in on every side, and we can call Him "friend."
—SUSANNA FOTH AUGHTMON

FAITH STEP: *What are the ways Jesus shows you He is your friend? How do you show Him that He is yours? Make it your goal today to be a true friend to Jesus.*

SUNDAY, JANUARY 6

I am convinced that neither death, nor life...nor anything else in all creation, will be able to separate us from the love of God in Christ Jesus our Lord.
Romans 8:38–39 (NRSV)

ONCE I WAS ASKED TO speak at a special anniversary service in my church. At the time, I was close to finishing my doctoral work in theology and was excited to share some of the fascinating things I had been studying. As I shared my thoughts with the team planning the service, they listened politely. Then one person gently said, "That all sounds very interesting. But I am thinking about the people we are doing this service for and how marginalized they have been. That is why we have chosen the readings we have. We hope everything in this service will reinforce the idea that"—and here he slowed down and emphasized every word with a decisive hand gesture— "nothing can separate you from the love of God."

His clarity stopped me in my tracks. How simple Jesus's message is! How accessible! And yet how often I can get pulled away from it by my own sense of unworthiness. I didn't need to prove myself. I just needed to stand there and enjoy the truth that brought us all together that evening: *Nothing* can separate us from the love of God.

My sense of unworthiness returns again and again, but Jesus is always there, continuing to come up with new ways of playfully bringing me back to the simple truth of an all-embracing, me-embracing love. —ELIZABETH BERNE DEGEAR

FAITH STEP: *Take some quiet time to yourself and call to mind a particular time when you felt really loved. What was the sensation? Now write down your answers to this question: What am I ashamed of? Once you've written your answers, give them to Jesus and let yourself feel how much He loves you.*

Monday, January 7

Therefore I tell you, do not be anxious about your life,
what you will eat or what you will drink, nor about your body,
what you will put on. Matthew 6:25 (ESV)

It wasn't what I expected to see at the store. Among the notebooks, locker mirrors, giant paper clips, and markers was a large display of fidget spinners. Everything a well-prepared child needs to head back to school, plus a little something for anxiety.

Worry rocks. Stress balls. Fidget spinners. Anxiety is big business. Even for children. Statistically, the percentage of children who rate their stress as high is shocking to those of us who once assumed childhood could be considered the least stressful season of life.

What message are our anxieties communicating to the generations coming after us?

Anxiety consumes time, energy, and emotions, no matter our age. It's no wonder that among the most comforting (and challenging) of the teachings of Jesus is this one: "Don't be anxious about your life."

What's striking is that when Jesus specified what He meant, it showed He knew we would often be frantic or overly stressed, not by wars and earthquakes and worldwide violence, but by what we would eat, drink, and wear. Our anxieties about relatively small things wreck us. For much of the world, having enough to eat is not a trivial matter. But even in the essentials of life, Jesus made it clear that if we're serving Him and trusting Him, we can—and should—cross worrying off our to-do list. —Cynthia Ruchti

---

Faith Step: *If you own a worry rock, stress ball, or fidget spinner—or perhaps you'll want to purchase an inexpensive one for this purpose—use a permanent marker to label it with "Jesus cancels anxiety."*

TUESDAY, JANUARY 8

Nor do people light a lamp and put it under a basket, but on a stand, and it gives light to all in the house. In the same way, let your light shine before others, so that they may see your good works and give glory to your Father who is in heaven. Matthew 5:15–17 (ESV)

AT DIFFERENT TIMES IN MY life, I've made myself smaller in a futile attempt to fit in, to not irritate others, and to remain invisible. Hiding my light has been exhausting and ineffective and, I see now, didn't glorify God. It's taken me fifty years to see that my self-protection was all about me.

Bottom line: It's not about me. It's about Him. It's not about my glory. It's about His. It's not about what I can do. It's about what He can do in me and through me.

Okay, so how do I get out of God's way? How do I remove the "basket"?

I can only do this by forgetting myself, by following the old adage to "not think less of myself, but think of myself less." And forgetting myself only comes when self-centeredness is pressed out of me— by failure, by hurt, and even by the eventual disappointment of so-called success.

There is exquisite freedom in being myself freely and trusting that the light of Jesus shines through me without my trying so hard.
—ISABELLA YOSUICO

FAITH STEP: *Sit down and shamelessly list the ways in which you are or could be a light—your qualities. Are you in God's way, either in pride or shame? Ask for help tossing the "basket."*

WEDNESDAY, JANUARY 9

I give you peace, the kind of peace that only I can give. It isn't like the peace that this world can give. So don't be worried or afraid. John 14:27 (CEV)

DO YOU EVER DOUBT GOD? Wonder if any of this belief system you've structured your life around is even real?

I do. The poet Christian Wiman said of his faith that sometimes he goes to bed a Christian and wakes up an atheist. I relate to that. I wish I were stronger, but I'm not someone who never wavers. That's just the truth.

In my seasons of doubt, there is a weird thing I hold on to. I'd like to sound more spiritual and say it's a verse or some profound insight from all the books I've read or some proof I've discovered of God's existence. But it's nothing nearly as objective as that.

Still, it's as real as real can be to me. And it came in the darkest time of my life: peace.

There was a time when everything I believed about my marriage was taken from me. It was not only taken—like a ball someone takes from your hands that remains intact and you have hopes of getting it back. No. It was obliterated. Like a crystal ball shattered by a hammer. Gone. Forever.

In those moments I should have felt lost, abandoned, in despair, like my life was out of control. And I did feel great pain. But underneath the shock wave of pain, there was peace. Strong, steady, fortifying peace that did not come from me. Peace I cannot explain. But I know it was Jesus.

When I would have let go of everything, Jesus held on to me.
—GWEN FORD FAULKENBERRY

FAITH STEP: *When in your life has Jesus come through for you with His peace beyond understanding? Purchase something small you can wear with the symbol of a dove that reminds you He is your peace.*

THURSDAY, JANUARY 10

---

*For the law was given through Moses; grace and truth
came through Jesus Christ. John 1:17 (NIV)*

RECENTLY, A TELEVISION NEWSCAST REPORTED a surprising annual increase of hit-and-run drivers. Many have wondered why the laws aren't reducing and discouraging crime and whether stricter punishment would help.

Those in Jesus's day may have thought the same thing. The chief priests and teachers of the law considered God's early laws to Moses the basis of morality, even adding their own graceless interpretations to endless ordinances and rules. Extremely harsh penalties served to discourage wrongdoers. Why would anyone dare break these rules?

Then Jesus entered the picture. Instead of abolishing the law, Jesus emphasized its fundamental purpose: to make us conscious of sin and wrongdoing (Romans 3:20). Knowing our hearts, He fulfilled those initial commandments by giving His life as payment for the ultimate death penalty. He initiated love, grace, and mercy as the supreme motivators for right actions (Romans 8:3).

In our society, we definitely need rules whether or not they influence people to do the right thing. We are all given a choice. But lasting change can only happen supernaturally, when Jesus steps in to transform the heart. We have all broken His laws (Romans 3:23), but Jesus's sacrificial love is the only thing that will ultimately change a heart and lower the statistics of criminal behavior.

That makes our job as followers of Jesus super important. Staying faithful to share the good news of Jesus's love, grace, and truth is not only our mission; it must become our passion. —REBECCA BARLOW JORDAN

FAITH STEP: *Pray today for those who enforce the laws of our country and also for those who break them—that Jesus's love would change their hearts forever.*

FRIDAY, JANUARY 11

But when you are arrested and stand trial, don't worry in advance about what to say. Just say what God tells you at that time, for it is not you who will be speaking, but the Holy Spirit. Mark 13:11 (NLT)

IT WAS MY FIRST TRIP to Ukraine. My husband and I had traveled there to teach a marriage conference, but we also anticipated spending time with two missionary couples associated with our organization.

Migraine headaches and chronic pain plagued one of the wives and limited her ministry activities. As a result, she felt as though she wasn't fulfilling her role. I wanted to encourage her, but what could I say without appearing nosy or giving her pat answers?

I recalled a conversation between Jesus and His disciples. He told them not to worry about what to say in their own defense while standing trial. He assured them that the Holy Spirit would give them the right words when they needed them most.

Jesus, remember Your promise to Your disciples. Fulfill it for me now. I need the right words, I prayed silently as I sat down in the woman's living room. We chatted briefly about her kids, and then two questions rolled off my tongue.

"How's your heart?" I asked.

Her eyes filled with tears. "Thank you for asking," she said. "That means so much." We talked for more than an hour and then prayed together. It was sweet and meaningful fellowship, because Jesus gave me the words I needed.

That experience has given me the confidence to trust Jesus in every situation—when sharing my faith with unbelievers, in a counseling situation, or preparing for a speaking engagement. He's the Living Word and always supplies the right words. —GRACE FOX

FAITH STEP: *For what situation do you need the right words today? Place one hand on your lips and tell Jesus that you trust Him to supply those words.*

SATURDAY, JANUARY 12

But the LORD said to Samuel, "Do not look at his appearance or at his physical stature, because I have refused him. For the LORD does not see as man sees; for man looks at the outward appearance, but the LORD looks at the heart." 1 Samuel 16:7 (NKJV)

CLEANING OUT MY BATHROOM CABINET the other day, I realized something. I have a ton of beauty products. Over the years, I've likely spent more time and money on my appearance than I care to remember and contributed heavily to the billion-dollar beauty market. From creams to mascara, I seem to have purchased enough to help keep the industry healthy. Part of the reason is I am among those who like to enhance their appearance. Who doesn't want to look younger and prettier? But this verse is a great reminder that our outward appearance doesn't matter at all to Jesus. He nurtures the beauty in our hearts.

During Jesus's ministry, He came across groups of people who were concerned with the way they appeared. In Matthew 23, he told the Pharisees, "Woe to you...hypocrites! For you are like whitewashed tombs which indeed appear beautiful outwardly but inside are full of dead men's bones and all uncleanness." Jesus recognized the deep spiritual deficiencies—ones that only He could fill. And Jesus let them know He didn't care about their presentation, but rather about the passion of their hearts.

Yes, in my time I have been passionate about my appearance, but I'm most grateful that Jesus only wants to look at and continue to nurture the goodness of my heart. —CAROL MACKEY

FAITH STEP: *Ask the Lord to give you eyes to see Him in the face of every person you meet.*

SUNDAY, JANUARY 13

Mary Magdalene went and announced to the disciples, "I have seen the Lord"—and that he had said these things to her. John 20:18 (ESV)

SOME SONGS TOUCH US so deeply that no matter how many years pass, we still "feel all the feels" the next time we hear them. When a tune from our youth airs on the radio or Scripture reminds us of an old worship song, we can't help immersing ourselves in what it meant to us when we first heard it.

When I read the above verse this morning, I was reminded of a song and impressed again by how many times Mary Magdalene's name appears at key moments in the life and ministry of Jesus. John 20 notes the following exquisitely compelling scenes, among others.

Mary Magdalene went to Jesus's tomb before dawn and saw the stone had been rolled away. She ran to tell Peter and John. Mary stood crying outside the tomb, assuming the body of her Lord had been stolen in the night, one more indignity for the One who had restored her hope.

An angel spoke to her. Significant by itself. She turned around to discover a gardener, who asked whom she was looking for and crying over. Then the "gardener" called her by name. It was Jesus. She was the first to whom He'd chosen to speak after His resurrection.

He tasked her with telling the others He was returning to His Father, their Father, His God, their God.

Mary Magdalene's announcement to the disciples will always remind me of the Sandi Patty and Larnelle Harris song "I've Just Seen Jesus." No matter how many times I hear that song, it always stirs in me the wonder of a risen Savior who conquers death but cares to speak tenderly to those who now await our turn to see Him alive. —CYNTHIA RUCHTI

FAITH STEP: *What music epitomizes the wonder you feel at serving a resurrected Jesus? Find that song and listen to it throughout the day.*

MONDAY, JANUARY 14

Then Jesus said, "Did I not tell you that if you believe,
you will see the glory of God?" John 11:40 (NIV)

"YOU HAVE CANCER." MY FINGERS tightened on the receiver as the receptionist spoke. Details spilled out like water from a dropped glass—the type, stage, and post-surgery possibilities. Depending on the tumor's size, I could lose a breast and require reconstructive surgery. I concentrated on keeping my voice even and held back tears, at least until I'd hung up. The only words that came to mind were, "Why me, Jesus? Why now?"

The weeks following that diagnosis were lost in a fog. Time alternately flew and dragged, as I waited to endure my procedure. My operation was a success, but ensuing radiation treatments left me confused, as if watching someone else's life through a pair of binoculars. I clung to Jesus, His abiding love my private sanctuary. My faith strengthened even as my body weakened.

Over several months, my self-confidence grew and my health returned. All five senses came alive, awakening a hunger for new experiences. Bit by bit, clarity of thought reappeared and, with it, a new wisdom and gratefulness. Little things no longer bothered me. I became more aware of the blessings surrounding me.

I learned that, like Lazarus, I wasn't alone. Friends, family, and Jesus had cried and prayed for me. And during that battle, I realized the true value of a life I'd taken for granted. I didn't have to die to rise again. Our Lord restored me, body and soul. At last, I have the answer to the question, "Why?" —HEIDI GAUL

FAITH STEP: *Every morning before rising, name one troubling problem and give it up to Jesus. Consider it dead to you and don't revive it. Replace it with a named blessing.*

TUESDAY, JANUARY 15

A cheerful heart is good medicine, but a broken spirit saps a person's strength. Proverbs 17:22 (NLT)

"WHAT IS GOING ON WITH this thing?" No matter what I tried, I couldn't get the self-checkout scanner off Spanish mode.

My son Nathan, who was nine at the time, tried unsuccessfully to wipe the smirk off his face. I looked around for an assistant but finally had to give up and scan my items in Spanish. My frustration mingled with laughter. *What must I look like?* Nathan laughed out loud as I finally inserted my money and took my change.

Wait...

"Nathan, did you hit the Spanish button?"

He grinned. "Yes."

"Why?"

"You needed to laugh."

I knew that some parents would reprimand such an embarrassing trick, but I gave my son a hug, laughed some more, thanked him, and thanked Jesus that Nathan had inherited my quirky sense of humor. My day had been stressful, but Nathan knew that laughter was the quickest way to improve my mood.

It is no wonder that Scripture tells us, "A cheerful heart is good medicine." I find that I feel closer to Jesus when I laugh and see the humor in circumstances. Seeing His sense of fun reflected in creation reminds me that He is the ultimate source of joy and that we serve a Lord Who understands that, with all life throws at us, sometimes the best thing we can do is laugh. —JEANETTE HANSCOME

FAITH STEP: *What makes you laugh? When has laughter been medicine to your soul? Ask Jesus to provide one thing—a funny movie, a silly kid moment—to cheer you or someone you love today.*

WEDNESDAY, JANUARY 16

Unless the LORD builds the house, those who build it labor in vain.
Unless the LORD watches over the city, the watchman stays awake in vain.
Psalm 127:1 (ESV)

IN MY WORK OVER THE years, I've seen Jesus guiding my path. He's brought writing and editing projects from unexpected sources. He's opened doors in mysterious ways. And He's nudged me to change direction sometimes.

I've also had times when I had a plan in mind and set out to make it happen. I've studied market trends, asked advice of experts, set a course, and plowed ahead with a big dose of stubbornness. I've designed spreadsheets to chart my progress and searched for an inside track to make my goals happen. None of those are bad techniques, but I've noticed that even though those plans require unending effort, they often fizzle.

Looking back, I've realized that during some of those periods, Jesus was pointing me to a different path, but I couldn't hear Him over my energetic determination. When I'm "building my house" (or my writing career, or my family, or my marriage, or my friendships) in my own strength and not inviting Him to do the building, I find myself laboring harder, not smarter.

These days, when I catch myself striving, growing resentful at the lack of progress, or confused by the way my building keeps crumbling, I stop and ask Jesus if I've grabbed the hammer from Him. Then I place it back in His carpenter hands and invite Him to show me a new way. What a blessing that He offers to be the Builder of our lives! —SHARON HINCK

FAITH STEP: *What are you building today? Put your tools in Jesus's hands and ask Him to be your Builder and Watchman.*

THURSDAY, JANUARY 17

I no longer call you servants, because a servant does not know his master's business. Instead, I have called you friends, for everything that I learned from my Father I have made known to you. John 15:15 (NIV)

I HAVE TAKEN A BREAK from social media this past year. Being on Facebook felt like hundreds of people were shouting their opinions at me and then showing me pictures of their delicious lunches. It distracted me from writing, and I would be sucked in for hours. I would worry about the prayer requests puzzle and puzzle over why someone had unfriended me. I would finally tear myself free only to feel unsettled, worried, and more than a little jealous of those fabulous lunches.

I am learning that social media, in small doses, can be a fun way to stay connected. But with my true friends, I need real face time. I want to hear the joy in their voices when they tell me how much they love their kids. I want to pray with them and buy them a cup of coffee when those same kids are driving them crazy nuts. Just clicking a "Like" button or pinning a sad face to their post doesn't satisfy.

Sometimes I think my prayers to Jesus are like social media posts. I am giving Him thumbs-ups and smiley faces, wanting His approval over my life, and He is saying, "Really? Is that all you want to share?" He is unsatisfied. And if I really stop and think about it...so am I. Aren't you? He loves us so much. He has called me and you His friends. He knows our need for face time with His Word and for real conversations in prayer. He wants us to know Him inside and out and find ourselves wrapped daily in His overwhelming grace and presence. —SUSANNA FOTH AUGHTMON

FAITH STEP: *Take a walk by yourself and tell Jesus about your day. Ask Him to surround you with His presence and be your friend.*

FRIDAY, JANUARY 18

But you are the ones chosen by God, chosen for the high calling of priestly work, chosen to be a holy people, God's instruments to do his work and speak out for him, to tell others of the night-and-day difference he made for you— from nothing to something, from rejected to accepted. 1 Peter 2:9–10 (MSG)

IT'S NOT A NEW PRACTICE to use clothing to make a statement. It actually happened in the Old Testament as well. When God established His tabernacle on earth, He set apart a high priest, choosing him as the holy one designated to bring the people's sins before the Lord. God gave detailed instructions about his duties and had requirements for the priest's clothing. The garments included an assortment of majestic colors: purple, scarlet, and blue. Skilled artisans carefully crafted and wove together the multicolored threads, stones, and fabric, and they attached a sacred emblem to the high priest's turban with a blue cord. The statement on this medallion of pure gold read, "Holy to the LORD" (Exodus 39:30). Peter explained it foreshadowed the time when Jesus, our great High Priest, would become the ultimate sacrifice for the sins of the entire world (Hebrews 5:8–10).

I read those passages recently and thought about my own wardrobe. It hardly makes any statement. But what if I "dressed" each morning, remembering that I am a "priest." I could even wear an invisible medallion of gold, reminding me that I, too, am chosen to be "holy to the Lord."

Our great High Priest became sin for us and dressed us in His holy righteousness (2 Corinthians 5:21). Wherever we go, whatever we do, our "clothing" can make a statement about who we are—royal priests, wholly dedicated to Jesus. —REBECCA BARLOW JORDAN

FAITH STEP: *Each morning when you dress this week, imagine you are wearing royal clothing. Ask Jesus to help you represent Him well.*

SATURDAY, JANUARY 19

Greater love has no one than this, than to lay down one's life for his friends. You are My friends if you do whatever I command you.
John 15:13–14 (NKJV)

MY SISTER JOYCE AND I decided to meet at a favorite restaurant one evening for some much-needed sister time. While enjoying our meal, we noticed sitting next to us two elderly and very stylish women. We exchanged glances, then smiles, and made small talk. I told one of the fashionistas it was my birthday. She asked me my age, and I told her the truth. She complimented me on how young she thought I looked and then told me she was eighty-six. She pointed to her friend and said, "We've been friends for over fifty years!" I marveled at the longevity of their sisterhood, which had lasted for decades. I've had friends for more than thirty-five years—mostly my college buddies who have seen me through the best and worst of times.

Friends are great. But Jesus is our ultimate Friend—the only One Who laid down His own life for us. I love my friends, but not enough to die for them. Nor do I expect that they will die for me. The Lord valued the friendships He made with the disciples. He invested in them. He was patient with them. He loved them. And after a certain time had passed, He said they were more than students—they were now friends (John 15:15). Even after Judas betrayed Him with a kiss, Jesus still addressed him as "friend" (Matthew 26:50). This was Jesus's final act of love toward the one who had sinned against Him. Jesus showed us what true friendship looks like; but most important, we'll never find a friend who loves us as deeply as He loves us. —CAROL MACKEY

FAITH STEP: *What makes a good friend? Read Proverbs 27:17, Proverbs 17:17, Proverbs 27:6, and Proverbs 18:24 to see if these characteristics ring true for you.*

SUNDAY, JANUARY 20

But he had to go through Samaria. John 4:4 (NRSV)

ONE OF MY FAVORITE STORIES recorded in the New Testament is about the woman at the well's encounter with Jesus. Maybe the story doesn't mean as much to you if you've never felt like an outsider or "less than." Or experienced the sting of prejudice or discrimination. Or carried around a weight of guilt over a wrong choice you've made. Or struggled with questions about spiritual matters that you didn't fully understand but didn't feel as though you could voice them. But then, can't we all identify with at least one of these emotions?

The core message of the story is found in one brief sentence: "But he had to go through Samaria." Although the shortest route from Judea to Galilee cut through Samaria, most Jews chose another way. They avoided contact with the Samaritans, a mixed race (of Jew and Gentile) who had been rejected by the Jews and had established their own temple and religious traditions. But not Jesus. His love compelled Him to go into Samaria to wait by a well for a woman who was emotionally and spiritually parched. A woman who desperately needed the living water He offered and would go on to introduce her village to their Messiah.

That same love compels Jesus to wait for each one of us today. Even when we're oblivious of our need for time with Him, He is there, gently prodding us to confess our failures and sins as the Samaritan woman did. Longing to heal us from our bruises and wounds. Ready to reveal His presence and power. Extending living water to refresh us and quench our thirst. The question is: Are we willing to meet with Him and receive all He desires to give us? —DIANNE NEAL MATTHEWS

FAITH STEP: *At the beginning or end of your day, imagine Jesus sitting and waiting for you to come by so He can talk with you. Will your love for Him compel you to respond?*

MONDAY, JANUARY 21

Since we are surrounded by so great a cloud of witnesses, let us lay aside every weight, and the sin which so easily ensnares us, and let us run with endurance the race that is set before us, looking unto Jesus, the author and finisher of our faith, who for the joy that was set before Him endured the cross, despising the shame, and has sat down at the right hand of the throne of God. Hebrews 12:1–2 (NKJV)

DO YOU EVER FEEL LIKE the path you're on is just too steep? Too rocky? Too rough? Dangerous? Maybe just too long? I've felt that way before. There have been seasons I've struggled in my marriage, with my job, my kids, my church, my weight, when I've felt like I couldn't keep going. I couldn't handle it anymore for one reason or another. What keeps you going in those moments?

In the movie *Selma*, Coretta Scott King has one of those times when she wavers, feeling crushed by the weight of the opposition in her path. Amelia Boynton Robinson says to her, "I'll tell you what I know to be true. It helps me when I'm feeling unsure.... I know that we are descendants of a mighty people who gave civilization to the world. People who survived the hulls of slave ships and tortures unimaginable. They are in our bloodstream. Pumping our hearts every second. They've prepared you. You are already prepared."

As Christians, we share a heritage with those who have gone before us and finished the race. They've been through the temptations, the hardship, and they didn't quit. It's like they are lined up along our path cheering us on. And at the finish line? Jesus. Standing with arms open wide to receive us. That's Who keeps us going, if we fix our eyes on Him. —GWEN FORD FAULKENBERRY

FAITH STEP: *Go for a walk, and list the things that are weighing you down and tell Jesus you give them to Him. Then trust Him for the endurance you need.*

TUESDAY, JANUARY 22

For this world is not our permanent home; we are looking forward to a home yet to come. Hebrews 13:14 (NLT)

YOU KNOW YOU'VE ENTERED A new season of life when it's your husband, Bill, who asks, "Are we there yet?" He prefers a paper map. I prefer my handy navigation app that lets me know exactly when we will arrive at our destination.

It's in our nature to wonder, "Are we there yet?" or "How much farther? How much longer?" We ask it while traveling and while sitting in the dentist's chair, when counting reps in out exercise routine and when longing for the scale to say we reached our goal.

We might grow weary of this world, our life's journey, as we continue onto our final destination. Our true home. Jesus said it and His followers repeated it in New Testament writings. In John 14, Jesus told us He's gone ahead to prepare a place for us. Where we live now is temporary housing. The body we live in is temporary.

We find this home uncomfortable most days and unbearably uncomfortable during seasons of distress and grief. The answer to our question, "Are we there yet?" isn't measured in miles or in how many good deeds we've done.

The length of our days was known from the beginning of time. He has the answer to the question, "How many more heartbeats?"

It's a question that isn't loaded with fear for those who trust Jesus rather than their accomplishments. It's loaded with longing. Imagine how glorious it will be when He answers, "You have arrived at your destination. Welcome home!" —CYNTHIA RUCHTI

FAITH STEP: *Do you give away Bibles to those who don't own one? Consider wrapping them in a no-longer-necessary map as a symbol of the journey with Jesus that ends in joy.*

WEDNESDAY, JANUARY 23

*"Come," he said. Then Peter got down out of the boat,
walked on the water and came toward Jesus. Matthew 14:29 (NIV)*

I HAVE A NICE SINGING voice. Mariah Carey need not worry, but I can definitely carry a tune. Even so, over the years, I've passed on several opportunities to sing publicly because of paralyzing stage fright. High school musical theater, college rock bands, coffeehouse folk singing with my own guitar...regardless of how much singing made my own heart sing, I was just too scared.

Still, I knew I wouldn't be passing up a Grammy-winning career, so I moved on from my singing ambitions and was content to join in congregational worship when I became a Christian. And even then, when asked to join the choir by a pew mate, I declined. Underneath, it was still fear.

Right before I turned fifty, I started to recount some of the if-onlys and what-ifs in my life, asking God to show me what He still had for me. Our God is not limited by age or timing, and I knew that my walk with Him had helped me overcome many fears. One answer came quickly when I noticed an invitation to choir rehearsal in our church's bulletin. I sensed the Holy Spirit coaxing me to just "suit up and show up."

Stepping into choir has been a healing joy. Not only because of answered prayer and the courage to confront my fear but also because lifting my voice in worship has power to neutralize the stress and sorrow of life and to change my heart. In turn, I can share my gift and joy with others, as I sing for an audience of One. —ISABELLA YOSUICO

FAITH STEP: *Make a list of some things you'd like to do where fear is the primary limitation. Ask God to remove the fear, and then choose to take a step toward your goal, feeling the fear and doing it anyway.*

THURSDAY, JANUARY 24

In the beginning was the Word, and the Word was with God, and the Word was God. He was in the beginning with God. All things came into being through him, and without him not one thing came into being. What has come into being in him was life, and the life was the light of all people. John 1:1–4 (NRSV)

WHEN I GET LOST IN my work, nothing is better. I open myself up to Jesus as Word and let His Spirit of creativity, love, and truth flow through me. But when I step out of this flow and look upon my work, nothing is worse. I judge the product of my efforts so harshly, worrying about how the words reflect on me.

This waltz between freedom and captivity seems to be one I am destined to dance. The way to heaven is to let myself be caught up in the "verb" of life—in the creativity and flow of it all. When I get stuck in the "noun" of life—like a passive viewer, watching the Story of Me—I find myself worrying again.

So often my mornings with Jesus need to bring me to that open dance of freedom. The two biblical passages that help me tap into this flow are the beginning of John's Gospel and the words of wisdom in Proverbs 8:22–31. God's delight in me, my delight in God's creation, the divine capacity to live and love through human experience—all this is the masterpiece, and my life can be a brushstroke. —ELIZABETH BERNE DEGEAR

FAITH STEP: *Sit with Proverbs 8. Ask Jesus to show you how to enter into life's creative flow so that you may let go of any self-consciousness holding you back.*

FRIDAY, JANUARY 25

The LORD appeared to us in the past, saying: "I have loved you with an everlasting love; I have drawn you with unfailing kindness." Jeremiah 31:3 (NIV)

"Jesus loves me, this I know..."

I'd grown up on the song and sung it to my children. But when my friend Jean spontaneously started singing "Jesus Loves Me" after our Bible study group celebrated Communion, tears welled up as if it were new to me.

I'd chosen a word for the year—*loved*—after feeling drawn to Jeremiah 31:3. I knew that, though I'd made a lot of progress in grasping my value in Christ, I still had work to do when it came to trusting that I was loved. I spent the year paying attention to what I privately called "love notes from Jesus"—special moments with friends; desires fulfilled after years of praying and hoping; returning to the church that had supported me as a newly single mom, this time as an author and speaker; seeing Him provide for needs; even allowing Him to reveal truths that were hard to accept about myself and realizing that He still adored me. As the year came to a close, I continued to notice His love notes. As I sang with my friends, I felt overwhelmed. I'd accepted Him as Savior at five years old, but today His love felt fresh.

"Jesus Loves Me." We sing the words and quote verses, but how often does the reality of His love sink in? How often do we take time to consider the countless ways He says, "I love you" every day?
—JEANETTE HANSCOME

FAITH STEP: *Find the words to "Jesus Loves Me." Print or copy them to keep handy. Sing the song to Jesus. Let the words sink in.*

SATURDAY, JANUARY 26

That's why Christ is the go-between of a new covenant. Now those God calls to himself will receive the eternal gift he promised. Hebrews 9:15 *(NIRV)*

THERE ARE TWO KINDS OF writers: plotters and pantsers. Plotters usually outline, planning their beginning, middle, and ending. Pantsers don't actually write first drafts "flying by the seat of their pants," as the name suggests. But they do often begin with a simple idea, writing as they go, unsure of the actual paths that will be involved or even the ending. In both fiction and devotional writing, I'm primarily a pantser, but I trust Jesus's leading to bring me to a satisfying ending. And He always does.

I've noticed that the practice of writing parallels some of the events of everyday life. When the Lord called Abraham to follow Him, Abraham had no idea where that path would end. At times, he must have questioned the Lord's plans and methods. But based on God's covenant, by faith Abraham would receive his promised inheritance (Hebrews 11:8).

At times, we may unconsciously think of Jesus as a pantser. When the path seems scary, uncharted, and difficult, we may ask, "Jesus, are You sure You know what You're doing?" We may even resist His methods, trying to rely on our own incomplete understanding. But Jeremiah 29:11 assures us that Jesus has a plan and a purpose for those He calls, one that He designed before our life stories ever began (Psalm 139:16). Jesus promises us an eternal inheritance with a beautiful, satisfying ending. Our job, like Abraham's, is simply to trust Him. —REBECCA BARLOW JORDAN

FAITH STEP: *As an act of trust, discard your to-do list for one day. Ask Jesus to write the agenda for your day.*

Sunday, January 27

Whoever brings blessing will be enriched, and one who waters will himself be watered. Proverbs 11:25 (ESV)

Years ago, I was at one of the lowest points of my life, weighed down by family and personal problems. Prayer support from friends kept me going, but I felt so useless, unfit for ministry—like I had nothing to offer anyone. During the three-hour drive to my usual writers' conference, I poured out my heart to God. I told Him how tired I was of being so needy. "Lord," I begged, "please just let me be a blessing to somebody this week." By the time I arrived at the busy conference, I'd forgotten about that prayer.

During registration, I met a young woman who shared how God had orchestrated her attendance. Even though she'd just started her teaching career, the public school principal gave her time off to go to the Christian conference and even obtained funding to cover all her expenses. Early the next morning, we chatted again and I explained how the sign-up sheets worked. Each time I saw her, I asked how things were going. After we spoke on the fourth day, she started to walk away, then hesitated. "I just want you to know what a blessing you've been to me this week," she said. "Every time I had a question, you were there. Each time I felt unsure or confused, I turned around and there you were."

All I remember from that conference is how her words revived me. What a privilege to be able to lift up another person's spirit. All that's required of us is simply to imitate Jesus. And the best part? The blessing bounces right back to us. Note to self: Sometimes when I feel like I need encouragement, what I really need is to encourage somebody else. —Dianne Neal Matthews

Faith Step: *Find a hymnal or go online to read the words of the old song "Make Me a Blessing." Sing or read the words to Jesus as a prayer.*

MONDAY, JANUARY 28

"For I know the plans I have for you," declares the LORD, "plans to prosper you and not to harm you, plans to give you hope and a future."
Jeremiah 29:11 (NIV)

I LOVE GETTING MYSELF ORGANIZED. I find a great deal of satisfaction in writing out to-do lists and checking off items one by one. I enjoy buying a new giant desk calendar for our fridge so that we can chart out the days and weeks ahead. At the beginning of every school year, I enter the dates of events on our shared online calendar so that my husband, Scott, and I can be in sync with each other and see what the kids have going on. I like knowing what is coming up next.

But no matter how organized I am, things always come up that shift those days on the calendar. I organize things based on my understanding, but my understanding is limited. That's true for everyone. Only Jesus can map out our lives. He is all-knowing. He is the true organizer. We want to write out our lives with permanent ink. He pries the pen out of our hands and drafts a different agenda.

Jesus wants us to trust Him with our paths, our plans, and our dreams. He has the power to overcome obstacles and the grace to navigate trials, but we have to put the pen in His hands. He is in the business of making our paths straight. He adjusts our lives with His mercy and an eye on eternity with Him. He will chart a different course for us to be sure. But when we invite Him into the details of our lives, we know we can trust Him because of His overwhelming love for us. —SUSANNA FOTH AUGHTMON

FAITH STEP: *Look at your calendar. What have you written in permanent ink? Where do you need to trust Jesus? Invite Him into the details of your life and ask Him to make your path straight.*

Tuesday, January 29

Once a religious leader asked Jesus this question: "Good Teacher, what should I do to inherit eternal life?" Luke 18:18 (NLT)

My husband, Gene, and I train and lead short-term ministry teams to Eastern Europe, where we host evangelistic family camps. As part of our morning routine, we break into small groups to discuss a Bible lesson based on the parables of Jesus. Team members with no experience often feel nervous. They ask, "As a group leader, what should I do if someone asks a question and I don't know the answer?"

"Be honest," we say. "Admit that you don't know the answer and then try to find it."

Our team members can't know every answer to every question their students ask. But Jesus—the Good Teacher—does.

Everywhere Jesus taught, people recognized His authority and marveled at His wisdom. Sometimes they posed questions to frame or stump Him, but they always failed. He consistently gave the right answer because He's the source of all wisdom.

Jesus extends an invitation with a promise: "Let me teach you, because I am humble and gentle at heart, and you will find rest for your souls" (Matthew 11:29). Are you in need of answers? Wondering how to relate with a difficult person? Seeking direction about selling your home? Wondering whether you should find a second opinion on a recent medical diagnosis? Questioning whether your prayers make a difference?

Ask the Good Teacher. He knows the right answer, and He'll share it with you. He'll also bless you with inner peace when you embrace His answer and shape your response accordingly. —Grace Fox

Faith Step: *What question would you like to ask Jesus? Write it down. Spend a few minutes in silence and listen for His voice. What is He saying to you?*

WEDNESDAY, JANUARY 30

I no longer call you servants, because a servant does not know his master's business. Instead, I have called you friends, for everything that I learned from my Father I have made known to you. John 15:15 (NIV)

JENNIFER AND I MET WHEN we were three years old. Our friendship has survived moves, our attendance at different schools, and major life changes. We shared a childhood obsession with *Little House on the Prairie*, and our junior high lip-gloss collections bordered on hoarding. We are proof that kids outgrow weird phases. We witnessed each other's awkward preteen years, big eighties hair, and less-than-stellar dating choices. When you've been friends this long, you have a unique window into each other's lives.

Cheryl is a friend who happens to be my cousin. Our friendship grew when I moved after my husband left. She supported me as I rebuilt my life, found my way at a new church and healed. I've lost track of how many times we've prayed together, and shared things that we each knew the other would keep private. Being family makes our bond all the more precious. She has become a friend that I trust in a deep way.

I often forget that while Jesus was on earth, His disciples became His friends. They traveled together, ate together, prayed together, and probably did a lot of laughing. Most important, Jesus shared secrets of His Father's kingdom with them—secrets that we now have access to. But it's still hard for me to think of Jesus as my friend. Verses like John 15:15 remind me that when Jennifer and I go months without contact, and Cheryl isn't available, I always have Him. —JEANETTE HANSCOME

FAITH STEP: *Write a letter to the friend you have known for the longest time or to one who saw you through a difficult season. Better yet, write both! Thank Jesus for being your most faithful friend.*

Thursday, January 31

I have hope in God. Acts 24:15 (NKJV)

I WAS IN A CONVERSATION the other day with a group of intellectuals who believe there is no God. One of them told me she thinks it is cruel to tell people God loves them—that marginalized folks are hurt by this kind of rhetoric because it implies God intends them to suffer. She also said it is damaging to make people believe if they just begged God enough, or did more of what He wanted, He would care more about their suffering and change the situation. Better to be free of this, take a scientific view, and recognize there is no God who sees or hears.

I agreed with her that this conception of God is undesirable. But what room is there for the marginalized in a purely scientific view of the world?

The idea my friends have of God is sad to me, in part because I think we Christians do a poor job of showing our God to the world. Otherwise, why would so many have the perception He's a taskmaster, unloving, and unkind? It's also sad because I see no hope in a purely scientific view. The marginalized are left to die or be eaten. It's survival of the fittest. No room for the weak.

Jesus turns this idea on its head. In His kingdom, the first are last and the last first. Little children are the leaders. His concern is for the least of these. Here's the God who says, "Blessed are the poor" and "I will never leave you nor forsake you." Here's a love that died so we can live. Here's the Savior whose story means hope for all the world. —GWEN FORD FAULKENBERRY

FAITH STEP: *Think of someone who needs a little hope today. Write a note of encouragement, reminding them Jesus redeems everything, and drop it in the mail.*

FRIDAY, FEBRUARY 1

The Son of Man has come eating and drinking, and you say, "Look, a glutton and a drunkard, a friend of tax collectors and sinners!" Nevertheless, wisdom is vindicated by all her children. Luke 7:34–35 (NRSV)

AS SOMEONE WHO BECAME RELIGIOUS as an adult, I can sometimes fool myself into believing there is a split: there is Church Lady Chaplain Lizzie, and then there is the person I was before my conversion. Last month, a dear friend invited me to her husband's fiftieth birthday party, where I knew I would see people I hadn't seen in more than a decade. As we approached their home, I was ambivalent. Would I have anything in common with these people now?

Well, it was a wonderful night. In this festive setting, there was plenty of room for genuine connection. It was so surprisingly delightful to see old friends again and to meet new people. The event wasn't a "holy" event in the way we might label such things, but it did feel like a gift from God. I was reminded that there is so much to be enjoyed in life. I think of the title of legendary producer Norman Lear's biography: *Even This I Get to Experience.*

When I fool myself into thinking that my life as a "good Christian" rules out enjoying myself in a wide variety of settings and communities, Jesus's wise words are there to remind me otherwise. Wisdom is a mother who has children everywhere. All communal moments are an opportunity for her family reunion. Jesus didn't turn down invitations to spend time with these brothers and sisters. He said yes with gusto. —ELIZABETH BERNE DEGEAR

FAITH STEP: *Pray with this Jesus Who went to events that caused other people to misjudge Him. Ask Him if there is some group or some experience that you have been unnecessarily shutting out. Ask Him to send an invitation your way if He wants you to enjoy something new.*

SATURDAY, FEBRUARY 2

I will not forget you! Isaiah 49:15 (NIV)

AN OLD FRIEND CALLS ME often but never remembers our conversation. In some ways, every day for her is like the movie *Groundhog Day*, in which a television weatherman finds himself caught in a time warp, living the same day repeatedly.

Every morning is a new day for my friend. She can rattle off long-term memories, especially those involving relatives and close friends, without any problems. But facts about recent events, people, and activities are lost within a few minutes. Her sweet testimony still radiates through her difficult and discouraging situation. She still boasts of the One she loves and Who loves her—the One Who will never forget her.

In my limited knowledge of my girlfriend's condition, I try to offer her encouraging suggestions, creative things she can do, or ways she can make a difference. Does she have a notebook? Can she paint or draw? Is she journaling? She'll forget those questions, but I try anyway, because I want so much to lift her spirits.

But Jesus reminds me often that He has not forgotten my friend. He is always with her. His promises to be with us always (Matthew 28:20) and never to forget us are ones we can take to our spiritual bank. I need that reminder often, but my friend already knows that and claims Jesus's words of truth. Jesus has been her best friend since childhood—and that's a long-term memory she can still celebrate daily. And because He is, I don't need to search for words to make my friend feel better. I can simply be a friend who will listen—like Jesus does. —REBECCA BARLOW JORDAN

FAITH STEP: *Write down the names of those who may simply need your presence and your listening ear this week.*

SUNDAY, FEBRUARY 3

Praise him with trumpet sound; praise him with lute and harp! Praise him with tambourine and dance; praise him with strings and pipe! Praise him with sounding cymbals; praise him with loud clashing cymbals! Let everything that has breath praise the LORD! Praise the LORD! Psalm 150:3–6 (ESV)

"YOU'RE RUINING CHURCH," A PARISHIONER told my then twelve-year-old son. My son had joined the contemporary praise team and played his electric guitar during a worship chorus. The music was respectful and uplifting, but some people find variety frightening.

The Psalms call us to explore endless ways to praise. Jesus is so amazing and so multifaceted, we need many different ways to express our praise. Kneeling in silent contemplation, we can offer our thanks for His suffering on our behalf. Arms raised in delight can welcome His presence into the deepest recesses of our hearts. Majestic organ pipes can rumble through our bones to declare the power of our risen Lord. A cappella voices remind us of our place within His Body. And all can reflect our worship of Jesus.

We can praise Jesus with other art forms as well. A watercolor painter can depict the beauty of creation illuminated because of His redemptive work. A dancer can convey our deepest struggles and the joy of relinquishing our lives to Him. A sculptor can form an image, remembering how we are formed in His likeness.

My son didn't ruin the church. He grew up encouraged to explore many musical styles and became a composition major in college. Today, he continues to write songs to worship Jesus. Let's join the psalmist in finding new and surprising ways to praise. —SHARON HINCK

FAITH STEP: *Offer Jesus your praise today using a musical style or an art form that is outside of your norm.*

MONDAY, FEBRUARY 4

Wait for the LORD; be strong and take heart and wait for the LORD.
Psalm 27:14 (NIV)

RECENTLY, I'VE BEEN STRUGGLING WITH a broken relationship. It's as if I'm stumbling along, blind and clueless. Last night, I battled insomnia, finally admitting defeat around three. I couldn't turn on my bedside light to read—it would disturb my husband, David— so I moved to the den and pored over a book until I felt drowsy.

Switching off the lamp, I strode back toward the bedroom. The pitch-black hallway loomed. After almost tripping over our black cat, I froze. My eyes were useless. I'd have to wait for them to adapt to the darkness. Seconds ticked by. Slowly, small glimmers of light became discernible—the red blinking dot on the phone, the clock's hands, stars in the onyx sky. Soon, mysterious shapes shifted into familiar furniture, and I crawled back between the sheets.

That experience was—pardon the pun—a wake-up call for me. As I stood motionless in the dark, I realized it mirrored my current situation. The helplessness, the impatience...the waiting. And the way everything became clear in good time.

Jesus is with us, even when we're spinning our wheels, going nowhere. He sees our challenges and will lead us through them, no matter how lost we feel or how many times we stumble. When we're willing to slow down and wait, He'll pierce the darkness and shed His light on the problem, so we can see. —HEIDI GAUL

FAITH STEP: *Tonight, after lights-out, lie still as your eyes adapt to the darkness. Focus your thoughts on a problem you're lost in. Ask Jesus to guide you to a solution. Be prepared to trust . . . and willing to wait.*

TUESDAY, FEBRUARY 5

He heals the brokenhearted
And binds up their wounds. Psalm 147:3 (NKJV)

I'VE HAD MANY HEARTBREAKS IN my fifty-plus years of living, but my divorce was by far the hardest to endure. The process was long and contentious, as well as financially and emotionally draining. The decision to split didn't come easily. I agonized over it. I prayed over it. I cried over it and then repeated the cycle. At the time, I was approaching my fiftieth birthday, and I felt like I was at a crossroads—death or life. I chose life. Actually, Jesus helped me choose. I had been praying and fasting for months and believed He would miraculously fix my marriage, which had been broken for years.

But He didn't.

So after almost four years, four lawyers, and thousands of dollars, my twenty-five-year marriage was legally over. The days and months that followed took a toll—the memories we shared in the house I now lived in alone haunted me. And it wasn't just the demise of my marriage that troubled me after my divorce was finalized. I had been laid off, my mom had died, *and* my marriage was ending. I didn't think I could take much more. But Jesus taught me to lean on Him—for support, for money, for peace. The verse "My grace is sufficient for you, for My strength is made perfect in weakness" (2 Corinthians 12:9) could not be more true. I had no strength for what was to come; I needed His. And He gave me a double portion so I could make it to tomorrow. —CAROL MACKEY

FAITH STEP: *Think about that next step you may lack the strength to take. Let Jesus carry you.*

WEDNESDAY, FEBRUARY 6

*Finally, brothers and sisters, whatever is true, whatever is noble, whatever
is right, whatever is pure, whatever is lovely, whatever is admirable—
if anything is excellent or praiseworthy—think about such things.*
Philippians 4:8 (NIV)

I COPIED PHILIPPIANS 4:8 IN white paint pen on black paper. I added
a few flourishes, took a picture of it, then emailed it to my Bible study
friends. That morning, we'd had a long talk about our attitudes and
how often they were rooted in what we chose to fill our minds with.
What might happen if we challenged ourselves to filter everything
through Philippians 4:8 for a week, even if that meant avoiding the
news, social media, and certain conversations?

As I kept my promise to make a pretty copy of the verse for
the women to set as wallpaper on their phones or computers, I
considered what it might mean for me to think on things that were
true, noble, right, pure....

But that afternoon, something happened that frustrated me.

The more I tried to apply Philippians 4:8, the more aware I
became of how often I allowed my mind to drift to unlovely places.
No wonder I had trouble sleeping, snapped at people I loved, and
felt anxious. Peace came when I asked Jesus to shift my thinking.

How different would our lives be if we tuned out everything that
contradicted Philippians 4:8? What would we talk about? What
would we watch and listen to? What would we think about at night?
As hard as it is some days, when we start to see it make a difference,
the peace becomes worth the effort. —JEANETTE HANSCOME

FAITH STEP: *Write Philippians 4:8 on a card or piece of paper and keep it
where you can see it often. Challenge yourself to filter your thoughts for a week.*

THURSDAY, FEBRUARY 7

"What do you want me to do for you?" "Lord, I want to see," he replied.
Luke 18:41 (NIV)

WATCHING THE MORNING NEWS AND its inevitable commercials, I saw another product warning that seemed unnecessary. A mascara company warned, "Do not use this product in a moving vehicle."

At first, I thought it joined the ranks of "Do not use this toaster in the bathtub" and "Do not put small animals in this microwave." But I *have* applied mascara as a passenger in the car with my husband, Bill.

On a bumpy country road not long ago, the mascara wand poked me in the eye. My eye recovered quickly, but what if...? What if I'd suffered permanent damage from such a trivial action?

If you've ever failed to wear safety goggles when woodworking or were splashed with hot oil from a cooking disaster, you might have entertained that unnerving thought.

Jesus often performed miracles for the blind. He never suggested over-the-counter eye drops. And He didn't suggest surgery. Both physically and spiritually, He restored sight by His power alone. Not even blindness was too difficult for Him.

The point Jesus made was that it didn't matter how the blindness happened—a birth defect, a workshop injury, or even a careless poke in the eye. What He cared about was restoring sight, because our ability to "see" matters to Him. He had the power and the "want to."

I pray that when my vision grows foggy—spiritually or physically—I will be quick to issue the invitation, "Lord, I want to see." —CYNTHIA RUCHTI

FAITH STEP: *Is your vision fogged by disappointment, disillusionment, or disobedience? It will take more than eye drops or surgery. Invite Jesus to add you to the list of those He healed from blindness.*

FRIDAY, FEBRUARY 8

Therefore, so that I would not exalt myself, a thorn in the flesh was given to me, a messenger of Satan to torment me so I would not exalt myself.
2 Corinthians 12:7 (HCSB)

STAGE FRIGHT PREVENTED ME FROM seizing opportunities to sing in my teens and twenties. If you've had stage fright, you know it's not only unpleasant, but also completely at odds with the act of singing. It chokes the joyous tune and stage presence right out of you.

The songstress in me often felt true rapture singing solo in my living room. Likewise, the diva in me longed for the spotlight. Yet the fear was so overwhelming and tangible, and my real life satisfying enough, I let singing slip away altogether.

I've asked God why He would give me talent but not courage.

Now years later, living a full life far from spotlighted stages, I see more clearly the mystical alchemy of Jesus in my heart.

I know I would have been very vulnerable to the licentious lures and crush of fame or failure. God protected me from myself.

Whether my insecurities or providence determined the road not taken is mercifully not the issue, because my God does indeed work in all things for the good. —ISABELLA YOSUICO

FAITH STEP: *Do you have an unfulfilled dream that won't be realized here on Earth? Consider the possibility that God protected you or had something better in mind. Thank Him.*

SATURDAY, FEBRUARY 9

We who are strong must be considerate of those who are sensitive about things like this. We must not just please ourselves. We should help others do what is right and build them up in the Lord. For even Christ didn't live to please himself. Romans 15:1–3 (NLT)

WHEN MY HUSBAND, GENE, AND I train our team of volunteers for missionary work overseas, we stress the need to practice cultural sensitivity. For example, we talk about how to behave when served foods that are new to us, cautioning against making facial expressions that reflect disdain. We encourage our volunteers to say thank you and to be open to new experiences for the sake of developing relationships.

Effective ministry happens in a cross-cultural setting when we set aside our personal preferences for others' sake, as Jesus did. The same principle works within our churches when the expression of someone's Christian faith looks different than ours. For instance, some folks feel contemporary worship music is the best; others prefer traditional songs. Some like services that follow a strict schedule; others prefer services that flow as the Holy Spirit leads. Some believers follow a conservative dress code for church services; others feel comfortable in blue jeans.

Who's to say which practice is best? Our heart attitude is the more important issue. Being willing to sacrifice our preferences for the sake of others' spiritual growth reflects Christ's attitude, and that's what really matters. —GRACE FOX

FAITH STEP: *Ask Jesus to show you whether you value personal preference over people. If the answer is yes, then ask Him to give you the grace needed to reverse that order.*

Sunday, February 10

For just as each of us has one body with many members, and these members do not all have the same function, so in Christ we, though many, form one body. Romans 12:4–5 (NIV)

My seventy-one-year-old dad has struggled for some time with depression. A new medicine seems to be working, and we are hopeful he's on the mend, but it has been a difficult season.

Dad is the song leader at our small country church, and I play piano. For several Sundays during his depressive episode, I watched him struggle, turning pages with shaky hands, tearing up more than usual or appropriate. Rock bottom for me was the morning he texted me before church that he could not be there. He had too much anxiety and asked me to manage without him. I was tearful that day—and for several Sundays to come—when I looked over at his empty seat.

Thank God he's back now. This week, on his way to the stage, he knocked over a music stand and papers went flying. I saw tragedy in this. From the piano, I motioned to my son to help him. But my son was laughing. At first this enraged me, until I saw my dad was laughing too.

This got me thinking about how the Body of Christ works. Maybe it's a gift that my first thought was concern for my dad, but in this case, concern was not what he needed. He needed my son's laughter, because he needed to laugh at himself.

Jesus is not one thing. He's all of the things we need—compassion, truth, power, strength, conviction, grace, courage, love—everything in one Person. And at just the right time. —Gwen Ford Faulkenberry

FAITH STEP: *Go online or ask your pastor for a test you can take to help you determine your spiritual gifts. Then look for a way you might use your gifts in the Body of Christ this week.*

MONDAY, FEBRUARY 11

They devoted themselves to the apostles' teaching and to fellowship, to the breaking of bread and to prayer. Acts 2:42 (NIV)

WHEN MY PRAYER PARTNER AND I had to stop our weekly routine, I thought my time for needing a special person to pray with had ended. I had plenty of friends that I exchanged prayer needs with. But I soon missed the sacred bond and sense of Jesus's love and presence that came with praying with someone on a regular basis.

"I miss having a prayer partner," I finally admitted to a friend.

"Maybe it's time to start praying for a new one."

While asking Jesus to send one, I considered what I wanted in a prayer partner. I'd had prayer and mentoring relationships that had turned into spiritual hierarchies. There were also times we did more chatting than praying. I didn't want to repeat either of those patterns. I knew that Jesus understood my need. A few weeks later, a longtime writer friend came to mind. We started a practice of texting our prayer requests every Sunday evening and lifting each other up throughout the week. Sometimes we share big needs over the phone, and we make a point of getting together every few months for lunch. I thank Jesus for her constantly.

From the time He left this earth, His people have been dedicated to prayer. It is no wonder that so many of us feel drawn to prayer partners. When we pray together, we have the beautiful opportunity to witness each other's growth, develop deeper friendships, and experience fellowship that few other relationships offer.
—JEANETTE HANSCOME

FAITH STEP: *If you don't have a prayer partner, ask Jesus to send you one. If you have one already, take time to send a note expressing why you are thankful for that person.*

TUESDAY, FEBRUARY 12

I have loved you with an everlasting love; I have drawn you with unfailing kindness. Jeremiah 31:3 (NIV)

"HOW DO I LOVE THEE? Let me count the ways." While dusting, I pulled a book of poetry off the shelf and thumbed through it. My eyes fell on the familiar opening lines of Sonnet 43 by Elizabeth Barrett Browning. And I immediately thought of a new friend, Gayle. When she introduced herself at Bible study, she shared that her husband had passed away two years before. She added that after being married fifty years, she missed him deeply every day.

Later, Gayle told me how loving her husband had been. He'd told her he loved her—not just every day, but a few times each day. And he demonstrated that love through actions like bringing her coffee each morning before she got out of bed. With tears in her eyes, Gayle remembered those last months as he battled illness. Often she'd asked how he was doing; he'd respond by saying, "No, how are *you*?" As I listened to Gayle, I regretted that I had never met this man who loved so well.

God tells us continually throughout the day how much He loves us. He's written it in His Word and demonstrated it through His creation that surrounds us. Most of all, He expressed His great love through His Son. Jesus demonstrated the supreme act of love by dying on the cross for us. When I think about that, I sometimes wonder, *How well am I loving Him?* Do I only verbally express my love when I sing with the praise team at church on Sundays? Do my daily actions reflect a desire to love and honor Jesus, or the pursuit of my personal agenda? I think I can do better. And maybe the first step is to count the ways that Jesus has loved me. —DIANNE NEAL MATTHEWS

FAITH STEP: *Start your day by telling Jesus one of the reasons you love Him.*

WEDNESDAY, FEBRUARY 13

Beloved, let us love one another, for love is from God,
and whoever loves has been born of God and knows God. 1 John 4:7 (ESV)

MY HUSBAND, SCOTT, AND I celebrated twenty years of marriage this year. The celebration didn't go quite as expected. We were going to drive to a little beach town that we love and wile away the hours in the sand. That was the plan, at least, until I proceeded to break two toes on each of my feet.

The beach was out. Crutches and sand don't mix. My personal toe catastrophe changed up all our plans. I couldn't take strolls downtown or browse through shops. I couldn't even carry my own cup of coffee to the patio outside our room. It was crazy. Scott didn't complain. He didn't say he was disappointed. He just loved me. I was limited in what I could do. And he met me there in that place. He drove me right up to the door of restaurants. He slowed his pace to walk beside me. He carried my coffee cup. In my weakness, he took care of me.

Love is patient. Love is kind. Love never fails.

There is a steadiness to real love. It doesn't waver or give out mid-toe-catastrophe. It doesn't break down when life gets difficult. When we love each other, we are living the life that Jesus created us for. It is because of His great love for us that we know what true love looks like. We are His beloved. When His life is lived out in us, we love like He does. And that is a beautiful thing.
—SUSANNA FOTH AUGHTMON

FAITH STEP: *Set out to show someone love today in a concrete way. Meet them right where they are with your words and your actions, just like Jesus does for you.*

Thursday, February 14

For this is how God loved the world: He gave his one and only Son, so that everyone who believes in him will not perish but have eternal life. John 3:16 (NLT)

Typically, we limit our gift-giving and special tokens of love to friends and relatives when it comes to celebrations like Valentine's Day, birthdays, anniversaries, or Christmas. But I love the example Jesus set for us. Through every word and deed of His entire three-year ministry, His life spelled love for everyone he encountered. He knew how to make all people feel special and important, especially the ones society had discarded. He healed outcast lepers, ate with hated tax collectors, and even forgave the ones who crucified Him.

Always creative in His approach, Jesus gifted others by affirming their uniqueness and invited all to enter His kingdom. He never compromised His beliefs. Yet because of His genuine acceptance and infinite grace, people were drawn to Him. Jesus, fulfilling His Father's mission, made love His passion, and He never limited His eternal gifts to a certain day or to a select people.

After reviewing Jesus's attitude toward people recently, I saw again how shallow my love can be at times in comparison to His. Selfishness can rise to the surface as easily as fresh cream. Without thinking, I can neglect opportunities year-round to show love to those beyond my inner circle of friends and family. But my desire is to search for ways to love others like Jesus did.

This year, I'm planning to start a personal love challenge, allowing Jesus's love full reign in my life. Valentine's Day is a good time to begin—and a good reminder to treat everyone specially, every day, all year long. —Rebecca Barlow Jordan

Faith Step: *This week, watch for those who especially need Jesus's love. Then ask Jesus to show you some unique ways to make these and others feel special all year long.*

FRIDAY, FEBRUARY 15

If the world hates you [and it does], know that it has hated Me before it hated you. If you belonged to the world, the world would love [you as] its own and would treat you with affection. But you are not of the world. John 15:18–19 (AMP)

YOUNG PEOPLE HAVE GROWN UP in a world unlike the one in which I was born. They've experienced hatred in realms that didn't touch small-town midwestern girls in the middle of the previous century.

But social media allows hatred to draw closer—as close as our phone screens. Many are unaware that people once thought before they spoke and were hesitant to share their opinions rather than eager to blurt them out, no matter how hurtful. "Hate crimes" once meant something different than it does in many circles today. The object of hate is sometimes the epitome of love—Jesus, His teachings, and His followers.

It shouldn't surprise us. For decades, we've skipped over the verses that record the heads-up Jesus gave millennia ago. "If the world hates you [and it does], know that it has hated Me before it hated you" (John 15:18).

We could be treated with affection by the world, but the cost would be too high a price to pay. We don't belong to this world. Hard as it is to swallow, our closeness to Christ makes us a target. But our closeness to Christ also affords us divine protection. —CYNTHIA RUCHTI

FAITH STEP: *How secure are you when the world—your coworkers, neighbors, social media followers—disrespect your faith? The further you are from Jesus, the harder those blows will land. Before you open social media today, pause to pray for protection and wisdom in your responses.*

SATURDAY, FEBRUARY 16

Do not forget to show hospitality to strangers, for by so doing some people have shown hospitality to angels without knowing it. Hebrews 13:2 (NIV)

MY DAUGHTER AND I ATTENDED a musical at a local dinner theater. A woman seated at our table struck up a conversation while we waited for the show to begin. We could easily have kept to ourselves, exchanged only a few pleasantries, and avoided engaging at a deeper level. Instead, as we chatted, we discovered some amazing connections.

She was a theater director, with many interests that my daughter and I shared. As we compared experiences, I learned she had a special passion for sharing faith through art. She was working on developing the drama ministry at her church but struggled with her desire to create excellent art—a struggle I'd also faced in my years of directing a Christian arts ministry.

We exchanged email addresses, and a few weeks later I had the pleasure of inviting her over for tea. Our conversation was rich with encouragement and peppered with gasps of recognition as we learned of the other's similar experiences and turning points in her walk with Jesus.

Discovering the surprise of kinship with a stranger may be why the book of Hebrews reminds us to open our hearts and lives to new people. Wherever this connection leads, I was blessed by the fellowship of a new acquaintance. She brought me a powerful message about Jesus's faithfulness through her stories. And her testimony rekindled embers in my heart that had grown cool. What joy I would have missed if I'd held back from embracing someone new. —SHARON HINCK

FAITH STEP: *This week, be aware of strangers around you—while running errands, in your neighborhood, at church, or at an event. Strike up a conversation and pray you can be an "angel unaware" to someone.*

SUNDAY, FEBRUARY 17

Now I plead with you, brethren, by the name of our Lord Jesus Christ, that you all speak the same thing, and that there be no divisions among you, but that you be perfectly joined together in the same mind and in the same judgment. 1 Corinthians 1:10 (NKJV)

RECENTLY, A PASTOR REMINDED ME of something. Sunday morning at eleven o'clock is the most segregated hour of the week. I took some time to think about that. I didn't grow up in the church and didn't come to know Christ until my early adulthood. But when I did attend and even join churches, they mostly had congregations that were like me: African-American. Segregation does have history in the pews. It was the law before the civil rights movement and subsequent legislation changed things. But since that change, Christian congregations remain largely separate.

I believe this grieves Jesus's heart. The Body of Christ, the church, is one body. And that Body has suffered many fractures because of race, culture, denomination, and even ideology. The Church at Corinth had this problem. Some of the people there thought they were better than others by birthright. No wonder Paul wasn't pleased.

Jesus knew that there would be these differences among His followers, but He didn't want us to focus on them. He wanted us all to focus on Him because we are all one in Christ. We may feel more comfortable in a congregation that reflects our own culture and style of worship. And there is a multitude of differences among believers—too many to list. But my hope is that we focus more on unity in Jesus Christ. —CAROL MACKEY

FAITH STEP: *Are there new members of your church? Make them feel welcome by showing the love of Christ. Remember the Lord's words: "By this all will know that you are My disciples, if you have love for one another" (John 13:35).*

MONDAY, FEBRUARY 18

I give you a new commandment, that you love one another. Just as I have loved you, you also should love one another. John 13:34 (NRSV)

LIVING IN THIS WORLD AS we do, sometimes things seem so complicated, don't they? On a macro scale, I see messes on every continent, things that worry me for now and for future generations; and in our own country, people I love fight on differing sides of political arguments. On a more micro scale, work often feels impossible, people hurt my kids' feelings, and my husband doesn't take out the trash when he is supposed to.

I tend to overthink my responses to problems. I was challenged about that recently when I learned of the Preemptive Love Coalition. Apparently this organization was formed by a Christian couple who were so dismayed by the conditions of some of the people in Iraq that they had to do something. Instead of overthinking what to do, they focused on one thing—the thing Jesus focused on—love.

Preemptive Lovers don't analyze who is worthy, who should be considered a friend or an enemy, who is likely to repay them, or even who believes in the same God. Their motto is "Love shows up." So they mobilize doctors to show up where care is needed. They mobilize teachers where kids need education. Food. Shelter. You get the picture.

I may never make a difference in the world on the scale they are, but I can learn from their obedience to Jesus's command to love. It's a great simplifier when things seem complicated. We don't have to overthink what Jesus would do. He would love.
—GWEN FORD FAULKENBERRY

FAITH STEP: *Show others your love for Jesus by volunteering at a local homeless shelter. Or, if one doesn't exist near you, take a meal to someone in need.*

TUESDAY, FEBRUARY 19

So the Lord himself will give you this sign: A virgin will become pregnant and give birth to a son, and she will name him Immanuel [God Is With Us].
Isaiah 7:14 (GW)

MY FRIEND HAD OFFERED TO help me out with a big PTA project the next week. But as I watched her walk away, I wondered if she would really keep her promise. She hadn't always kept her word in the past. Would she let me down again? We've probably all been disappointed by someone not keeping a promise. Maybe we were counting on them to help out on moving day, or pick us up at the airport, or babysit for an important event. Many people have suffered the excruciating pain of having a spouse break the promises made in their wedding vows.

The Bible has recorded a number of promises that Jesus made to us. He will extend forgiveness to anyone who repents of sin. He will give us rest if we come to Him and let Him lead us. We will have troubles in this life, but He will empower us to live as overcomers. He will never leave us and no one can snatch us from His hand. He is preparing an eternal home for us where he will take us one day to live with Him forever.

I may have good reason to doubt the word of a few people, but never Jesus's. I know this because of Who He is. Jesus wasn't only the fulfillment of hundreds of Old Testament prophecies about the Messiah; He was a promise kept. The words of Isaiah were even repeated in Matthew 1:21 after Mary conceived. So the question is never, *"Can* I believe Him?" but, *"Will* I believe Him?"
—DIANNE NEAL MATTHEWS

FAITH STEP: *Which promise of Jesus means the most to you right now? Write out a brief prayer telling Him why. Thank Him for always keeping His word.*

WEDNESDAY, FEBRUARY 20

---

*Teach them to your children, talking about them when you sit in your house
and when you walk along the road, when you lie down and when you get up.
Deuteronomy 11:19 (HCSB)*

IT'S HABIT NOW. A HARD one to break. And I wouldn't want to. I habitually make improvements along my life's daily journey.

It's what Jesus did—watch for needs and offer His healing touch or a word of encouragement along the way.

When I get the mail from the mailbox across the road, I look for weeds in the flower bed. Even plucking two or three improves the presentation.

When I leave the family room, first I scan for empty popcorn bowls, bits of paper destined for the garbage, or folded laundry headed for a dresser upstairs.

After I brush my teeth, I run the hand towel over the countertops to wipe away any water spots.

If I pass someone in need, I attempt to brighten their moment, even if I have no power to change their circumstances.

When I'm working on a project, along the road to completion, both distractions and opportunities abound. Knowing the difference between a distraction and an opportunity is something I can only discern by watching and listening for Jesus's clear direction.

But if I can pull a weed from someone's life, clean up a small mess before it becomes a large one, point out where Jesus is figuratively standing near, or offer a cup of Jesus-water to a thirsty soul, what a great day it's been! —CYNTHIA RUCHTI

FAITH STEP: *Don't walk past the picture that needs straightening or the weed that needs pulling today. And take note of the people around you who are thirsty for what you're carrying in your soul's canteen.*

THURSDAY, FEBRUARY 21

So they called to the blind man, "Cheer up! On your feet! He's calling you."
Throwing his cloak aside, he jumped to his feet and came to Jesus.
Mark 10:49–50 (NIV)

MANY YEARS AGO, I SPENT a year in a volunteer corps, sharing a home with seven other young volunteers. We came from all over the country. The surprising complaint of two housemates used to make us all laugh: they hated layering their clothes. These young women were from Louisiana, and it drove them crazy that, in the harsh Alaskan climate, every time they went outside they had to take the time to put on multiple layers. And every time they came inside they had to take the time to peel them off. Those of us who had experienced a cold winter every year of our lives didn't give it a second thought. For us, the challenges that had us griping were the darkness that descended at two o'clock in the afternoon and being so many time zones away from our loved ones that it was hard to find a time to call them.

I wonder if our souls are like that. We come into this world as unencumbered spirits, and then the harsh circumstances of our lives force us to put on layer upon layer as protection from the world's realities. This layering is something we get used to and think of as perfectly normal, until Jesus calls us and we feel the original truth and freedom of our own being. The Good News makes us feel those layers of worldly protection are a burden that is no longer relevant to our circumstance. Being called by Christ makes us throw our cloak aside without a second thought, trusting that wherever we are, we live in freedom, light, and love. —ELIZABETH BERNE DEGEAR

FAITH STEP: *What is a defensive layer you are "wearing" in your life right now? Ask Jesus to be with you as you feel the burden of carrying this layer with you. Ask Jesus to lead you to the time and place when you can cheerfully cast off this layer without a second thought.*

FRIDAY, FEBRUARY 22

You, Lord, are forgiving and good, abounding in love to all who call to you. Hear my prayer, LORD; listen to my cry for mercy. When I am in distress, I call to you, because you answer me. Psalm 86:5–7 (NIV)

I NEED FORGIVENESS AND MERCY daily. This is because I make mistakes regularly. Being a mom of three boys tends to exacerbate the problem. Any time you are living in close proximity with others, they will get to experience your weaknesses firsthand. When I am stressed out with deadlines or bill payments or a lack of sleep, my weaknesses seem to grow. I get frustrated more easily. My perfectionism and pride come bubbling up.

This week, I have had to apologize repeatedly to my children as my emotions have gotten the better of me. *Yesterday when I said I would try to do better and not yell at you, I meant it. Right up until that time that I yelled at you today. Can you forgive me...again?*

Forgiveness and mercy are an integral part of following Jesus. Our lives are a process of coming undone and Jesus putting us back together. We won't get it right every day. But we can learn from our mistakes. We may be a mess, but if we can offer that mess to the One Who loves us the most, He can begin to heal our brokenness. He loves us and tells us that, even though we are a mess, He is not leaving us that way. He has a plan. A way to bring us closer to Him. He steps into our weakness and brings His strength. He offers mercy and forgiveness and reminds us who we are in Him. New creations...being transformed into His likeness and image a little more every day. —SUSANNA FOTH AUGHTMON

FAITH STEP: *Write your most recent "mess" on a piece of paper. Offer it to Jesus. Now erase it and, in its place, write, "Jesus forgives me and offers me mercy."*

SATURDAY, FEBRUARY 23

Because of our faith, Christ has brought us into this place of undeserved privilege where we now stand, and we confidently and joyfully look forward to sharing God's glory. Romans 5:2 (NLT)

As I WRITE THIS, I'M about twenty hours away from boarding a Boeing 747 bound for Frankfurt. I've flown internationally nearly forty times in the past decade, always in economy class. This trip will be no different. I'll scrunch my knees up and pull my elbows in, and I'll eat from plastic dishes and cups.

My friend Connie recently returned to Canada from Europe with her husband. Connie told me that the airline goofed on their reservations. To maintain good customer service reviews, the airline bumped them from economy into first class.

"There's no comparison," said Connie. "Imagine eating from china dishes and sleeping under a quilt. I felt like royalty! How can I ever be content in economy again?"

Queen Connie's fairy tale turned me a light shade of green. Perhaps someday I will experience a place of privilege on a Boeing 747. In the meantime, I enjoy an undeserved privilege of another sort, and it far surpasses china and quilts at thirty-seven thousand feet.

I'm seated in a place of peace with Jesus. When I placed my faith in Him, He moved me from a life without hope and an eternity without Him to a place of forgiveness, freedom, and assurance of heaven.

I don't just *feel* like royalty; I *am* royalty. Jesus, in His kindness, has seated me in a place I don't deserve but for which I'm exceedingly grateful. I could never be content elsewhere. —GRACE FOX

FAITH STEP: *Draw a simple airplane. Place an X near the front of the plane, representing your position in first class, spiritually speaking. Thank Jesus for paying the price so you could experience this highest and undeserved privilege.*

SUNDAY, FEBRUARY 24

In the same way, I tell you, there is joy in the presence of the angels of God over one sinner who repents. Luke 15:10 (AMP)

MY YOUNGEST GRANDSON CRUSHED ME with his nine-year-old hug Sunday morning after church. In his burly-boy way, he told me he'd made a decision the night before. He'd realized that at least some of the anxieties he'd been wrestling with since toddlerhood were related to a much deeper issue than fear of non-Velcro shoes and vegetables that don't taste like corn.

His young heart sensed his need to give his life to Jesus, to ask forgiveness of his sins and recognize Jesus as Savior and Lord.

When my son-in-law called my grandson's other grandparents to share the happy news, Grandpa M. asked, "What time was that?" Grandpa M. broke into tears. "I was praying for him that very moment."

The complete verse of Luke 15:10 reads: "I [Jesus] tell you, there is joy in the presence of the angels of God over one sinner who repents [that is, changes his inner self—his old way of thinking, regrets past sins, lives his life in a way that proves repentance; and seeks God's purpose for his life]."

Joy certainly broke out in our household when my grandson told us his news. Imagine a sea of angels joining the party!

It was a true and certain decision on my grandson's part. Imagine the confusion or disappointment in heaven if someone changes only his heart and not his life, or makes only life change and not a heart change?

Repent is not a word to be taken lightly. Watching its wonder in my grandson still makes my heart sing. —CYNTHIA RUCHTI

FAITH STEP: *Post this note in a spot where you'll see it frequently: Repent = Changed heart and life.*

MONDAY, FEBRUARY 25

I have told you these things, so that in me you may have peace. In this world you will have trouble. But take heart! I have overcome the world.
John 16:33 (NIV)

AS A BREAST CANCER SURVIVOR, I find that health concerns can overtake my thoughts. My anxiety level is like a tide rolling in and out when it comes to any medical challenges I face. This month I'm due for my annual mammogram. Already, butterflies flutter in my stomach.

One thing that helps calm me is remembering I'm not alone. No matter what the outcome, I have Jesus standing beside me. If the test comes back negative for cancer, I'll rejoice and carry on. However, if I receive the opposite answer, I'll have no choice but to accept it as God's will. When I get scared, I'll lean hard on Jesus. And if the going gets rough and I fall, I can trust Him to carry me through the journey, just as He has done many times before. He knows me better than anyone and understands my weakness.

I've come to expect and accept life's ups and downs. Suffering and trials are all part of the refining of my soul. Without pain, I might not appreciate—or even recognize—the blessings I've been given. Paul, in Romans 5:3–4, tells us that our sufferings produce perseverance, which in turn builds character. The end product is hope.

I don't welcome trials, but I know they're necessary. The woman who emerges from the other side of these struggles is stronger, more caring, and a closer reflection of Jesus. An individual of high character, filled with a hope in Christ that defies circumstance. A survivor.
—HEIDI GAUL

FAITH STEP: *What challenge are you facing today? Are you overwhelmed? Pray for insight to see how God is using this trial to mold you into a better person.*

TUESDAY, FEBRUARY 26

A cheerful heart is good medicine, but a crushed spirit dries up the bones.
Proverbs 17:22 (NIV)

LAUGHING IS MY FAVORITE THING to do. I like funny movies. I love funny books. I share funny videos. If someone else starts laughing, I have to join in. We place a high value on humor in our family. I love it when my kids get tickled and break out in giggles. If I can make my husband and kids laugh? I feel like I have won the lottery. The best moment is when my husband, Scott, laughs until he cries. None of us can keep it together when he is laughing that hard.

What is it about joy that is so contagious?

I have a hunch that we love to laugh so much because Jesus created us for joy. His Word is full of joy references, such as *You shall go out with joy and be led forth with peace. Weeping may endure for the night, but joy comes in the morning. In His presence there is fullness of joy. The joy of the Lord is my strength.*

Life can be hard. There is brokenness and grief to contend with. There are dark days in all of our lives. But the truth is that we were formed with joy in mind. Joy heals us and restores us like good medicine. Joy lifts our spirits and ushers in hope. If we can laugh, if we can find joy, even in the dark moments, we know that we are not alone. He is there. The One in whom joy resides. Jesus, with all His hope and goodness and love, is the joy-bringer. Embrace that joy-filled person that He created us to be! —SUSANNA FOTH AUGHTMON

FAITH STEP: *Get together with a joyful friend. Laugh as much as you can and thank your friend for being like Jesus, the joy-bringer.*

WEDNESDAY, FEBRUARY 27

For by the grace given me I say to every one of you: Do not think of yourself
more highly than you ought, but rather think of yourself with sober judgment,
in accordance with the faith God has distributed to each of you.
Romans 12:3 (NIV)

I ENJOY SINGING. SO WHEN God graciously delivered me from my
paralyzing stage fright, urging me to take the stage with my church
choir, I rejoiced.

The first week, I sang along with my rehearsal app at home, eyes
closed in raptured reverence—and more than a little imagination.

Won't be long before they'll move me to the worship team, I thought.
Who knows where that could lead? I envisioned myself belting out
Gospel like some unlikely combo of Shirley Caesar and Amy Grant.

Well, at that first rehearsal, I stood with fifty faithful men and
women to practice six worship songs, most of which I knew. Five
minutes into it, I was humbled to the tips of my tonsils.

My fellow altos chatted about how best to render our parts on the
twelve-bar; I don't read music. They captured the choir director's
vocal instructions on the first try; uncertain, I sounded like an
injured duck. The worship team's voices rose in flawless praise; I
was too busy thinking to soar.

Romans 12 says each of us is an equal part of a whole, endowed
by God Himself with gifts for His glory alone.

Knowing my place frees me to join with my brethren in humble
praise, whatever part I sing. —ISABELLA YOSUICO

FAITH STEP: *In what part of your life could pride be hindering you in some*
way? Ask God to search your heart and consider the freedom of knowing
your place.

THURSDAY, FEBRUARY 28

But of Him you are in Christ Jesus, who became for us wisdom from God—and righteousness and sanctification and redemption—that, as it is written, "He who glories, let him glory in the LORD." 1 Corinthians 1:30–31 (NKJV)

A FRIEND FROM OHIO RECENTLY asked me if I was proud of my Southern heritage. I told him a Southern heritage is complicated, but I do love the South. I'm proud of things commonly associated with us, like great hospitality, modest means, appreciation for the simple things, unspoiled natural beauty, inexpensive fun, strong family ties, friendliness, a slower pace, front porches, resourcefulness, good food, hugging, showing emotions, working hard, living close to the land, etc.

However, I'm ashamed that the South has a history of slave ownership. I'm also ashamed of the terrible statistics we often show in regard to education, teenage pregnancy, poverty, obesity, etc. I am ashamed of people in the South who are proud of these things and/or won't take responsibility for making them better.

This all got me thinking about what it means to be proud of something. Proud Southerner. Proud American. Proud parent. Proud sports fan. Proud Christian. Pride can be a good thing, but it's tricky, isn't it? Pride in good things can sometimes blind us to the evil that's just as real. Just like my Southern heritage. All of the good can't take away the problems. And Jesus should never be used as a cover for the abuses committed in His name.

The truth is, we followers of Jesus have nothing to be proud of. Not really. The good we do and are comes from Jesus—all glory goes to Him. —GWEN FORD FAULKENBERRY

FAITH STEP: *Consider whether you have misplaced pride in your life. If there's something good you use to cover sin, repent and let Jesus help you make it right.*

FRIDAY, MARCH 1

*Be strong and courageous. Do not fear or be in dread of them, for it is the
LORD your God who goes with you. He will not leave you or forsake you.
Deuteronomy 31:6 (ESV)*

AROUND AGE TWELVE, I CHANGED from a bubbly, outgoing girl into a
shy person with no self-confidence. In high school, I remember waiting
for someone to choose me for their team during PE class. Wondering
if someone would want me for their partner for the biology project.
And that awful day when my last class walked to the football field for
a pep rally. I didn't have any friends in that class, so I walked alone
while everyone else around me talked and laughed in pairs or groups.

Although I overcame my shyness as an adult, that feeling of
isolation has come back each time my husband and I have relocated,
especially since we moved away from our kids and grandkids. It's
a lonely feeling to go shopping or run errands and know that no
one knows your name. That insecurity intensified when I walked
into the new ladies' Bible study at the church I recently joined. The
ladies were divided into small groups, and I was told to sit at any
table. But looking around, I saw a roomful of old friends chatting
and laughing. Was there a place for me?

Feeling left out leads to isolation, which leads to loneliness, which
can lead to depression. The only thing that helps me in this struggle
is knowing that Jesus has promised to never leave me. No matter how
many times I move, He's right there with me. And if I step out, He
leads me to kindred spirits—like the eight precious women I ended up
sharing a table with at that Bible study. —DIANNE NEAL MATTHEWS

FAITH STEP: *The next time you're out in public or at church, ask Jesus to show
you someone who is feeling lonely or left out. What can you do to make them feel
valued and included?*

SATURDAY, MARCH 2

We have different gifts, according to the grace given to each of us.
If your gift is prophesying, then prophesy in accordance with your faith;
if it is serving, then serve; if it is teaching, then teach; if it is to encourage,
then give encouragement; if it is giving, then give generously; if it is to lead,
do it diligently; if it is to show mercy, do it cheerfully. Romans 12:6–8 (NIV)

MY YOUNGEST SON, ADDISON, ASKED me, "Mom, what did you want to be when you grew up?"

I said, "Well, I thought I wanted to be a counselor."

Addie laughed. "Mom, you would be horrible at that."

"Why do you say that?"

"You can't stand hearing about sad things."

It took me four semesters of college psychology to figure that out. "I've always wanted to help people. It just took time to figure out how."

"How?"

"I encourage people."

"Oh."

"With my writing."

"Okay."

He wasn't impressed, but it got me thinking. As a young adult, I was a nurse's aide, a financial aid assistant, and a short-term missionary. None of these careers were a good fit for me. Sometimes we have to recognize who we aren't before we can embrace who we are. We all have a certain kind of light to share. We are each created with innate gifts and a purpose. Jesus wants us to spread all that light and creativity around. We need each other's brightness and beauty. When we step into all that Jesus has for us and let Him use us, the world gets better. So as soon as you figure it out? Shine your light right over here. —SUSANNA FOTH AUGHTMON

FAITH STEP: *How do you shine Jesus's love into the darkness of your world?*

SUNDAY, MARCH 3

*So Sarah laughed to herself, saying, "After I have grown old,
and my husband is old, shall I have pleasure?" Genesis 18:12 (NRSV)*

IT MAY COME AS A surprise that the Bible covers issues including the
desires of women-of-a-certain-age. But here, in Genesis, we have
just such a situation. God is promising fulfillment of a long-held
desire, and when Sarah hears it, she laughs. *At this age!* she thinks to
herself. *No way.*

I am embarrassed to admit how often a similar dialogue goes on
between me and Jesus. I feel some sort of longing, or have a vision
of what is still possible in my vocation or in my personal life, and
I feel Jesus with me, nodding and smiling. And then immediately
my own skepticism and insecurity intrude: *Too late. Too old. Not in
these circumstances.*

Despite Sarah's laugh, God said, "Yes, indeed." What might have
started out as Sarah's sarcastic laugh of disbelief transforms into
another, fuller, more joyful kind of laughter. When Sarah's long-
prayed-for desire comes to pass, she names the fruit of this desire
"Isaac," meaning "laughter." She exclaims, "God has brought laughter for me; everyone who hears will laugh with me" (Genesis 21:6).

I need to embrace this story more fully so that my own dismissive
self-mockery can turn into delight. So that I can laugh the kind of
laughter that draws the world into a celebration of the miracles Jesus
continues to work through all of us. —ELIZABETH BERNE DEGEAR

FAITH STEP: *Pray that Jesus opens an opportunity for a genuine, full-bellied,
wholehearted laugh. And then take the opportunity to enjoy! Become aware of
the ways you laugh at your own dreams and desires, and trust that Jesus takes
these same deep desires to heart.*

MONDAY, MARCH 4

But Jesus looked at them and said, "With man this is impossible, but with God all things are possible." Matthew 19:26 (ESV)

IT IS POSSIBLE TO EAT oatmeal with chopsticks.

Knowing the hotel I was staying in didn't provide a complimentary continental breakfast, I'd brought several envelopes of my favorite ancient grains cereal and dried dates. I knew I could heat water in the coffee maker in the room. Imagine my joy when I discovered that the hotel room's coffee setup stocked half-and-half instead of powdered creamer. The cereal, dates, and half-and-half would suffice.

If I'd only had a spoon.

I found a pair of thin bamboo stir sticks for the coffee. Short, flimsy chopstick wannabes. But they worked. I figured out if I cut back on the prescribed amount of hot water, I could make a breakfast cereal thick enough to eat with two short sticks.

Conditions were rarely perfect—okay, never—for Jesus, but oh what He accomplished with what the world would consider not enough! When all He had was water, He turned it into wine. When all He had to offer was five small fish and two small loaves of barley bread, He fed thousands, with food to spare.

He rocked the world with His ability to make something out of nothing, to see impossibilities and turn them into answers.

Jesus, when my faith is small, don't let me forget what You can do with practically nothing. —CYNTHIA RUCHTI

FAITH STEP: *What are the crumbs in your life that need His touch? Empty bank account? Crumbling relationship? A doctor's low-percentage prognosis? Lay it before the One who doesn't even need a crumb to create a feast.*

TUESDAY, MARCH 5

Do nothing out of selfish ambition or vain conceit. Rather, in humility value others above yourselves. Philippians 2:3 (NIV)

MY HUSBAND, DAVID, JUST RETIRED. Now he helps around the house. The inside's always been my territory and the yard his, so we had to adjust. I say that with a smile on my face because Jesus has given me not only a wonderful mate but also a learning opportunity.

For instance, when David "does the kitchen," the dishwasher is loosely filled, with all the cutlery carefully divided into separate compartments. I never waste an inch of space, and I always wipe down the counters.

I've noticed differences in other areas as well. Vacuuming, social interactions, even his relationship with Jesus. In my opinion, he doesn't spend enough time in prayer.

I've always believed my techniques are better. *Why can't he see that? How long before he gives in and does things right?* Days have passed with no change. He keeps approaching tasks in his own style.

Finishing up the dishes yesterday, I noticed an empty space on the top rack and I wedged in one more bowl. *The right way.* I dried my hands and walked past the dining room where my husband sat at the table. His eyes were closed, but he wasn't sleeping. His lips moved in quiet prayer.

That instant, I realized I needed to change my perspective. I scrutinized the kitchen. But it looked fine. It always did. And there was more than one way to do chores. I silently thanked the Lord for the revelation. Because as He teaches us, Jesus is the only way to God, but our personal paths to Christ are as unique as the lives we lead. —HEIDI GAUL

FAITH STEP: *Pray for Jesus's wisdom to help you perform a task in a different way but with acceptable results. Then watch for other jobs or opinions that might need changing up.*

WEDNESDAY, MARCH 6

Simon, son of Jonah, you are blessed! You didn't discover this on your own. It was shown to you by my Father in heaven. So I will call you Peter, which means "a rock." On this rock I will build my church. Matthew 16:17–18 (CEV)

I AM WORKING ON A curriculum for ninth-grade students called Story Boss. The idea is that we all have a story, and there may be parts of that story we haven't chosen, but our story doesn't have to be the boss of us. I'm challenging them to take control of their own narratives as they grow.

One of the lessons asks students, "Who do others say you are?" The answers vary. *Class clown. Brainiac. Band geek.* On and on they go. Then I ask them who they want to be. It's interesting how those answers take more time. Some kids know, but others have no clue. They've never thought about trying to be anything other than the label assigned to them.

If you can get kids to write out a vision for their future, they may begin to believe in it. Jesus did this when He changed Simon's name to Peter. Before this, Peter was certainly no rock. Look at the power of Jesus's name change. Peter went from the person afraid to step out of the boat when Jesus called him to the foundational leader of the first church.

One reason I'm so passionate about Story Boss is that I know Jesus is the true Boss of my story. There have been times I thought my story was over and He showed me a new direction. Times I saw no way out but He made the way. And just like He made the way for Peter, He can make the way for you. —GWEN FORD FAULKENBERRY

FAITH STEP: *If you feel stuck in a certain role in your life, turn the page. Pray for direction and then write down what you want the next chapter to be. Trust Jesus to show you the way.*

THURSDAY, MARCH 7

Whoever does not love does not know God, because God is love. 1 John 4:8 *(NIV)*

WE CALL MY SON, ISAAC, the ambassador of love. Isaac has Down syndrome. While I'm not fond of any stereotypes—including those that paint people with Down as 24/7 happy—our boy undeniably oozes love.

Mind you, he expresses all the emotions any of us do, but when it comes to loving, Isaac is an expert. He can feel, foster, and elicit love with conspicuous awareness, eye-gazing focus, and generosity. Some of you know what I mean.

I've often wondered why this is, Down syndrome mythology aside. No doubt, it helps that our family is joyous and warmly affectionate a lot of the time. Surely Isaac's guileless and admittedly simpler experience of life contributes to his unbridled love. He is not fearless, so fearlessness is not what makes him so open-hearted. And contrary to popular belief, he is not loving with all people or all the time. Still, his love light is brighter than most.

I've heard that some ancient cultures revered children with Down syndrome as special, divine gifts. I am convinced this is true, believing I glimpse the Source of the loving spirit my son possesses. The Word tells us that God is love. As a mom blessed with a child with Down syndrome, I can confidently say that Isaac's love for me and my love for Isaac help me better understand God's boundless love.

Just as God sent Jesus as a tangible expression of His love for us, God sent us Isaac. Like Jesus's love, Isaac's love is generous and deeply personal. I see Jesus in and through Isaac, His earthly ambassador of love. —ISABELLA YOSUICO

FAITH STEP: *Consider some of the challenges you're facing in light of God's love. Though God is never the author of evil, how can you view these challenges as instruments of love rather than of harm?*

Friday, March 8

May God, who gives this patience and encouragement, help you live in complete harmony with each other, as is fitting for followers of Christ Jesus. Romans 15:5 (NLT)

I'VE COLLECTED POTTERY FROM POLAND since my husband and I began doing ministry there in 2008. My collection now contains a variety of mugs, dessert plates, serving bowls and trays, and a tea set. Each piece bears a stamp that verifies authenticity.

Only a few pieces match. Floral patterns adorn some; geometric patterns or polka dots decorate others. Setting the table presents an eclectic look, but I like it. It reminds me of the Body of Christ.

All who follow Christ bear His name, but we differ from one another in appearance, experience, and giftedness. Unfortunately, these differences can cause divisions within the Body. When we allow them to irritate us, we fail to see their collective beauty. That's why Scripture encourages us to work together for harmony.

Striving for harmony within the Body doesn't mean we lose our individuality or deny who God created us to be. It does, however, require that we love and respect believers who differ from us. We learn to work together, being willing to serve one another for Christ's glory rather than going our separate ways when we can't agree. Behaving in such a manner offers a worthy example to those who don't yet know Christ. "Your love for one another will prove to the world that you are my disciples," said Jesus (John 13:35).

Each of Christ's followers is a unique individual. Collectively, we're a beautiful, eclectic bunch. Let's appreciate the diversity, knowing that's the way Jesus likes it. —GRACE FOX

FAITH STEP: *Set your dinner table using dishes that don't match. Enjoy the variety, and thank Jesus for creating His family members uniquely.*

SATURDAY, MARCH 9

The diligent make use of everything they find. Proverbs 12:27 (NLT)

BECAUSE OF MY PASTOR-FATHER'S MEDIOCRE salary, I understood the value of a dollar. Daddy built porch add-ons with lumber scraps and recycled numerous "treasures" from his walks through back alleys. We learned to "use it up, wear it out, make it do, or do without."

That principle followed me through lean years of my own marriage as I tried to stretch our one-income minister's salary. But sometimes I took it to a new level, which occasionally brought conflict. One year, I filled up the trunk of our old Chevrolet with assorted lumber pieces that I had scraped together from a nearby home construction site—with permission, of course. Unfortunately, those scraps ended up in the garbage. I did succeed in furnishing our home with baskets and secondhand décor from garage sales, however.

Then a few years ago, I fell in love with yard art. Pinterest only fueled my creative desire to recycle and extend the life of useful items. I repurposed old chairs into flower containers and added a discarded headboard to a garden bed. I even rescued two doors, numerous patio posts, and bathroom cabinet fronts from our recent home remodel.

Recently, I counted the treasures I'd collected that were still waiting for a makeover. Obviously I needed to find a balance in saving and releasing. That's when Jesus reminded me of a spiritual truth. *Are there too many discards sitting idly in my heart waiting for a final home? Worn-out habits? Useless thoughts? Outdated beliefs?*

Jesus is teaching me additional meaning: "For everything there is a season....A time to keep and a time to throw away" (Ecclesiastes 3:1, 6 NLT). That goes for my yard—and my heart. —REBECCA BARLOW JORDAN

FAITH STEP: *Ask Jesus for wisdom to show you what needs discarding—and what needs keeping in your life.*

SUNDAY, MARCH 10

So why are you now challenging God by burdening the Gentile believers with a yoke that neither we nor our ancestors were able to bear? We believe that we are all saved the same way, by the undeserved grace of the Lord Jesus.
Acts 15:10—11 (NLT)

IN MY PAST WORK WITH a Christian arts ministry, and also with my writing work, I've been blessed to get acquainted with believers of many different denominations. Within each different part of the Body, various rules are engrained into living out faith. Some people don't eat meat during Lent. Some reject watching any television or movies. Some change the altar vestments only while wearing gloves. Rules may be codified by a church, but many are unspoken traditions that have found a firm footing over the years.

I've always tended to be a rule-follower. I enjoy the security of traditions that can be a lovely expression of our devotion to God.

The problem arises when we impose our traditions and preferences onto others—or trust in them instead of our Savior. In the early church, as recorded in Acts 15, some of the Christians were insisting that Gentile converts obey all the ceremonial laws. Even the most rigorous Pharisee wasn't truly able to follow them. Peter's speech reminds us that our regulations cannot save us.

Our rules can encourage choices that prevent unneeded temptations. They may preserve our religious symbolism. We can honor traditions that have been passed down through the generations. But they aren't a way to earn salvation. Jesus has already provided that through His love. —SHARON HINCK

FAITH STEP: *Is there a tradition that has become burdensome for you? Ask Jesus to show you if you're following that rule for the wrong reasons.*

MONDAY, MARCH 11

If you go the wrong way—to the right or to the left—you will hear a voice behind you saying, "This is the right way. You should go this way."
Isaiah 30:21 (NCV)

WHEN I BOUGHT A NEW GPS, the improved and added features impressed me. But I did miss the voice that notified me whenever I missed a turn by repeating, "Recalculating...recalculating..." until it revised the route. At first I found that announcement annoying, but at least it reminded me that the GPS was looking out for me by helping me stay on the right path.

During His earthly ministry, Jesus helped people reevaluate, recalculate, and revise the trajectory of their lives. He called some fishermen to leave their nets, follow Him, and fish for something bigger. He freed a woman charged with adultery, urging her to live a new life. After meeting Jesus, a wealthy tax collector named Zacchaeus did a 180-degree turn: he vowed to give half of his possessions to the poor and reimburse anyone he had cheated fourfold. One conversation with Jesus turned the woman at the well from a shame-filled outcast who avoided others into an energetic evangelist who brought her fellow villagers to the Messiah.

Jesus still offers guidance to those who want to know the best path to take in life. If we're headed in the wrong direction, He may let us know with gentle nudges in our spirits or conviction when we read His Word. So while I love that little box in my car, I have a better GPS, God's Perfect Son, to guide me in this journey of life and let me know when I need to recalculate the route to my ultimate destination. —DIANNE NEAL MATTHEWS

FAITH STEP: *Prayerfully examine the path your life is taking and ask Jesus if you need to make any course corrections.*

Tuesday, March 12

In their hearts humans plan their course, but the LORD establishes their steps.
Proverbs 16:9 (NIV)

I HAVE BEEN WRESTLING WITH the idea of going back to work full-time. With our kids headed to college in the next few years, the time has come. Writing for the past decade has been my dream come true. So taking a step back from writing, in some ways, feels like the death of a dream. But Jesus has been speaking to my heart. First, He has been reminding me that *He is the dream giver.* Writing was His dream for me. Second, He is reminding me that chasing the dream is not the goal. *Chasing Him is.*

A few weeks back, I spoke at a women's retreat about expectations, and one of the Scriptures I touched on was Proverbs 16:9: "In their hearts humans plan their course, but the LORD establishes their steps." I encouraged the women to pray, "God, I don't know what today holds for me. I have some plans, but I would like you to establish my steps." Let's be honest. I was speaking to myself. I needed to pray this prayer.

Two days ago, I opened up *Mornings with Jesus,* and the devotion's Scripture for the day was…Proverbs 16:9. Yesterday, a letter from my mom to my three boys ended with…Proverbs 16:9. Jesus was making a point. When we try to control our destiny, it's never a good outcome. But when we cling to Him, there is a present peace in the midst of uncertainty. When we invite Him into our lives, He brings Himself. Wisdom. Clarity. Love. Mercy. Strength. And that is what we have needed all along. —SUSANNA FOTH AUGHTMON

FAITH STEP: *Write down your expectations for today and pray, "Jesus, here are my plans, but I would like You to order my steps."*

WEDNESDAY, MARCH 13

But now thus says the LORD, he who created you, O Jacob, he who formed you, O Israel: "Fear not, for I have redeemed you; I have called you by name, you are mine." Isaiah 43:1 (ESV)

MY YOUNG ADULT SON, CHRISTIAN, lives two hundred miles away, so I don't see him as often as I would like to. I worried about him for a long time. *Is he okay? Why won't he move closer to me and his brother?* I constantly reminded myself that he was an adult on his own journey with Jesus. It was time to let him grow up. At his age, I was already a wife and mom. Still, it hurt not to have him close and be involved in his everyday life.

While searching a website that sold Scripture art, I found a frameable graphic with one of my favorite verses written in beautiful flowing script against a starry sky background: "I have called you by name, you are mine." My heart leaped. *That's for Christian!* It was also for me—a reminder that Jesus had His eye on my son even when I couldn't be with him. I heard Him telling me, *He's Mine. I'm taking care of him in ways that you can't.* I ordered three prints—one for each of my sons and one for myself—so each of us would have a visual reminder that the Lord of the universe was watching over us, and I would remember Who my sons really belonged to.

Parental concerns don't end when our kids hit adulthood; they just change. Thankfully, even when they are far away from us, we can trust the One Who calls them by name and watches them constantly. We can remember that the same Jesus who carries us through our journeys also carries them through theirs. —JEANETTE HANSCOME

FAITH STEP: *Find a verse that reminds you of someone you love, are concerned about, or are praying for. Create (or order) a frameable copy for them and another for yourself.*

Thursday, March 14

*In my Father's house are many mansions: if it were not so,
I would have told you. I go to prepare a place for you. John 14:2* (KJV)

Two longtime friends from Poland recently visited us. It was their first trip to Canada, and I wanted them to feel welcome. So I invested extra time and energy into preparing for their arrival.

I bought their favorite tea and coffee and stocked up on food that would be a good representation of typical Canadian meals. I also planned an open house so those who'd met this couple while volunteering at our Polish camps could come and greet them.

I vacuumed and dusted the entire house. A vase holding fresh carnations and baby's breath added a special touch to the guest bedroom. So did the copy of *Mornings with Jesus* I placed on the nightstand. Outside, Gene used a leaf blower to clean the driveway.

Preparing for our friends' visit brought me joy. None of the tasks felt burdensome because I value our relationship. I hoped that the results of my labor would help these weary travelers to rest well, find every physical need met, and feel that my home was their temporary haven.

Two thousand years ago, Jesus said He had to return to heaven to prepare a place for us. He knows the dates of our arrivals, and He's making things ready. My imagination can't fathom what this entails, but without a doubt, it will exceed our wildest expectations.

If we, as human beings, invest time and energy into preparing for houseguests because we want them to know how special they are to us, we can only guess what Jesus is doing for us. —Grace Fox

Faith Step: *Dust or vacuum one room in your house. As you do, thank Jesus for preparing a place for you in heaven. Marvel at His measureless love for you, His precious child.*

FRIDAY, MARCH 15

I will praise You, for I am fearfully and wonderfully made; Marvelous are Your works, And that my soul knows very well. Psalm 139:14 (NKJV)

I LOVE TO WATCH POLICE procedurals on TV. The analytical methods the detectives use for catching criminals and the dramatic way the stories unfold keeps me glued to the screen. But what intrigues me the most is the use of forensic evidence, such as DNA samples and other genetic material left behind by the perp. By the end of the show, the criminal is apprehended because of the overwhelming evidence—always the DNA—that doesn't lie.

God, in His infinite wisdom, created us to be uniquely different. Our fingerprints prove that none of us are alike. Similar, yes. Identical matches, no. Even identical twins have a different set of prints.

When Jesus chose the twelve disciples, He knew each man was unique—with his own virtues and flaws. Can you imagine if all of the disciples were like Peter—impulsive and hotheaded? Or like Judas, whose name is often used synonymously with betrayal or treason? I think the Lord was trying to show us that individuality matters. Jesus loved each disciple for who he was because He knew each man would be useful in ministry in his own way. The Lord embraced the disciple Thomas despite his doubt and unbelief (John 20:25). In much the same way, He accepts us just as we are, imperfections and all. Each and every one of us, His children, are different, but we are all special to Him. The proof is in the way Jesus loves us completely. The overwhelming evidence is in the cross.
—CAROL MACKEY

FAITH STEP: *Think about what you consider to be a personal flaw, physical or otherwise. Replace it with this thought: God created you to be uniquely "you." You are made in His image, so don't go changing—you are perfect the way you are!*

SATURDAY, MARCH 16

Therefore, if anyone is in Christ, the new creation has come: The old has gone, the new is here! 2 Corinthians 5:17 (NIV)

WE'VE BEEN PREPPING THE HOUSE for painting. It's challenging work because our home is more than a hundred years old, and the siding has seen better years. The first step was to scrape any loose chips free. I had thought it would be easy. But the farther I moved along the wall, the more bits came off, until more bare wood than painted planks remained. Then we cleaned the siding and applied caulking to the window frames. Soon, the base coat and charming yellow paint will be applied.

All these different steps remind me of the work Jesus has to do on us—and in us—as He draws us closer to His likeness. Over time, the Lord has scraped off a lot of my earthly habits and selfish mind-sets. Every time I think He's done, I find new facets of my personality that need stripping. There's always something to improve on, so He might never be finished with us this side of heaven. But Jesus's blood has washed me clean, and now my sins are white as snow. I'm a new person in Him, ready to apply my "base coat," by strengthening my Bible knowledge and refining my faith.

All my life, Jesus will continue my restoration. Every day, I'll become more beautiful, as I grow to resemble Him in nature and give Him the glory He deserves. Like our newly painted house shining in the sunshine, in heaven I'll glow, transformed in His radiance. —HEIDI GAUL

FAITH STEP: *Which of your personality traits need chipping off so Jesus can shine through? As imperfections come to mind, think of Christlike qualities you can replace them with.*

SUNDAY, MARCH 17

I looked again and could hardly believe my eyes. *Everything above me was new. Everything below me was new.* Everything around me was new *because the heaven and earth that had been passed away . . . . He will wipe away every tear from their eyes. Revelation 21:1, 4 (VOICE)*

THE INCREDIBLE BEAUTY OF GOD'S creation always takes my breath away: the majesty of Colorado's mountains, the magnificence of Alaskan glaciers, and the Eden-like shorelines of Kauai, Hawaii. I cry joyful tears as I watch, amazed at His wonders.

But I've also shed sad tears when I've seen the disasters in our world: earthquakes, fires, floods, and tornadoes—those things that can destroy the earth's beauty. There's something about the intricacies of God's creatures and beautiful creation that takes me to another place and another time and creates a simple longing in my heart for something bigger, something better—and yes, something even more beautiful.

A Bible study that my husband, Larry, and I are doing together on heaven further nourishes that desire. It's easy to confine our view of heaven to angels and golden streets. But the Bible reveals so much more. My earthly enjoyment of God's beauty is really a yearning for our final resting place on the New Heaven *and* the New Earth. There, as Jesus promised, we'll experience a restored Eden forever.

Despite some of the ugliness and even some of the beauty on our temporary earth, I'm choosing to focus upward. The appeal of the New Heaven and the New Earth will far surpass anything we could ever imagine. But the best part of forever is the beautiful face of Jesus. —REBECCA BARLOW JORDAN

FAITH STEP: *Research Bible verses on the New Heaven and the New Earth online or in a commentary, and record your findings. Thank Jesus for giving you a future in eternity.*

MONDAY, MARCH 18

O LORD, you have examined my heart and know everything about me.
Psalm 139:1 (NLT)

I HAVE BEEN COMPLETELY COLOR-BLIND since birth, so I see the world like a black-and-white movie. Attending a class at church about using coloring to deepen my prayer life might seem like an odd choice for me. But when I saw the blurb for Colorful Prayer, I knew I needed to sign up. It sounded like fun, and I had labeled pencils. I appreciated anything that could allow me to weave creativity into my time with Jesus.

"This isn't about artistic ability, and it isn't about the colors," the instructors assured us. "It's about meditating on a Scripture and letting the picture flow from that." Still, when it came time to spend a few moments in prayer with our coloring page, verse, and pencils, I became insecure about being the only one in the room who couldn't see the colors and was afraid I might put two together that didn't match. Then a kind voice whispered, *I don't care if your colors match. I created them all. Choose colors that mean something to you.* The knowledge that Jesus could see what had always been a mystery to me and that He would know exactly why I chose red, purple, ocean blue, and lavender liberated me to create a prayer bursting with the colors of my gratitude to the One who knew and loved me.

"O LORD you...know everything about me," including the fears that so often get in our way, even when we're trying to focus on Him. When we trust Jesus's love for the heart He knows so well, we find the freedom to worship and love Him from a deeper, more honest place. —JEANETTE HANSCOME

FAITH STEP: *Which colors have special meaning for you? Use them to create something that represents Jesus's deep knowledge of you and love for you. Ask Him to free you from the fears that restrict you from trying new things.*

TUESDAY, MARCH 19

All a man's ways seem right to him, but the LORD evaluates the motives.
Proverbs 21:2 (HCSB)

YOU CAN'T SEE ME SQUIRMING, but I am. Without Jesus, this verse—and many others—would have me running for shelter from the divine lightning bolt that would otherwise surely come.

I do a lot of good things. And I do a lot of good things in Jesus's name. When I lay my head down at night, I can recount quite a few deeds I think I've done right that day, along with a few not-so-nice ones.

Cooking a meal for a sick friend, mentoring at-risk students, saying yes to sacrificial quality time with my kids. Surely a lot of the good I do comes from Jesus living through me.

Jesus is a powerful flashlight, and I am blessed to see a deeper truth to my good deeds: even the good I do is often self-serving. Sure, I do want to help my ailing buddy, but it makes me feel great to see her tearful appreciation. Yes, I revel in encouraging a troubled child, but I don't mind the reputational capital I'm earning either.

And while I enjoy spending time playing with my kids, I am sometimes motivated by guilt rather than love. My motives are often mixed.

Sometimes I recognize how delusional I am! The work, whatever it is, isn't about me; it's about Him. Or at least it should be. Thank God that Jesus is the Light and the Truth. Thankfully, Jesus is also the Savior, who loved me enough to die for me, a sinner still.
—ISABELLA YOSUICO

FAITH STEP: *When in doubt, self-check your motives: Are they motivated by love for God or others? Do they glorify God? Shake off any shame about your mixed motives and thank Jesus for the loving grace that saves you and enables you to do good, even with mixed motives.*

WEDNESDAY, MARCH 20

The Spirit of the LORD is upon Me, Because He has anointed Me to preach the gospel to the poor; He has sent Me to heal the brokenhearted.
Luke 4:18 (NKJV)

WHEN I LOST MY JOB, the timing couldn't have been worse. I was in the middle of a bitter and costly divorce. And without that salary, I wasn't sure how to support my newly single self. *Lord, what's going on?* I wondered.

Months passed, and I decided to hire a résumé writer, beefed up my LinkedIn page, and started to apply for jobs. But nothing happened. It had been over a decade since I had even refreshed my résumé. Now I was like a fish out of water. I was over fifty, unemployed, and getting divorced—what a trifecta. I became frustrated and angry. Angry at my employer for letting me go. Angry at my soon-to-be ex for our divorce. Angry at the world. I sank into a depression. Once I got out of my funk, I tapped into my network and got a few freelance gigs, which made me feel better. When you've been hurt, it's easy to become bitter and resentful. But I learned that while it's okay to be angry, it's not okay to stay angry.

Jesus knows our fragile condition, and He is always patient through the healing process. He wants us to be emotionally whole. Throughout the Gospels, Jesus was as concerned about those who were emotionally distraught as He was about the physically wounded. "He heals the brokenhearted and binds up their wounds" (Psalm 147:3). God has a perfect plan for our lives, and He wants our full participation. We can do so much more for others (and for God!) once we let go of the pain and embrace the blessing of forgiveness. —CAROL MACKEY

FAITH STEP: *If you're enduring a season of brokenness, pray this prayer: Lord, please heal the broken places in my heart. Some things I have never spoken, but You know what they are. Help me release the pain so I can be a better witness for You.*

THURSDAY, MARCH 21

The Spirit of the Lord GOD is upon me; because the LORD hath anointed me . . . to comfort all that mourn . . . to give unto them beauty for ashes.
Isaiah 61:1–3 (KJV)

THE OTHER DAY, MY FRIEND Stephanie posted something on Instagram that said, "In Japan, broken objects are often repaired with gold. The flaw is seen as a unique piece of the object's history, which adds to its beauty. Consider this." Stephanie is full of these little nuggets of wisdom and she admonishes us to consider them. So I did.

With a little research, I found that the concept is called "kintsugi." It's a process by which artists take cracked pottery and pour gold into the cracked places. What comes out is this new piece of pottery that has gold veining, kind of like marble. The gold highlights where the broken places were. It's beautiful—often more beautiful than the original piece of pottery was before the breaking.

I've lived kintsugi, and I bet you have too. We tend to focus on how bad it feels to be broken, but in Jesus, that's no ending place. It's a new beginning. Jesus's hands are the hands of an artist. He doesn't just toss us out like I would a broken bowl or cup. He sees opportunity. The potential for beauty. Jesus pours out His love and grace and truth into the broken places—our pain, our mistakes, our fears, our failures—and fills us up with Him until we are whole.
—GWEN FORD FAULKENBERRY

FAITH STEP: *Google images of kintsugi pottery. Keep those images in your mind as a picture of what your life looks like in Jesus.*

FRIDAY, MARCH 22

Walk in the light, as he is in the light. 1 John 1:7 (ESV)

MANY OF THE ROOMS IN our home are dark, even on sunny days. After the sun has risen over the trees, the house itself blocks sun from flooding those rooms. Others are shaded by towering pines that cool the home, keeping sun rays from penetrating.

I love light. If I had my way, I'd choose windows for walls. We're told, after all, to walk in the light, as Jesus is in the light (1 John 1:7).

In other passages of Scripture, we're told that those who follow after evil prefer darkness, falsely assuming it hides their deeds (John 3:19).

But I could live in a home where every room is flooded with light and still live in internal darkness. The light in my soul is more important than what pours into the rooms of my home.

Jesus is the light of the world—the internal world—as we're told in John 8:12: "Again Jesus spoke to them, saying, 'I am the light of the world. Whoever follows me will not walk in darkness, but will have the light of life.'"

How much time do I spend in gratitude for the light in my soul (because of Jesus) compared to the amount of time I spend noticing how dark the corners are that remain within me rather than rejoicing at the light Christ is bringing day by day? Time to change some attitude lightbulbs. —CYNTHIA RUCHTI

FAITH STEP: *Leave one small lamp or electric candle burning when you're home today, even if it seems unnecessary, as a reminder to thank Jesus for the gift of His light that floods your soul.*

SATURDAY, MARCH 23

Do not worry about anything, but in everything by prayer and supplication with thanksgiving let your requests be made known to God.
Philippians 4:6 (NRSV)

THIS MORNING, THERE WAS A story in the paper about a long-lost relative of mine. She is the widow of my grandfather's favorite cousin. Her unusual last name—also my mother's maiden name—is what caught my eye, but the story about her was even more of a surprise. A few days shy of her ninety-ninth birthday, she was marrying a ninety-four-year-old man she met at the gym! This couple has been an inspiration to all who know them—and, probably, to all who read about them in the paper. When asked what the secret was to their energetic happiness, she said, "We live worry-free lives; we do not let anything we cannot control bother us in the least."

I aspire to share something beyond a family name with this woman. I hope to share her life philosophy. My mornings with Jesus often remind me that I need not get bogged down by the cares of the world. But, truth be told, by midafternoon, I am often caught up in the stress of my own life and bombarded by an endless stream of breaking news that makes me worried sick about our world. The thing is, we can't attribute this couple's attitude to a stick-your-head-in-the-sand approach to life. My long-lost cousin was actually mayor of her town when she was in her seventies and ran for state senate in her eighties! Apparently, she doesn't worry about all the things she can't do anything about, while also fully embracing all the ways she can make a difference. This is a balance I ask Jesus to help me find. —ELIZABETH BERNE DEGEAR

FAITH STEP: *Recognize that worries wear us down. Ask Jesus to help you find balance between serenity and productivity.*

SUNDAY, MARCH 24

A certain moneylender had two debtors. One owed five hundred denarii, and the other fifty. When they could not pay, he cancelled the debt of both. Now which of them will love him more? Luke 7:41–42 (ESV)

I COME FROM A LITURGICAL church background, and every Sunday the rhythms of worship include a time for confession of sins. One week, my heart resisted. "Why do I have to take time to focus on the thoughts, words, and deeds that hurt You and others?" I asked Jesus silently. "After all, I know You forgive me, and thinking about all the ways I missed the target this week is just depressing."

He gently reminded me of this story in Luke. He wants to deepen my understanding of His love. This understanding grows from appreciating His grace and forgiveness. My appreciation increases when I fully see how big the debt is that He has forgiven.

It would be easy to gloss over the time I complained, the way I gossiped, and the selfish choices I made throughout the week. A time of confession challenges me to confront my sins instead of hiding them or brushing them off. Taking time to reflect and confess isn't an exercise in feeling bad. It's a valuable chance to remember how much I need Jesus. As I realize anew the hugeness of the debt He has canceled, my heart swells with a deeper love for Him.

Sometimes I use the Ten Commandments as a tool, thinking through ways I put other things before Christ. Other times, I let the Holy Spirit bring memories to light from the past days. Tears often fill my eyes, but they give way to tears of joy as I hear the familiar words from my Savior: "Your sins are forgiven." —SHARON HINCK

FAITH STEP: *Spend time in confession today. Thank Jesus for the reminder of your need for Him and His great and complete love for you.*

MONDAY, MARCH 25

Jesus answered, "Everyone who drinks this water will be thirsty again,
but whoever drinks the water I give them will never thirst. Indeed, the water
I give them will become in them a spring of water welling up to eternal life."
John 4:13–14 (NIV)

I LIVE IN THE NORTHWEST, near the Cascade Range. Last week, I visited Multnomah Falls in the Columbia River Gorge. The waterfall there is magnificent—three and a half times as tall as Niagara Falls. The water races over a towering cliff to pound the rocks below. It reminded me of Jesus's vast power. When the torrent settles into quiet pools and a soft mist tickles my nose, I see and feel Jesus's gentle touch. Feeling His presence in nature delights my spirit.

But it's the source of waterfalls, especially when there's no snowpack nearby, that fascinates and puzzles me. *Where and how does all that water originate to create such a massive flow?* I hike to the top of various falls and follow creeks or riverbanks as far as I can, searching for answers. Most of the time, I'm forced to turn back when I'm confronted by overgrowth. But in some cases, I'm blessed with a clear path all the way to a river's starting point—a spring.

Springs don't flash with drama like waterfalls do. They rarely gush and spurt with the force of a geyser. They don't amaze onlookers or draw a lot of attention. But they're just as awesome and mysterious. From quiet, hidden places, water bubbles forth, lots of it, until a stream or river grows from the flow. I want to reflect those headwaters—the rivers of living water that are now a part of me. I'd like faith to flow through me like a mighty current, strong enough for others to feel the rush of Jesus's power and tenderness when we meet. —HEIDI GAUL

FAITH STEP: *Travel to a waterfall. Think about the powerful spring that lives within you and new ways to share its flow.*

Tuesday, March 26

Then Samuel said, "Is the Lord as delighted with burnt offerings and sacrifices as he would be with your obedience? To follow instructions is better than to sacrifice. To obey is better than sacrificing the fat of rams." 1 Samuel 15:22 (GW)

I ONCE VISITED A CLASSROOM where the students thought of the teacher more as a buddy than an authority figure. They liked his personality and enjoyed being around him but saw no reason to obey his instructions; this attitude led to an unproductive and chaotic environment. If we're not careful, we can slip into that mindset toward Jesus. Yes, He is our closest friend, but the Bible makes it clear that He is also our Lord and Master, to be revered and obeyed.

In the Old Testament, God pointed out the hypocrisy of performing the rituals without an obedient spirit. What was intended as a picture of His holiness often dissolved into empty, meaningless rituals. Jesus later highlighted the same problem when He asked, "So why do you call me 'Lord' when you won't obey me?" (Luke 6:46 TLB).

Our church attendance, ministry service, Bible studies, and charitable giving all lapse into meaningless actions if we don't have an obedient spirit. It doesn't matter how generous we are with our time and money if we don't obey Jesus and His Word. That obedience includes parts that seem too hard, like forgiving others even when they don't deserve it. And trusting Him so much that we patiently wait on Him to act even when we feel like panicking or taking matters into our hands.

Sometimes we act like *obey* is a four-letter word to be avoided. But Jesus equated it with another four-letter word: "If you *love* me, you will obey my commands" (John 14:15 NCV). —DIANNE NEAL MATTHEWS

FAITH STEP: *Ask Jesus to reveal any area of your life where you are not fully obeying Him. Do you love Him enough to make any needed changes?*

WEDNESDAY, MARCH 27

Don't worry about anything; instead, pray about everything. Tell God what you need, and thank him for all he has done. Then you will experience God's peace, which exceeds anything we can understand. His peace will guard your hearts and minds as you live in Christ Jesus. Philippians 4:6–7 (NLT)

AS A SINGLE MOM, I shoulder most of the financial burden when it comes to raising my teenage son, Nathan. So after sending the deposit for his band trip, I started to feel guilty over not being able to afford braces for him without going into debt. It sent my heart reeling. *Maybe I should have said no to the trip.* But trips were part of the fun of band, and I wanted my fifteen-year-old, who'd never been outside the two states we'd lived in, to experience air travel and a competition in Hawaii. I prayed. *Jesus, how am I going to afford college if I can't keep up with the costs of high school? What does it say if I pay for a band trip but am afraid to go into debt for braces? If Nathan has self-esteem issues because of his teeth, it'll be my fault!*

Don't worry.... I didn't know whether the command I was remembering was from Matthew or Philippians, only that my fears were crippling. But just as I'd learned to trust Jesus to provide for my necessities, I needed to trust Him to help me provide for my teenage son.

Life is expensive no matter how frugal we are. Sometimes all we can do is our best. "Don't worry" takes on new meaning when we trust Jesus for whatever is overwhelming us. That is when we get to experience the release of letting Him handle it and the joy of seeing what He'll do. —JEANETTE HANSCOME

FAITH STEP: *Which expense are you most worried about? Write your concern in a letter to Jesus. Ask Him to help you trust Him. Keep the letter as a record of how He works.*

THURSDAY, MARCH 28

The LORD hears his people when they call to him for help.
He rescues them from all their troubles. Psalm 34:17 (NLT)

RAINDROPS PELTED MY CAR WINDSHIELD recently as I headed out of the dentist's parking lot to finish my errands. *Not a good day to shop for groceries!* Ah well, my trusty umbrella rested beside me.

But just as I pulled onto the highway, the skies exploded with rain. I made a split-second decision to go for it and not return home, hoping the deluge would let up. Bad decision. As I turned onto the main street, water almost flooded the sides, sloshing near the curb. I could barely see the street. I slowed down, but pickup trucks raced by me, drenching my windshield and blinding my view. Entering the grocery store parking lot, I inched my way through a parade of other cars.

I've got to get home! Panic rose as the rain descended harder. I circled the parking lot, then exited onto the interstate service road. Through the blurred windshield, I could see nothing but a thin veil of light. I didn't know what to do. There was no place to turn around or pull over.

Remembering the Bible promise I had just read earlier that morning in Psalm 34:17, I began crying out one word: *Jesus! Jesus! Jesus!* The more it poured, the louder I cried. My yells continued as I inched through the blinding rain, focusing only on the faint red taillights of a car that suddenly appeared in front of me.

The rain never stopped. About twenty minutes later, I arrived home and walked into the arms of my husband. I realized then what could have happened. But Jesus had heard my cries, delivered me safely out of my troubles, and filled me with peace—and a huge amount of gratitude. —REBECCA BARLOW JORDAN

FAITH STEP: *Think about the times when Jesus heard your cries to Him. Offer a prayer of gratitude for His timely rescues in the midst of difficult circumstances.*

FRIDAY, MARCH 29

Even before he made the world, God loved us and chose us in Christ to be holy and without fault in his eyes. God decided in advance to adopt us into his own family by bringing us to himself through Jesus Christ. This is what he wanted to do, and it gave him great pleasure. Ephesians 1:4—5 (NLT)

A FAMILY IN MY COMMUNITY has adopted more than twenty children. All of them have physical challenges. One girl was born without arms. Another is blind. Two have required numerous plastic surgeries after suffering burns. Several have club feet.

They gave me a tour of their home when I interviewed the family for a magazine article. Every room was designed to create an environment in which the kids could thrive. One room held a hospital bed with an IV pole on which hung a teeny wind chime. A breeze wafted through the open window beside the bed and set the chimes ringing.

"My daughter who's visually impaired sleeps here. She can't see, but she can hear and smell," said the mother. Then she told me about planting a flowering bush outside, beneath the window, so the breeze could carry its perfumed scent into the bedroom.

"And this," she said as we approached a wall featuring a framed picture of each child, "this is our VIP photo gallery. The family you see here isn't perfect, but being part of it brings me great pleasure."

I drove home marveling at this couple's compassion in action and the way in which their family models the family of God—a unique blend of individuals with their own unique challenges, loved and adopted into His family thanks to Jesus's selfless love, and bringing great pleasure to Him. —GRACE FOX

FAITH STEP: *Write a note of thanks to Jesus for making your spiritual adoption into God's family possible.*

SATURDAY, MARCH 30

His divine power has granted to us all things that pertain to life and godliness, through the knowledge of him who called us to his own glory and excellence, by which he has granted to us his precious and very great promises, so that through them you may become partakers of the divine nature, having escaped from the corruption that is in the world because of sinful desire. 2 Peter 1:3–4 (ESV)

"THE CLOCK WILL START WHEN I leave the room. You'll have one hour to escape," the game guide told us. I looked around at our group and the elaborate set and props surrounding us, my heart beating fast.

Our youngest daughter worked at this new facility where families, friends, and corporate groups pitted their wits against puzzles and clues to find their way out. In order to succeed, we had to solve riddles and figure out codes that would lead us from room to room. My head spun from all the contraptions and secrets that various group members found. We had loads of fun and, eventually, we managed to escape.

Although that game was entertaining, when I consider the game of life, I'm glad that our escape from sin and death isn't as complicated. Sometimes we think we have to solve complex riddles or search for our Savior. Throughout the generations, various people have designed harsh rules and plans to try to win God's favor, as if we have to find our own way out of sin and its consequences. But Jesus invites us to be partakers in His nature, and that makes our escape a simple and straightforward gift from His hand.

When I feel as if following Jesus is too complicated and difficult, it's usually because I've tried to walk in my own power instead of inviting His life and godliness to fill my heart. Instead, I'm going to thank Him for granting me all that I need. —SHARON HINCK

FAITH STEP: *Unlock a simple lock as a reminder that Jesus has allowed us to escape the world's corruption.*

SUNDAY, MARCH 31

Watch and pray, lest you enter into temptation. The spirit indeed is willing, but the flesh is weak. Mark 14:38 (NKJV)

HOW MANY TIMES HAVE YOU eaten a sweet treat while on a diet? Or bought an expensive dress because it was "calling your name"? Or told "a little white lie"? I know I have. Temptations can be hard to resist. Truth is, as long as we are living, we will be tempted. And if we're not careful, we can fall into temptation.

In Mark 14:32–40, Jesus prays fervently in the garden of Gethsemane. It was time for Him to go to the cross to fulfill His destiny. He needed His disciples to pray now more than ever, but they were napping. The temptation of sleep won them over, much to Jesus's dismay.

Prayer can be a tool against temptation. Jesus warned Peter specifically about the pitfalls of not praying and falling into temptation (v. 37). Just as Jesus had prophesied, Peter denied Him three times. He gave in to temptation. He lied. Of course he was devastated for falling prey to the devil's bait, and he "wept bitterly" (Matthew 26:75).

Like Peter, we can be blindsided by Satan's temptations. And many times we aren't prepared. Eve wasn't in the garden. David wasn't with Bathsheba. And certainly Judas wasn't. All these Bible characters listened to the wrong voice at a most crucial time. The only sure defense we have is prayer. We should pray without ceasing (1 Thessalonians 5:17) and keep God's Word in our hearts and minds. Jesus was tempted too (Matthew 4:1) and resisted the devil by quoting Scripture. God has prepared a way for us to ward off temptation. It's up to us to take it! —CAROL MACKEY

FAITH STEP: *Next time you're tempted, read or recite Mark 14:38. And remember that Jesus was tempted too—and He never gave in! We have the power to "just say no" too (1 Corinthians 10:13).*

MONDAY, APRIL 1

Now to Him who is able to do above and beyond all that we ask or think according to the power that works in us. Ephesians 3:20 (HCSB)

MY SURROGATE FATHER FIGURE DIED recently, and our family traveled to his memorial in New Jersey. His wife bought several large forsythia for all the children to plant in his name. Since I live in Florida, she gave me the money to buy and plant some kind of memorial at home.

I live in a condo, and our landscaping is managed by the homeowner association (HOA), but I had an inspiration—an answer to prayer. I called our quaint town hall to ask if I could donate a plant for a public space. They didn't have a tree-dedication program in place, but they were receptive to my proposal. After checking with their team, they suggested a showy tropical shrub. The price well exceeded our budget, but I didn't want to be cheap. I asked if they had another option within my budget.

My contact soon wrote that their horticulturist was inspired to research a beautiful, flowering native tree within my budget. It would be the only one of its kind in our town's beautiful new waterfront park, planted in a small, waterside meditation garden. The plant they'd originally proposed was nearby, and looked rather mundane compared to the unique tree's stature and location.

To top it off, the city offered to install a plaque at the spot, which meant the tree would inaugurate a new tree-dedication program, inspired by my father figure. Wow!

I was moved to tears by how Jesus had once again exceeded my expectations —ISABELLA YOSUICO

FAITH STEP: *Are you exceeding your budget and limiting God by your own fixed idea about what's best? Have faith in what you feel He is leading you to do.*

TUESDAY, APRIL 2

Looking unto Jesus the author and finisher of our faith. Hebrews 12:2 *(KJV)*

MY DAUGHTER GRACE IS SEVENTEEN. She just started her junior year of high school. Somewhere in the middle of her sophomore year, about the time mail from colleges started rolling in, I had a bit of a panic attack. What will I do when she leaves the nest? How will she survive? Have I taught her everything she needs to know? Given her everything she needs? What about laundry? Parallel parking? Budgeting money? Creating healthy boundaries in relationships? What about challenges to her faith? Have I been all she needs? Has she seen enough Jesus in me?

I've spent the months since then taking deep breaths, praying a lot, and exercising to reduce my level of stress. I've also meditated on the above verse.

Jesus has had to remind me that He was there when Grace was born, and He'll be there when she leaves the nest. He's been there all along for us both, guiding and nurturing, shaping and molding, helping us grow as mother and daughter. He's not finished with us yet.

If I take my eyes off Him, anxiety creeps in. My fears, my not-enough-ness, my worry about her well-being can siphon the joy out of the time she remains under my roof. But as long as I look to Him, I can rest in His sufficient grace. It was enough to get her here and enough to bring us this far. He'll be enough to lead us on.
—GWEN FORD FAULKENBERRY

FAITH STEP: *Make a timeline of your life starting with the moment you became a Christian. List the significant events Jesus has brought you through. Now draw an arrow at the end that points into the future. Write the name Jesus in the space where the arrow points to help you visualize Him as the author and finisher of your faith.*

Wednesday, April 3

You will open the eyes of the blind. You will free the captives from prison, releasing those who sit in dark dungeons. Isaiah 42:7 *(NLT)*

I STARED OUT THE WINDOW as my friend drove me home from cataract surgery, amazed at how easily I read words and numbers on signs that had looked blurry just hours earlier. Later, I gazed out my kitchen window, shocked at how sharp and clear the outlines of the houses across the field looked. When my husband came home, I was mesmerized by the decorative stitching on his belt, which I didn't remember noticing before.

Old Testament prophets predicted that when the Messiah came, He would open the eyes of the blind. Jesus did far more than give physical sight to people who had been born blind or had lost their eyesight. He helped people see how to find joy, meaning, and purpose through living in personal relationship with their Creator. He opened their eyes to the transforming power of sacrificial love. Today, Jesus still wants to give us sight, to help us see truths in the Word, to understand the needs of those around us, or to see the way to heal a broken relationship.

Before I read my Bible, I often pray, "Open my eyes to what you want to show me." And I'm amazed when I see new things I hadn't noticed before or when I understand a verse more clearly. Now I'm working to develop the habit of praying for my eyes to be opened at other times: before a dreaded conversation or interaction, as I wrestle with a difficult decision, or just to begin a new day. While I consider myself an observant person, I know that Jesus can open my eyes to see things I have no idea I'm missing. —DIANNE NEAL MATTHEWS

FAITH STEP: *What is it that you need to see for the first time or understand more clearly? Talk to Jesus about it, and ask Him to open your eyes.*

THURSDAY, APRIL 4

But now even more the report about him went abroad, and great crowds gathered to hear him and to be healed of their infirmities. But he would withdraw to desolate places and pray. Luke 5:15–16 (ESV)

"THERE'S NOT ENOUGH OF ME to go around," I told my husband. A friend's father had died, and I wanted to make her a meal. I hadn't talked to my grown kids in several days and wanted to check in with them. Another friend was facing tough medical issues, and I wanted to visit with her. In fact, everyone I knew was in a place of need. My longing to help others soon transformed into worry, panic, and stress.

Jesus must have felt similar pressure. People clamored for His help, and His compassionate heart never wanted to turn anyone away. He spent long days teaching, healing, comforting, and feeding those who came to Him. Yet when the needs arrived in a never-ending flood, He didn't push harder, longer, or faster. He didn't complain or draw attention to how exhausted and burdened He felt. Instead, He withdrew to pray.

When I'm feeling overwhelmed, I can remember Jesus's example. I can step back to a place of quiet and pray. As I do that, He equips and strengthens me and brings new wisdom, showing me how to prioritize my efforts. He reminds me that the Body has many members, and together we can do His will. Most important, He deepens my reliance on Him. Of course there is not enough of me to help in every way I'd like. I'm not the Savior; He is.

When we fret as if the burden of every human need is on our shoulders, let's withdraw to a quiet place with our Lord. We don't have to be enough. Jesus already is. —SHARON HINCK

FAITH STEP: *Today, withdraw to a quiet place and talk to Jesus about the needs of your family and friends.*

Friday, April 5

For assuredly, I say to you, whoever says to this mountain, "Be removed and be cast into the sea," and does not doubt in his heart, but believes that those things he says will be done, he will have whatever he says. Mark 11:23 (NKJV)

I ADMIRE THE GARDEN CULTURE in the suburban area in which I live. Life is blossoming all around. That's probably a reason why I love the theme of nature Jesus uses in the New Testament. He references nature and agriculture many times in His parables and messages to us—mountains, trees, vines, branches, fruit, soil, crops, seeds, and so on. When I first came to Christ, I took these verses at face value. Some were pretty straightforward, like planting seed in good soil (Mark 4:8) and the fact that He is the True Vine as we are the branches (John 15:5). Those make sense. But there are others that are harder to understand.

For some reason, Mark 11:23 was a stumbling block. I took several Bible study classes later and came to some clarity. I had to come to understand that Jesus used the word *mountain* as an example of all the things that seemed too big to handle in our lives, things that often have rough terrain and are steep—not easy to climb or navigate. The really scary stuff. He doesn't want us to be scared. He wants us to stand boldly in faith and tell our "mountains" to be removed from our lives and cast them into the sea, knowing they are gone forever. That can happen if we have faith that He can do it. I can now say boldly, "I have mountain-moving faith, and I thank you, Lord, that this mountain is removed and cast into the sea!" —CAROL MACKEY

FAITH STEP: *Which mountains in your life do you want the Lord to move? Write them down and have faith that He will remove them. When He answers your prayer, write that down too.*

SATURDAY, APRIL 6

But Jesus said, "Foxes have dens and birds have nests, but I, the Messiah, have no home of my own—no place to lay my head." Matthew 8:20 (TLB)

I'VE BEEN NOTING FOR SALE signs popping up in front yards of houses between ours and those in town. *Someday?*

What home would offer the eclectic blend of must-haves for my husband Bill and me? Hunting land for him, a great view for me, a machine shed for him, a roomy dining room for me, a place for a large television for him, places for conversation groupings for me....

As we pray about our casual house search, we're reminded that we aren't on the hunt for a move from homelessness to having a roof over our heads. We're not—as so many across the world are—longing for a discarded piece of corrugated metal to replace the cardboard for our roof. We're not growing weary of a dirt floor, hoping for something more solid. Gratitude swells at how much we have been given.

Jesus—the fulfillment of God's promises to us—had no home of His own, because of His devotion to the task ahead of Him. When others hinted at wanting to follow Him, Jesus said, "Are you ready to rough it? We're not staying in the best inns, you know" (Matthew 8:20 MSG).

Jesus didn't have time to worry about mowing His lawn or fixing clogged eave troughs or repainting the mailbox. He couldn't expend His energy on landscaping or replacing worn carpeting. He had a single-minded goal from which He could not be distracted—telling the truth about His Father's love and inviting us to embrace that Good News.

What discomforts am I willing to endure to walk that same path?
—CYNTHIA RUCHTI

FAITH STEP: *Tonight, when you nestle your head into your pillow—whether it's perfect for you or not—thank Jesus for all He was willing to give up on your behalf.*

SUNDAY, APRIL 7

And I will ask the Father, and he will give you another Advocate,
who will never leave you. He is the Holy Spirit, who leads into all truth.
John 14:16–17 (NLT)

YEARS AGO, MY HUSBAND AND I completed a three-week Bible study tour of the Holy Land, a generous gift from a church member. From early morning until late at night, a Messianic Jewish scholar drove us through the land of Israel in a VW bus that didn't have air-conditioning. We heard the stories behind every biblical patriarch and every ruin from Jewish history. We crossed the Sea of Galilee where Jesus calmed a raging storm and walked on water. We hiked through lush mountain paths, floated in the Dead Sea, and sang lively Jewish music.

We especially enjoyed our tour of Jerusalem. We walked the streets where Jesus walked, viewed the Temple remains where He taught and worshipped, and gathered in the garden where He prayed and sweat drops of blood the night He was betrayed. We gaped at Golgotha, the site of Jesus's crucifixion, and bowed our heads when we walked into a tomb similar to the one where Jesus had been buried. Every place we set our feet felt hallowed. Jesus's presence and a holy hush surrounded us throughout the tour.

Ever since that trip, I've longed to go back. However, I realize that even if I never return, I'll find Jesus's presence wherever I am. Not only did Jesus walk before me, preparing the way, He also gave me His Spirit as a child when I asked Jesus into my heart. Since that moment, just as the disciples experienced with Jesus, His presence has lived in me.

Through time with Him, Jesus is teaching me that every place is a holy place when He lives within us and walks beside us.
—REBECCA BARLOW JORDAN

FAITH STEP: *Where do you feel Jesus's presence the most? Wherever you go today, thank Jesus that He is walking with you.*

MONDAY, APRIL 8

For this very reason, Christ died and returned to life so that he might be the Lord of both the dead and the living. Romans 14:9 (NIV)

I SAT AT THE TABLE, spooning jelly beans into bright-colored plastic eggs and filling Easter baskets with chocolate bunnies. My gaze settled on the carton of dyed eggs. How difficult would today's hunt be? It all depended on who did the hiding.

I hide things well. Many of my secrets I keep locked away from others. Some I try—unsuccessfully—to keep hidden from myself. But I can't conceal anything from Jesus.

At the crucifixion, Jesus absorbed every sin ever committed. To save the thieves hanging beside Him, Jesus took on their sins. For Judas, He bore the guilt of His own betrayer. For Martha, Mary's sister, He carried her critical nature. Murderer, drunk, blackmailer—the list is endless. The magnitude of His sacrifice overwhelms me. For One who'd never sinned, the burden must have been horrendous. But it hasn't diminished the pile of sins I've heaped at the base of the cross.

He's borne the weight of all my sins as I stumble through life. He asks only that I repent and make Him my Lord. That's the beauty of the resurrection. He uncovers the darkness we try to hide and exposes it to light. And through His blood we can throw off all our sins and become like Him.

What sin has Jesus helped you overcome? You can rest knowing He's risen far above the hate, hurts, and pain we've inflicted on one another—and on Him. He plays only one role now, Lord of lords and King of kings. He is risen! —HEIDI GAUL

FAITH STEP: *Make a list of the sin-titles that you've worn in life. Tear it up and throw it away. On a clean sheet of paper, write forgiven. Celebrate Easter as a child of the King.*

TUESDAY, APRIL 9

The next day he saw Jesus coming toward him, and said, "Behold, the Lamb of God, who takes away the sin of the world!" John 1:29 (ESV)

WHEN I SERVED AS A leader for the international youth ministry Awana years ago, I noticed that some of my little Sparkies (kindergarteners through second graders) had a lot of trouble reciting their verses and simply mouthed the words in a monotone. I encouraged them to memorize Scriptures in phrases and to recite them with expression. Later, when they learned John 1:29, some of them spoke it in an excited voice, while others recited it with a firm authority. But they all put the emphasis on the word *behold*.

This verse profoundly affects me. I visualize John the Baptist looking up to see Jesus approaching. In that moment, he's overcome by the enormity of what the Messiah's presence on earth means. He utters this sentence that sums up the core message of the Bible.

Sometimes I enjoy a deep, theological discussion, but I find comfort in the simplicity of verses like John 1:29. It reminds me that as long as I grasp this basic concept, I have all I need to share Christ with others. People unfamiliar with the Bible might not know about the Passover lambs or the daily sacrifices at the Temple. They may not yet fully understand why Jesus had to die. But I can still point them to Jesus.

Every day, we have people watching our behavior and listening to what we say. If we stay faithful to the Lamb, they may want to know more about the One Who takes away their sins. Who knows how many souls will come into the kingdom when we live each day in a way that says, "Behold Jesus!" —DIANNE NEAL MATTHEWS

FAITH STEP: *Think of someone you know who needs to meet Jesus. Decide how you will show Him to that person.*

WEDNESDAY, APRIL 10

Simon, Simon, Satan has asked to sift each of you like wheat. But I have pleaded in prayer for you, Simon, that your faith should not fail.
Luke 22:31–32 (NLT)

I PARTICIPATE IN A WEEKLY online Bible study. At the end of each session, our leader assigns prayer partners. It's our responsibility to connect, share our prayer requests, and then be faithful to intercede on each other's behalf for the next seven days.

Sometimes prayer partners connect only once, at the beginning of the new week. Depending on circumstances, we might connect several times to exchange texts containing brief updates and additional requests. Regardless of how often we touch base, knowing that someone else is praying for me every day fills me with strength and courage. I know I'm not traveling the road alone.

Several years ago, my pastor encouraged our congregation to tell people when we're praying for them rather than assuming they know. If they're grieving or feeling alone, hurt, confused, or desperate, this awareness might breathe hope and life into their situation. It could provide them with the ability to persevere when they're tempted to give up.

Jesus prayed for His twelve disciples in private (John 17), but He took it a step further and told them that He did so. He wanted them to know they weren't fighting their battles alone. He knew the strength His reassurance would infuse into their weary hearts.

It only takes a moment to encourage others in the same way. Our reassurance of prayer support could make all the difference in the world. —GRACE FOX

FAITH STEP: *Send an email or a card to a missionary, a sick loved one, or a lonely senior and tell them of your prayer support. Your words might be a game changer.*

THURSDAY, APRIL 11

The Pharisee stood by himself and prayed this prayer: "I thank you, God, that I am not like other people—cheaters, sinners, adulterers. I'm certainly not like that tax collector!" Luke 18:11 (NLT)

WE CHRISTIANS DO THE GOSPEL an awful disservice. We look down our noses at a skeptic's sin or frown on a sister's misstep, so easily forgetting the grace we receive every day.

I was recently not pleased with my husband. My displeasure was fueled in part by epic stress and my own self-centeredness. Troubled and desperate, I awkwardly confessed my disillusionment to an older widow from my faith circle. I watched her eyebrows rise and her lips purse in judgment. With a few words, she leveled me with shame, citing chapter and verse to support her stance.

It didn't make me love my husband more, but I did resolve never to confide in her again.

As I processed the exchange, I recognized that I've done the same thing to others, unbelievers and believers alike.

There is a better way. The way of compassion modeled by Jesus on the cross.

The further I've come in my Christian journey, the more clearly I see the distance left to travel. I will never be perfect here, but I can enjoy the perfection of God's unconditional love and acceptance in my imperfect state.

This is good news for everyone. —ISABELLA YOSUICO

FAITH STEP: *Take a walk, keeping your own Christian journey in mind. Find a nice stone along the way to carry in your pocket as a reminder of the Gospel.*

FRIDAY, APRIL 12

See, I am doing a new thing! Now it springs up; do you not perceive it?
I am making a way in the wilderness and streams in the wasteland.
Isaiah 43:19 (NIV)

"DOES ANYONE HAVE A PRAYER request?" our worship director asked after choir rehearsal.

I raised my hand. "I hit send today." Tears filled my eyes. My choir friends knew exactly what I meant—I'd finally finished my book and sent it to the publisher. The ink had barely dried on my contract when I joined the choir, so they'd prayed me through every chapter.

My friend Terri wrapped her arm around me while everyone in the room cheered. I thanked them for supporting me through six months of writing that required me to revisit being abandoned by my ex-husband, adjusting to life as a single mom, and starting over in my childhood hometown. I'd never expected to recover from the trauma of those painful years, let alone write a book about everything. I'd also never expected to find a church family as loving and precious as the one I left behind when divorce forced me to move. But the warmth of Terri's arm reminded me of what I sensed Jesus telling me all week long: by hitting send, I was moving out of my old story and into the one He had for me now.

Loss changes us forever, but with Jesus, we have the hope of a new thing to come. This doesn't mean we make less of what has happened, and we might still have healing to do, but when we can focus on His faithfulness, each day holds promise. —JEANETTE HANSCOME

FAITH STEP: *Write down at least one thing that you never expected to recover from. How has Jesus helped you move forward? What new thing is He doing in your life now?*

SATURDAY, APRIL 13

You were saved by faith in God, who treats us much better than we deserve. This is God's gift to you, and not anything you have done on your own. Ephesians 2:8 (CEV)

IF I'M HONEST, I HAVE to admit I struggle to understand the cross. We live in a world where, at least in modern countries, there is little concept of blood sacrifice. In ancient times, it was the way things were done. People sinned, then brought sacrifices to atone for their sins. The sins were symbolically placed on the animals, which were then killed for the sins. Gory? Yes, but I'm sure it made sense to ancient people.

The cross would have made sense to them as well. In fact, it had to be done this way to make sense at all. Jesus was the perfect sacrifice, once and for all, for the sins of the world. I can talk about this all day, but do I really get it? No.

A little Tozer helps illuminate. A. W. Tozer writes, "We please Him most, not by frantically trying to make ourselves good, but by throwing ourselves into His arms with all our imperfections and believing that He understands everything—and still loves us."

I think what the cross means is that I don't have to be good for Jesus to save me. He already did. I don't have to sacrifice anything, or clean myself up, or atone for the evil things I've done and am. When I try to do those things, not only is it useless, but it takes away from the cross—it insults what He did. The way I show my appreciation is to run to Him and let myself be loved, with all my imperfections. It's free. I don't get this either. But I'm so thankful.
—GWEN FORD FAULKENBERRY

FAITH STEP: *Find the song that reminds you most of Jesus's love on YouTube. Close your eyes and listen to it, meditating on the lyrics that speak to your heart.*

SUNDAY, APRIL 14

Some women were there watching from a distance—Mary Magdalene, Mary
(the mother of James the Younger and of Joses), Salome, and others. They
and many other Galilean women who were his followers had ministered
to him when he was up in Galilee, and had come with him to Jerusalem.
Mark 15:40–41 (TLB)

PALM SUNDAY LAUNCHES US INTO Holy Week. Often, we begin this sacred time by embodying the crowds who welcomed Jesus into Jerusalem with a great deal of hoopla. We grab our palm leaves and start waving. And yet we know where this is all leading; on Palm Sunday, we also hear the story of the crucifixion.

This year, I want to spend Holy Week with the women who stayed with Jesus through it all. Long after the cheering crowds dispersed, after even the closest of Jesus's male friends scattered in terror, His Galilean women friends stayed with Him. These were the women who had known Jesus and ministered to Jesus throughout all those years when He was ministering to others on the road.

This year, something struck me that I never really noticed before: it isn't until Jesus has died on the cross that the Gospel writer Mark even mentions Mary Magdalene. And yet, when we are introduced to her in this tragic moment, when "it's over," we also learn that she was with Jesus and the ministry from the very beginning. So let it be with us this Holy Week. During this sacred time when our prayer practice revs up and gets more attention, let's stay with the relationships that have been building all along and let them carry us through to the end. —ELIZABETH BERNE DEGEAR

FAITH STEP: *The Greek word used to describe the women ministering to Jesus is* diakoneo. *This year, who has ministered to you? In their care for you, who have been the deacons in your life? Can you bring those relationships into your Holy Week and see where they lead?*

MONDAY, APRIL 15

Many women were also there, looking on from a distance; they had followed Jesus from Galilee and had provided for him. Among them were Mary Magdalene, and Mary the mother of James and Joseph, and the mother of the sons of Zebedee. Matthew 27:55–56 (NRSV)

TODAY, THE MONDAY OF HOLY Week, I continue to sit with the women who stayed. I am struck by the fact that those who were closest to Jesus during His ministry, providing for Him out of their resources while He spent his energies focused on healing others, are here, kept at a distance. The culture dictated that their place, as women, was at a distance. Pushed to the margins of this crucifixion scene, they are also pushed to the margins of the Gospel stories that have been passed down to us. But as I pray with these women during Holy Week, I know their hearts were as intimately entwined with the heart of Jesus as is humanly and divinely possible.

Today I am reminded that, even while these women are marginalized by official protocol, Jesus lived and ministered at the margins. He helped people transform their world so that "official" was no longer synonymous with "most powerful" or "true." Joining these women who are looking on at a distance, who are experiencing the power of it all within their own beings, we can be inspired to step into our story of Jesus Christ. —ELIZABETH BERNE DEGEAR

FAITH STEP: *Pray with the women who stayed with Jesus through the crucifixion. Note how the powers that be are marginalizing them, keeping them at a distance. Feel how the love between them and Jesus crosses that distance, making it disappear.*

TUESDAY, APRIL 16

As soon as they left the synagogue, they went with [James] and John to the house of Simon and Andrew. Now Simon's mother-in-law was lying sick with a fever. Right away, they told [Jesus] about her. He came and raised her up by taking her hand. The fever left her, and she began to take care of them. Mark 1:29–31 (TLV)

GOD HAS BLESSED ME WITH not one but *two* mothers-in-law. My husband was adopted at birth, and he is connected to both the mother who birthed him and the mother who raised him. Whenever family descends on the home of either of my mothers-in-law, I always notice that they are often stuck in the kitchen, while the rest of us get to enjoy fun together out in the yard.

But then I learned that the Greek word used to describe what Simon's mother-in-law does in Mark 1 is *diakoneo*. This is the same word used to describe church ministry. Healed of her ailment, she is free to minister! As grateful as I am to my mothers-in-law for their delicious family meals prepared and served over the years, that is not what I am going to remember them for. It is the way they have ministered to me from their faith and life experiences, the stories they have shared about their own hardships and triumphs, their prayers for our family, and the ways their love has shaped who my children have become—that is what I will always remember and be grateful for.

This Gospel vignette is about mutuality between one man and one woman. When she needed someone, He cared enough to minister to her, and He raised her up. Then, in return, she cared enough to minister to Him too. —ELIZABETH BERNE DEGEAR

FAITH STEP: *Trust that there is more to preparing for Easter than meal preparation this year. Pray with Jesus and see if there is a new way for Him to raise you up and for you to celebrate that He is risen.*

WEDNESDAY, APRIL 17

It is by your holding fast to the word of life that I can boast on the day of Christ that I did not run in vain or labor in vain. But even if I am being poured out as a libation over the sacrifice and the offering of your faith, I am glad and rejoice with all of you—and in the same way you also must be glad and rejoice with me. Philippians 2:16–18 (NRSV)

I SPENT TWO DAYS VISITING the priest who baptized and confirmed me, who presided at my wedding, and who has inspired my faith for decades. Now he's battling lung cancer, and it looks like the cancer is winning. We sat in a church service together in the chapel of his residence, and the first reading was this passage from Philippians. He is someone who has truly poured himself out as a libation, laboring for Jesus in ways that have had a powerful impact on communities long after he has moved on to his next assignment. So, of course, the reading rang true as we sat in prayer. But it was doubly poignant because, before we entered the chapel, he had described his treatment, which involved draining fluid from his lungs. How could I heed Scripture's call—"you must be glad and rejoice with me"—when illness was causing this wonderful person to suffer? It is one thing for disciples to pour all their faith and energy into their work for Jesus, but it is quite another to do so in a bodily way. I wondered, *Are we truly asked to be drained like this?*

And then I remember that image of water pouring from Jesus's side as He hung on the cross. And I remember my beloved priest's message during the last Easter Vigil he presided over: "Even in the resurrection, you can't forget the crucifixion." —ELIZABETH BERNE DEGEAR

FAITH STEP: *Have courage this Holy Week. Instead of just hoping to rejoice at Easter, sit with the mess of life. Trust that the mystery of Christ's death and resurrection will take it from there.*

THURSDAY, APRIL 18

And when Jesus had cried out again in a loud voice, he gave up his spirit. At that moment. . . . [t]he earth shook, the rocks split and the tombs broke open. The bodies of many holy people who had died were raised to life. They came out of the tombs after Jesus' resurrection and went into the holy city and appeared to many people. Matthew 27:50–53 (NIV)

HOLY THURSDAY IS MY FAVORITE day of the year. To me, it may be the most Christian day in our liturgical calendar—because the Last Supper is about community. It is about sharing a meal and about the pivotal moment when Jesus trusted that His ministry was transforming into something much longer-lasting. It was the moment when a movement led by one man became a transcendent reality available to any and all.

You may be wondering, if the Last Supper means so much to me, why I'm quoting a Scripture passage about the crucifixion. Because, in these verses, we see the communal nature of Jesus's life, His ministry, and even His last meal coming alive in the moment of His death. It is not just Jesus who rises from the grave. His commitment to humanity *and* divinity somehow frees *many* holy people to loose themselves from death and to appear to *many* people.

I read this passage at the funeral of a cherished member of our church community. And I said I believed that, along with Jesus, our friend had been raised to life and had the power to appear to us in any holy place where his loved ones kept his memory alive. Indeed, people have shared stories with me of how this friend continues to be in their lives, strengthening their own faith while surprising them with the realness of His presence. —ELIZABETH BERNE DeGEAR

FAITH STEP: *This Holy Week, be open to the ways your cherished loved ones who have died may appear to you. What is the essence of the message they wish to share with you?*

FRIDAY, APRIL 19

After the sabbath, as the first day of the week was dawning, Mary Magdalene and the other Mary went to see the tomb. And suddenly there was a great earthquake; for an angel of the Lord, descending from heaven, came and rolled back the stone and sat on it. His appearance was like lightning, and his clothing white as snow. For fear of him the guards shook and became like dead men. Matthew 28:1–4 (NRSV)

EVERY YEAR, AS LENT BEGINS, I wonder if Easter will really "happen" for me again this year.

And every year, I am surprised that Holy Week can feel *this* new and *this* real. There is always more of me that can wake up to the dawn of Christ's resurrection.

Finding these new places in myself that need resurrection rests in the fact that I can always relate to the guards in this story. They are the ones who have been placed there to guard Jesus's body. They are the ones who experience the resurrection as a great earthquake. They are the ones who shake and become like dead men in the presence of the angel at the empty tomb.

There is always some part of my own faith life that relates to the guards. Some part of me that has become comfortable with protecting authority—whether it's the authority of the institutions I put my trust in or my own. And then sometime during Lent and Holy Week, something happens to challenge that comfort and to show me the empty nature of it all. It usually feels like an earthquake, a disruption that terrifies my defenses. During this sacred week, I am given the grace to let this part of me—this "guard," this defensive posture—be shaken off in the presence of the angel of the Lord. —ELIZABETH BERNE DEGEAR

FAITH STEP: *Assess your faith life. Which parts guard beliefs or practices that are no longer genuinely alive for you? Try shaking them off to make room for some new aspect of Christ to enter your life, even if it feels like an earthquake or a bolt of lightning.*

SATURDAY, APRIL 20

But the angel said to the women, "Do not be afraid; I know that you are looking for Jesus who was crucified. He is not here; for he has been raised, as he said. Come, see the place where he lay. Then go quickly and tell his disciples, 'He has been raised from the dead.'" Matthew 28:5–7 (NRSV)

THE EXPERIENCE THAT MAKES THE guards of Jesus's tomb shake and act like dead men is the same experience that makes these wonderful women rush to declare the impossibly good news: Jesus has been raised!

And just as we all have those parts of ourselves that are like those terrified guards—trying to protect that which is empty and no longer alive in the Spirit—so we all have those parts of ourselves that are like these courageous women. Mary Magdalene had the resources to build the ministry behind Jesus's ministry. She had the courage to stand witness with her friends as they all lost a friend to crucifixion. She had the consciousness to experience the resurrection and speak joyful truth in a time of fear and despair. Oh, how I want to be with Mary Magdalene this Easter!

There is plenty going on in the world today—and perhaps in your personal life as well—that seems as earth-shattering as the crucifixion and the earthquake some experienced back then. With dramatic change, sudden loss, and world events we cannot control, can we tap into the Mary Magdalene within each of us? If we can, we will find ourselves experiencing a truly inspired faith. Surrounded by a world steeped in fear, we will also experience true peace, and we will be quick to share news of this peace with others. —ELIZABETH BERNE DEGEAR

FAITH STEP: *In your search for Jesus before Easter dawns, spend some time with Mary Magdalene, the first to experience and proclaim the resurrection. Find inspiration in her vision and courage, so that you, too, may find the heart to share good news, even when all seems dire.*

EASTER SUNDAY, APRIL 21

Near the cross of Jesus stood his mother, his mother's sister, Mary the wife of Clopas, and Mary Magdalene. When Jesus saw his mother there, and the disciple whom he loved standing nearby, he said to her, "Woman, here is your son." John 19:25–26 (NIV)

FOR SEVERAL YEARS, A CHURCH in our town presented a massive production that included hyperrealistic scenes depicting issues teenagers and adults face, such as the consequences of drug use, drinking and driving, suicide, relationship collapse, and disinterest in the Gospel.

As the Easter season approached this year, I thought about the volunteers who were part of the most heart-gripping scene—the crucifixion of Jesus.

The church had no trouble getting volunteers to play the part of the grieving mother of Jesus. Hands went up to volunteer to play the part of Mary Magdalene. The part of John, the disciple Jesus loved, was an easy role to fill.

Few said, "Hey, sign me up to play Jesus. I want to be the one to wear a crown of thorns, hang for hours on a splinter-ridden cross, be mocked, spit upon, held up to ridicule. Sign me up to be bound to that cross."

Jesus had no discussion with His Father that included "Could I be John instead of Me? How about one of the soldiers? I like their uniforms." Instead, He voluntarily laid down His life for what we needed most—forgiveness of our sins. It's no cliché to say He died so we could live.

I can put myself in the scene at the foot of the cross. But I can't fully imagine it from His viewpoint, because that part could only be played in real life—real *Life*—by Him. —CYNTHIA RUCHTI

FAITH STEP: *Consider celebrating the impact of the crucifixion through the eyes of each of the characters we're told were "nearby." Imagine their emotions and responses, then compare them to the intensity of your response to Christ's sacrifice.*

MONDAY, APRIL 22

Jesus said, "Father, forgive them, for they do not know what they are doing."
Luke 23:34 (NIV)

FORGIVENESS IS A PROCESS, NOT an emotion that oozes instantly from our hearts. A child who is being verbally or physically attacked or a parent angry at the bullying of her teenager at school may not want to forgive immediately. As a mom and a grandmom, I've experienced a few situations of my own that brought knee-jerk reactions. Justice may be necessary, but revenge only makes us bitter.

Lately, however, I've read about Christians in other countries who have experienced family persecution and even agonizing deaths. Yet I've been amazed to hear about those who have openly granted forgiveness to their persecutors. Was it instant? Maybe. Maybe not. But neither was it a long, drawn-out process. Most of them claimed they were secure in their devotion to Jesus and followed His example of loving and forgiving their enemies. They got it.

Jesus is our ultimate role model. As He hung, crucified on a splintered cross, Jesus's words to His enemies and persecutors were immediate: "Father, forgive them, for they do not know what they're doing." His devotion to His Father gave Him the strength to forgive.

My initial reactions have mellowed since I was an elementary school girl fighting over something trivial on the playground. And hopefully, I've matured since the years of trying to tackle offenses against my kids. In some particularly hard issues of my life, forgiveness has seemed more like...a process. But what I want most is to mirror Jesus's response: to love and forgive—no matter what. —REBECCA BARLOW JORDAN

FAITH STEP: *When you or someone you love is hurt, do you respond or react? Ask Jesus to help you love and forgive—no matter what.*

TUESDAY, APRIL 23

Then he said to Thomas, "Put your finger here; see my hands. Reach out your hand and put it into my side. Stop doubting and believe."
John 20:27 (NIV)

I GO BACK TO THE story of "doubting Thomas" often. There's something about his character that intrigues me. Did his actions speak of a certain personality type, not just hardened cynicism? He seems pragmatic and envious of the other disciples' claim to have seen Jesus—Thomas hadn't been included. I don't judge him, because I share a few of his traits.

Jesus recognizes our weaknesses and loves us just as we are. He wants our faith to grow, and as part of the triune God, His will always wins out. Knowing this helped me yesterday, as a friend on social media messaged me privately. Sharing her thoughts on Jesus, she debated His holiness and value in her life. While I read her questions and doubts, Thomas came to mind. Did my friend matter to Jesus? Yes, He died for her. What could I say to help her? How could I address her fragile faith to draw her closer to Him? I settled in for a long instant-messaging session. Jesus knew her exact needs and simply used me to communicate.

Jesus knows everything about us, all our strengths and failures. With infinite wisdom, Jesus understood Thomas's requirements for belief—tangible proof—and He supplied it. Just like He took great care in helping me reassure my friend. Jesus doesn't waste time on justifiable anger. He reaffirmed Thomas's faith because it was necessary. He offered guidance to my friend for the same reason. And we can be certain He will do the same for us when we need assurance. —HEIDI GAUL

FAITH STEP: *Write down your traits, good and bad. Think of ways Jesus meets you where you are, to strengthen your walk with Him.*

WEDNESDAY, APRIL 24

For one will scarcely die for a righteous person—though perhaps for a good person one would dare even to die—but God shows his love for us in that while we were still sinners, Christ died for us. Romans 5:7–8 (ESV)

"GRANDMA, I KNOW IT'S NOT good to be mean to our friends, but it's okay to be mean to bad guys, right?"

I marveled at the theological discussion generated by this precious four-year-old. "No, honey. Jesus tells us to love even our enemies."

Her forehead wrinkled. "Grandma, isn't God strange?"

Yes, yes, He is. I thought about her question all week. Jesus showed us the amazing strangeness of His love because He came into a world that scorned Him. He embraced "bad guys" like tax collectors who cheated their countrymen. He patiently corrected disciples who squabbled and doubted. He chose a road of suffering and death, praying forgiveness over the ones who crucified Him. Most wonderful of all, He defeated death for us by dying and then rising victoriously.

We can celebrate the bewildering and generous love of Jesus every day. He comes to us when we're prickly, cranky, and rebellious. He reaches out even when we turn from Him again and again. He sends gifts into our lives even when our mouths are full of complaints. And He invites us to offer this strange and unconditional love to others: the grumpy neighbor whose dog barks all night, the coworker who slacks off and causes more effort for us, the relative whose criticisms cut us to the core. Jesus reminds us we are all "bad guys" apart from Him, and He dwells in us to teach us how to love the way He does.

—SHARON HINCK

FAITH STEP: *Think of one "bad guy" causing irritation in your life and choose a loving deed to do for him or her.*

Thursday, April 25

You keep track of all my sorrows. You have collected all my tears in your bottle. You have recorded each one in your book. Psalm 56:8 (NLT)

I FOLDED THE SOFT VINTAGE handkerchief and tucked it into the card it arrived in. My friend Judy had a beautiful tradition of sending them to women who'd lost someone they loved. She'd sent me one when I was going through a divorce, knowing from experience that divorce felt like death and brought just as much grief.

This is for your precious tears, she'd written in the card. The handkerchief caught a lot of them. At first, I was afraid to mess up the delicate embroidered cloth, until one emotional night when a tender voice whispered, *I think that's what she sent it for.* Every time I held it, finally letting go of the sadness of the day, I felt the love of my friend and the nearness of Jesus, Who kept more of my tears than any handkerchief could hold. The next morning, I would rinse it out, hang it to dry, tuck it back inside the card, and put it in my nightstand drawer for the next time I needed it.

Judy's handkerchief is now in my Blessings Box as a reminder of the many times it soaked up healing tears that Jesus cared enough to collect. It reminds me that He is with us in every moment of grief, whether we're weeping over the death of a marriage or a loved one. "You keep track of all my sorrows...." David experienced it and so can we. Some of our bottles are more like fifty-gallon vats, but He keeps them anyway, because our tears are precious to Him.
—JEANETTE HANSCOME

FAITH STEP: *Pray for a friend who is grieving right now (over anything). Ask Jesus how you can encourage her, whether it's through a card, a visit, or taking the time to listen and share her tears.*

FRIDAY, APRIL 26

This is the day that the LORD has made. Let us rejoice and be glad today!
Psalm 118:24 (NCV)

"LET'S CHOOSE TO HAVE A good day." I've heard my daughter, Holly, say that to her older children on more than one occasion. Maybe they had brought a bad attitude to the breakfast table, grumbled about the family's plans for the day, or complained about how long a car trip would take. Personally, I don't feel able to criticize anyone for the habit of complaining; sometimes it seems as though I've taken complaining to a whole new level.

I cringe when I read about how harshly God reacted to the Israelites' grumbling in the Old Testament. I feel convicted when I read the New Testament admonitions to do everything without complaining. And yet it's so easy to slip into that mind-set. Am I supposed to slap on a smile regardless of how I'm feeling? The answer can be found in the book of Psalms. Many chapters begin with the writer pouring out his negative emotions: grief, disappointment, sadness, anger, depression. Then the writer shifts the focus to God: His character, His past provision, His promises. By praying with such honesty and trust, the writer is able to end on a note of praise.

Complaining is contagious; it affects those around us. It keeps us from seeing the many blessings we've already been given and from looking toward the promise of more. Worst of all, it makes us miss out on the full, abundant life that Jesus wants to give us (John 10:10). Every day, we have a choice: we can give in to negative thinking, or we can acknowledge that Jesus has given us this day and choose to embrace all that it holds. —DIANNE NEAL MATTHEWS

FAITH STEP: *The next time you're tempted to complain, go to Jesus in prayer instead. Honestly tell Him how you feel; end by reciting Psalm 118:24. Then choose to smile for Him.*

SATURDAY, APRIL 27

Give thanks to the LORD, for he is good; his love endures forever.
Psalm 107:1 (NIV)

IN A HOUSE OF BOYS, most material possessions do not last long. Even as I type, my computer is leaning on the diagonal and the left side is completely open, revealing its mechanical innards. *How can this be?* I have pretty strict rules regarding the use of my computer. The computer stays on the table at all times. *Do not lift it. Do not carry it. Definitely, do not run with it. Don't try to balance it on your knee.* So many rules. And yet here I am, with my computer yawning open on one side. It needs fixing. But I don't have much hope for it.

That's because the shelf life of modern technology is short. The truth is that nothing much in this life lasts. Not even when we try to take care of it. Not even when we make sure not to balance it on our knees. But one thing that does last is Jesus's love for us. His love is put to the test…over and over again.

We mess up? *He loves us.*

We doubt Him? *He loves us.*

We pull away from Him in anger and hurt when life doesn't go our way? *He loves us.*

We get bogged down in despair and discouragement? *His love keeps going.*

It endures. Forever. Until we see Him face to face. This is what He promises. This is what is true. His long-suffering, strong, faithful, trustworthy love surrounding us on all sides for all of our days. And that is something we can be truly thankful for.
—SUSANNA FOTH AUGHTMON

FAITH STEP: *Spend some time thinking of all the ways that Jesus has shown you His love throughout your life. Thank Him for His enduring love.*

SUNDAY, APRIL 28

And I am sure of this, that he who began a good work in you will bring it to completion at the day of Jesus Christ. Philippians 1:6 (ESV)

MY PRINTER SOFTWARE HAS THIS nifty photo-editing tool that allows me to significantly improve my looks with a single mouse-click. Suddenly, my skin is silky, vibrant, and wrinkle-free. How very nice! If only it were so with my spiritual life.

While we are sanctified or freed by Christ's blood (Acts 13:38–39), sanctification also refers to how we're transformed over time. That's definitely not a one-click job.

In my own life, being transformed into Christ's likeness has involved nearly relentless and sometimes painful chiseling. The shaping tools have varied: People who've challenged some obstinate defects in me. Circumstances beyond my existing skill set that have compelled me to grow. Problems so overwhelming I could only surrender to God's chosen solution.

In retrospect, I see much of the pain was rooted in my resistance. Rather than wisely taking God at His Word, I fought what I knew God was asking of me and doing in me.

It's taken me a long time, possibly longer than most folks, to realize that the wisest and, ultimately, the easiest path to holiness is to submit fully to the Potter's hands.

Humbly, faithfully, and, yes, thankfully. —ISABELLA YOSUICO

FAITH STEP: *Set aside quiet time to inventory known areas of resistance. Ask the Potter to help you let go in faith.*

MONDAY, APRIL 29

You also must be ready all the time, for the Son of Man will come when least expected. Luke 12:40 (NLT)

WHEN MY HUSBAND, GENE, AND I decided to sell our house years ago, the real estate agent made suggestions about how to prepare it prior to listing.

"Take personal photos off the walls," she said. "Anyone who views the house needs to visualize their family, not yours, living here. Empty your closets of storage boxes so they'll look more spacious. Make sure the kitchen counters are clean and uncluttered, and keep nice-looking, fresh bathroom towels handy to replace damp ones."

The agent wanted to sell the house as much as we did, so she stressed the necessity of being ready to show it at a moment's notice. This was a tall order considering our family's busy schedule, but we did our best to cooperate. Our mutual goal was to keep the house presentable at all times, lest we be caught off guard and miss a possible sale.

How much more ought we pay attention to our heart's condition in light of Jesus Christ's imminent return! When He appears, there'll be no time for last-minute spiritual housecleaning. It'll be too late to seek reconciliation for a broken relationship or resolution to anger and unforgiveness. There will be no point to scurrying about, trying to hide secret sins from His gaze.

We know Jesus is coming soon, and He's given us ample time to get ready for His arrival. Let's not be caught off guard. The time to prepare our hearts is now, so that we might welcome Him with joy. —GRACE FOX

FAITH STEP: *What sinful attitudes or behaviors might Jesus find in your life if He returned today? Ask Him to cleanse you and determine to take whatever steps necessary to deal with them.*

TUESDAY, APRIL 30

Though the LORD is exalted, he looks kindly on the lowly;
though lofty, he sees them from afar. Psalm 138:6 (NIV)

I ADORE FLOWERS, AND MY husband, David, enjoys working the soil, so every year our yard comes alive with blossoms, from crocuses to irises to roses. You can almost tell the month by what's blooming. Maintaining our garden requires regular attention, so I spend a lot of time watering as David trims, plants, and weeds.

One day, as I lowered the hose into the well we'd dug around a favorite floribunda, I noticed a blotch of color near the dirt. Pulling the hose aside, I knelt beside the bush. There, just two inches above the ground, a delicate bud waited, sprouting from the base of an older branch. Growing at a ninety-degree angle, the petals almost touched the dirt. Though ordinary in its appearance, it was an unexpected, and welcomed, surprise. This hidden rose touched my heart more than all the flowers adorning the rosebush's crown.

It reminded me of my relationship with Christ, so hidden until it was ready to come to bloom. How had my faith been worthy of Jesus's notice? How could I share it? I remembered the flower as it stretched bravely toward the sun.

I asked my clippers-bearing husband to snip the bud free. I put it in a vase and set it in a place of honor on our kitchen island where I could admire its singular beauty.

Whenever I entered that room, I thought of how Jesus saw me from afar and pulled me from my struggles into His unwarranted grace. He valued my soul's worth and put me in a place of honor. —HEIDI GAUL

FAITH STEP: *Write a note letting a friend know how highly you value him or her. Cut a flower from your garden, or purchase one from the store, to present along with the note.*

WEDNESDAY, MAY 1

You are like whitewashed tombs, which look beautiful on the outside but on the inside are full of . . . everything unclean. Matthew 23:27 (NIV)

As SOON AS THE FROST disappears and the daffodils appear, I'm ready to garden. A couple of years ago, I determined to simplify the work but still make the garden as beautiful as possible. Perennials would return on their own, but I planned to cut back on annuals significantly. I bought a few petunias to add color in the empty spots. My husband, Larry, and I also planted low-maintenance and disease-resistant roses, replacing the struggling vegetable garden.

But the simplified gardening grew into hours of beautification. The new roses required mulch. So did the other areas. Seventy-seven bags of mulch, to be exact—on sale, of course. Spreading all those brown sprigs, along with weed-pulling, stretched into two months' worth of work.

When we finished, the outside gardens were indeed more beautiful. But inside the house, I noticed the dust had gotten a little thicker, the bathrooms a little dirtier, and there were more smudges on the floor. I had been so focused on keeping the outside yards beautiful that I had neglected the inside of the house.

I read Matthew 23 recently, where Jesus used a whitewashed tomb, a cup, and a dish to illustrate the legalistic and hypocritical habits of the Jewish leaders He encountered. Evidently they worked hard at obeying rules—cleanliness and beauty on the outside— while neglecting the inside (their hearts).

My own experience, along with Jesus's powerful words to the teachers of the law and Pharisees, was a sober reminder: Jesus loves for us to add beauty—inside and out—but He's most concerned with the cleanliness and purity of our hearts. —REBECCA BARLOW JORDAN

FAITH STEP: *Leave a clean cup on your desk or counter this week as a reminder to ask Jesus to keep the inside of your spiritual home (your heart) more beautiful.*

THURSDAY, MAY 2

Now finish the work, so that your eager willingness to do it may be matched by your completion of it, according to your means. 2 Corinthians 8:11 *(NIV)*

I'M A GREAT "STARTER." I instigate enthusiastic ideas, whether they involve cleaning a closet, canning jam, or planting a huge garden. However, I often get in over my head. Once all the items are pulled from the closet, the mess overwhelms me. After I get my canning supplies assembled, the many steps involved become daunting. And that huge garden? By midsummer, the weeds win the battle as I tire of the project.

Follow-through is also difficult as a disciple of Jesus. Like James and John, I might boldly leave everything to follow, then end up squabbling about who is the greatest. Like Thomas, I may walk faithfully alongside the Savior, but then doubt His presence. Like Peter, I enthusiastically proclaim my loyalty to my Savior. Yet when confronted with social pressure, I shrink into myself, unable to even admit I serve Him.

Sometimes we think life should get easier as time goes by, but it's often during the last stretch of the race when the muscles scream to quit. It's the last contractions of childbirth that are the fiercest.

Are you in a place of exhaustion, feeling unable to finish the work of serving Jesus where He has placed you today? Take heart! Even as He calls us to endure, He also promises to work in and through us. "Being confident of this, that he who began a good work in you will carry it on to completion until the day of Christ Jesus" (Philippians 1:6). —SHARON HINCK

FAITH STEP: *Look at a goal, mission, or task you haven't completed. Ask Jesus to carry on the work in you and prayerfully take one more step toward finishing.*

FRIDAY, MAY 3

Woe to you, scribes and Pharisees, hypocrites! For you tithe mint and dill and cumin, and have neglected the weightier matters of the law: justice and mercy and faithfulness. Matthew 23:23 (ESV)

MY HERB GARDEN IS A series of hanging baskets. I step onto my back deck to snip basil and thyme for the sauce simmering on the stove. Often, I pick rosemary for no other reason than the aroma it leaves on my hands. A few leaves of mint tossed into my giant water jug with fresh cucumbers and a squeeze of lime is more refreshing than anything the beverage aisle or soda machine can offer.

I know better than to plant mint in my raised beds or flat on the ground. Mint takes over. It grows—as they say—like a weed. It fares well in the hanging basket in which I keep it. Contained.

Having been counseled about mint's wild exuberance, I find it curious that the scribes and Pharisees—law keepers in Jesus's time who peered over their reading glasses at Jesus and His spirit-of-the-law mentality—were faithful to give 10 percent (or a tithe) of their mint and dill. Not exactly a sacrifice on their part. Mint no doubt grew like a weed in those days too.

They neglected what Jesus called "the weightier matters" of the law, however, which they claimed to follow with exacting diligence—justice and mercy and faithfulness. The Faithful One, Jesus, recognized unfaithfulness in their stinginess with the important things.

When I pass my basket of mint, I'm reminded of my responsibility to be generous with justice, mercy, and faithfulness. Am I giving abundantly of the things that matter to Jesus? —CYNTHIA RUCHTI

FAITH STEP: *The next time you're offered a mint following a restaurant meal, or the next time you reach for a breath mint, stop for a moment of self-examination and pray, "Jesus, show me where I'm neglecting the weightier matters."*

SATURDAY, MAY 4

Others fell on good ground and yielded a crop. Matthew 13:8 (NKJV)

I GREW UP IN INNER-CITY New York where the only greenery around was the shrubs and grass surrounding our public housing project. After I got married, we bought a house in the suburbs with a small backyard. It was a dream fulfilled. I'm a nature lover, and I've always admired houses accented with beautiful gardens and foliage, so when we moved, I decided to try my hand at gardening. I'd never done it before and was a little nervous. I bought the prettiest blooms and a pair of gloves and got to work.

A few weeks later, I noticed one area was burgeoning, bursting with color, but the other was not. Certainly not for lack of care; I watered both sets of plants, added fertilizer to each, and yet one set of blooms looked neglected. What was I doing wrong?

"Your soil is no good. It's like sand," my landscaper answered, pushing the toe of his shoe into the grainy dirt.

I had planted good flowers in bad soil. Jesus's parable of the sower (Matthew 13:1–9) immediately came to mind: The same seed placed in different environments will yield different results. If the environment is not right, there will be no growth. What began as a practical lesson in gardening morphed into spiritual food for thought.

As I read and study His Word, the seed of faith He placed in me continues to grow and blossom. However, when I allow my heart to harden, there is no spiritual growth. I must keep the soil of my heart soft and become a receiver of "good seed"—God's Word. It's imperative for growth. —CAROL MACKEY

FAITH STEP: *Pray this prayer: Lord, help me to realize when my heart is becoming like hard, dry dirt. Make my heart a fertile place so You can use me for Your service. Amen.*

SUNDAY, MAY 5

Then the women said to Naomi, "Praise the LORD, who has not left you without
a family redeemer today. May his name become well known in Israel.
He will renew your life and sustain you in your old age." Ruth 4:14–15 (HCSB)

I IMAGINE THAT NAOMI HAD a picture in her mind of how her life would turn out. She probably assumed that her family would ride out the famine in Moab and then return to Bethlehem, where her sons would marry hometown girls and fill her life with grandchildren. Instead, Naomi's husband died, and her sons married Moabite women. Later, Naomi's sons died, leaving her a destitute widow. She did return to Bethlehem, but as a woman beaten down by life, telling the women who greeted her by name to call her "Bitter" instead.

But God was working behind the scenes, and oh, what a difference a few short chapters can make! The book of Ruth ends with Naomi filled with joy and a new zest for life. Boaz took on the role of family redeemer and protector and promised to provide for Naomi for the rest of her life. Even better, the union between Boaz and Naomi's daughter-in-law Ruth produced a baby boy for Naomi to care for and love.

I don't know about you, but some parts of the picture I had envisioned for my life are now missing or distorted. Maybe you even feel beaten down by the grief and sorrow of losses you've suffered. If we trust in God and cling to Him, He will give us new meaning and zest for life. And it all goes back to that baby boy in Naomi's lap. Because little Obed was an ancestor of Jesus, our own family Redeemer Who has promised to protect and provide for us throughout our lives. —DIANNE NEAL MATTHEWS

FAITH STEP: *Do you feel disappointed about some ways your life doesn't match the picture you had in mind? Tell Jesus you're ready for Him to write a new chapter.*

MONDAY, MAY 6

Being confident of this, that he who began a good work in you will carry it on to completion until the day of Christ Jesus. Philippians 1:6 (NIV)

THIS PAST MARCH, OUR FAMILY of five moved into a cute cottage with a small front yard. I have a thing about front yards. They need flowers. This yard was covered in weeds. So I yanked them up. They grew back. I yanked them up again. Weeds are crazy persistent. But I am relentless.

I had a vision of what I wanted this yard to look like. Once the ground was finally bare, I prepped the soil for seeding. I seeded it with wildflowers, because how fun would it be to open the door each morning to that kind of beauty? I raked the soil, added compost, and watched videos about casting seed. I mixed the sand, dirt, and seed and broadcast it all over the yard. I've been watering it faithfully twice a day. And I am waiting. For flowers. And for the beauty to show up. I know it will.

Three weeks in, there is one lonely poppy clinging to the edge of the sidewalk. I love that poppy so much. I know that soon its brothers and sisters will show up. I can't wait.

Jesus is the relentless Gardener when it comes to our hearts and lives. He has a vision for us, the ones whom He created. He longs to unearth the beauty in us that He created us for. So He goes to work: weeding, pruning, trimming, and yanking. Sometimes it is uncomfortable. Other times it's downright painful. But He has promised to work in us and through us, until the day when His glory and beauty are fully revealed in our lives. —SUSANNA FOTH AUGHTMON

FAITH STEP: *Place a cut flower on your kitchen counter. Each time you see it, remind yourself that Jesus is doing a good work in your life, revealing more of His beauty each day.*

TUESDAY, MAY 7

Put not your trust in princes, in a son of man, in whom there is no salvation.
Psalm 146:3 (ESV)

IF I'M COMPLETELY HONEST WITH myself, I have, at times, entrusted my "salvation" to other people. I've wanted someone to bail me out of an emotional or practical bind or looked to people for quick, decisive answers. Most especially when I'm feeling overwhelmed or overwrought, I'd rather call someone or consult a professional, even before I call on God. In my drive for immediate relief, I more quickly turn to flesh-and-blood people when what I really need to do is pause, pray, and wait.

I recently faced a financial crisis after a series of bad decisions and large unexpected expenses.

The Bible itself tells us that trusting God and seeking human help are not mutually exclusive. Like the old joke about the man who prays for rescue from a flood and then refuses the physical help God sends his way. But seeking God first often leads to unexpected answers or directs us to the best person to help us.

Pray and wait.

There are few things in life as difficult as waiting on God when the need seems—or truly is—urgent.

God's help is often just in time and just enough.

This verse speaks of lowercase princes and sons of man. If I put my trust in *the* Prince and Son of Man, I will find the salvation I seek. —ISABELLA YOSUICO

FAITH STEP: *Next time you face an urgent need to pick up the phone for advice, first stop and pray.*

WEDNESDAY, MAY 8

---

*You chose Israel to be your very own people forever, and you,
O LORD, became their God.* 1 Chronicles 17:22 (NLT)

"THE WEATHER'S TOO NICE TO stay indoors," said my sixth-grade teacher. "Let's go outside and play soccer."

My heart sank. *Oh no. Not again.*

The teacher appointed two boys as captains. They took turns choosing the peers they wanted on their teams. As their options waned, so did my self-confidence. I was a skinny girl with glasses, more skilled in writing book reports than in playing sports. When neither captain chose me, I joined the team my teacher assigned me to.

As an adult, I've experienced the disappointment and shame that come from not being chosen—like when my fiancé broke our engagement to pursue a different woman. And when publishers have passed over my book proposals.

Dwelling on such experiences embeds within me a negative message: "You're not good enough. Nobody wants you." I have to be intentional about rejecting the lies.

Instead, I meditate on Jesus's words: "You didn't choose me. I chose you. I appointed you to go and produce lasting fruit, so that the Father will give you whatever you ask for, using my name" (John 15:16).

Knowing that Jesus has chosen me lessens the pain of rejection, and knowing that He's given me a specific purpose makes me feel special.

The King of the universe has chosen me to be His friend, His daughter, His bride. He's chosen you too. —GRACE FOX

FAITH STEP: *Read John 15:16 aloud and personalize it by adding your name.
"I chose you, Grace, and appointed you to go and produce lasting fruit. . . ."*

Thursday, May 9

Praise be to the God and Father of our Lord Jesus Christ, the Father of compassion and the God of all comfort, who comforts us in all our troubles, so that we can comfort those in any trouble with the comfort we ourselves receive from God. 2 Corinthians 1:3–4 (NIV)

I WAS JUST GETTING TO know the woman sitting across from me, but we'd connected and found we had some painful things in common. I was on the other side of my crisis; she'd barely begun hers.

It felt strange to be having this conversation in the same place where I'd confided a devastating secret to a friend several years earlier. Her comfort had strengthened me to face what came next and provided me with an example of how to minister to others.

I had an opinion about what my new friend should do but thought I should leave the decision to her and Jesus alone. I could pray with her as others had prayed with me, hug her, share her tears, and keep my promise to stay in touch. Jesus had comforted me through friends, and now it was my turn to be there for someone else.

When we are in the throes of a life-altering trial, it is all we can do to cling to belief that we will one day use our experiences to help others. We may listen to a story that is eerily similar to ours and know that this is our chance to offer comfort. We can empathize in ways that are impossible for those who haven't been there and know when to speak and when not to. In those moments, we feel surprisingly grateful for the hard thing that we thought we'd never survive and the comfort that came through Jesus and those He placed in our path. —JEANETTE HANSCOME

FAITH STEP: *Consider how a past trial has equipped you to help others. Who do you have compassion for now? Who have you helped already?*

FRIDAY, MAY 10

The greatest of these is love. 1 Corinthians 13:13 (NIV)

I ATTENDED A FUNERAL SERVICE today. It was emotional just stepping in the door of First Baptist Church, the church where I grew up. Funny how smells, creaking stairs, a shiny black piano, and banners with the names of God can just take you home. Suddenly, I was five years old, with my former preacher and his wife loving on us, and then ten years old watching a friend from church, Larry Johnston, stand to yell amen. I could imagine my piano teacher at the piano, younger versions of my mom and dad teaching Sunday school, my grandpa's funeral, my wedding, and my brother's a few years later.

Beyond those memories, remembering my friend Debbie made me cry, though I'm not much of a crier. I thought of how much calmer I instantly felt whenever she walked into a room. How I never saw her be anything but kind. In many ways, she seemed so simple in her faith, but not simpleminded. Her life wasn't really simple or easy. I think it was her daily choice to trust Jesus that fueled her quiet strength.

Her service reminded me again of how short life is, really, and that the people we spend our lives with are what matters. At the end of Debbie's life, no one cared about her education or lack of it, or how much money she made, or anything else. But they cared how she touched their lives with the love of Jesus. I want to be remembered that way. —GWEN FORD FAULKENBERRY

FAITH STEP: *Think of a person in your life who showed you the love of Jesus in some way (big or small). Write a note thanking him or her that conveys how much it meant and send it.*

SATURDAY, MAY 11

When Jesus therefore saw His mother, and the disciple whom He loved standing by, He said to His mother, "Woman, behold your son!" John 19:26 (NKJV)

TODAY, I'M SIFTING THROUGH FAMILY photos, remembering and missing my mom. She was my best friend. Because of our mutual love and trust, I tried my best to obey her. As I followed her wishes, I could see the delight in her eyes and knew she was proud of me.

When I read the story of Jesus changing water into wine (John 2:1–10), I can almost feel Mary's excitement as she directs the servants to follow Jesus's bidding. It's as if she couldn't bear to wait one more day for the world to know how incredible her son was. I wish I could've witnessed the looks they exchanged during those key moments, when Jesus declared that His time hadn't yet come, and yet He honored her wishes. Their bond was tight, their intimacy complete. I like to think I would've responded in obedience to my mother's encouragement, just as Jesus did.

Even as He hung on the cross, Jesus sought to protect Mary, telling her to look on John as her son. The two probably built a strong relationship, from their mutual adoration for Christ. But still.…

During the years since my mom's passing, I've spent many hours with wonderful older women. They've doled large servings of wisdom, guidance, and love on me. But they're not my mother.

I've never met a substitute for my precious mother. I don't want to. But I've found a bond just as meaningful, a love as deep. There is One who believes in me, as I depend on Him. I'm not alone. He's pushing me to do more, to be more in Him. His love covers my loss. And that's enough. —HEIDI GAUL

FAITH STEP: *Ask Jesus to lead you to someone who needs motherly love and support. Give thanks for the chance to serve Him as you walk in obedience to His wishes.*

MOTHER'S DAY, SUNDAY, MAY 12

"Jerusalem, Jerusalem . . . how often I have longed to gather your children together, as a hen gathers her chicks under her wings, and you were not willing."
Matthew 23:37 *(NIV)*

I LOVE IT THAT IN a moment when Jesus is concerned with a whole nation of people He is trying to save, He feels like a mother. That is a Jesus I could spend *every* morning with! What a relief it is to know that Jesus has had that feeling so familiar to me in my daily life. Whether I'm trying to gather everyone to get out the door on time on a typical day, or I'm in one of those more poignant Big Moments when I want to gather one of my growing children under my protective wing and shield them from the painful life lesson their own willfulness will inevitably teach them, I love praying to this mother-hen-Jesus.

This mother-hen-Jesus is with me when I am feeling the frustrations of motherhood, and this mother-hen-Jesus is also a mother to me, when my own willfulness keeps me from easily falling into Christ's love. Jesus knows the pain of loving someone so much that your heart sees clearly what they need, *and* He knows that each of us has the free will to make our own choices, even when that means rejecting what we need. As we see in this moment when He is crying out to Jerusalem, His ability to "let go and let God" did not come without pain and frustration, but what an example of motherly love He leaves us with! —ELIZABETH BERNE DEGEAR

FAITH STEP: *Imagine yourself as a chick and Jesus as a Mother Hen, trying to gather you under her wing. What parts of you are not willing to be protected and loved? Can you love those parts of you today?*

Monday, May 13

*You have given me your shield of victory. Your right hand supports me;
your help has made me great. Psalm 18:35 (NLT)*

I LOVE MY MOM'S HANDS. They are capable and hardworking. Veins line the top of them. They are weathered from years of working in her garden. But these are the hands that felt my feverish forehead when I was little. I reached for them in the middle of a crowd so that I could feel safe. They showed me how to clean, make chocolate chip cookies, and write my name. When my boys were born, my mom's were the first hands to give my babies a bath. They taught me how to swaddle and hold and nurture. My mom's hands are my favorite. They are the embodiment of care and love.

Lately, my hands have begun to look more like my mom's. My hands find a great deal of joy being in the dirt, planting flowers, and holding the hands of my growing boys. My hands cook and clean and take care of my family. And they write stories and mark the years as they fly by. I want my hands to be the embodiment of care and love.

The most amazing hands of all time were Jesus's hands. His hands performed miracles and brought the dead to life. His hands broke bread and fish and fed thousands. His hands healed the sick and even helped the blind to see. His hands helped the lame to walk. Jesus's hands are the true embodiment of care and love. When we use our hands to care for those around us, our hands are like Jesus's hands. And those are the hands that will change the world.
—SUSANNA FOTH AUGHTMON

FAITH STEP: *Look at your hands. These are the hands of Jesus, showing love for the world you live in. Remember that throughout the day as you care for those you love.*

TUESDAY, MAY 14

[He] richly supplies us with all things to enjoy. 1 Timothy 6:17 (NASB)

I'M ONE OF MANY WHO have made a conscious decision to adopt the Jesus Meal Plan. Its actual name may be something different, but from my perspective, it means taking no more than my body needs, savoring each morsel as a gift from Him, listening to signals He built into my systems to inform my body when I've had enough, and building most meals with foods that came from the ground, trees, and bushes with minimum human distortion.

The primary element of my Jesus Meal Plan is Jesus. For years, I ate without involving Him in decision-making. I asked Him to *bless* what I was eating. But I didn't ask if what I prepared was worthy of His blessing.

It impresses me that whatever was on His plate—little or much—He thanked His Father for it. At the feeding of the five thousand, plus women and children, Jesus didn't wait to thank God *after* the five small loaves and two sardines became enough to satisfy the crowd. He blessed the meal when it was still too little in everyone's eyes but His. He knew that the crowd's satisfaction ultimately would come from the miracle, not the portion size.

The Bible tells us we've been given all things "richly to enjoy." I once assumed that meant He provides great volumes of food to enjoy. But "rich" isn't one potato chip after another until the bag is gone.

Rich may be closer to the tasting spoon of delicacies prepared by a world-renowned chef. Rich for its flavors and satisfaction, not its volume. Ultimately, only Jesus completely satisfies. —CYNTHIA RUCHTI

FAITH STEP: *At your next meal, savor the morsel above the mouthful, the flavor over the volume, and ask if what you've put on the plate before you is worthy of His blessing. I will too.*

WEDNESDAY, MAY 15

Then He looked at them and said, "What then is this that is written: 'The stone which the builders rejected Has become the chief cornerstone'?" Luke 20:17 (NKJV)

NO ONE LIKES REJECTION. UNFORTUNATELY, it's a part of life. Diligent employees get passed over for promotions. Husbands leave loyal wives. The list goes on.

In high school, I was never good at team sports. So gym was my least favorite subject—especially basketball. I remember one day in my gym class, it came time to choose players for the basketball game, and fear and panic overcame me. Everyone knew I wasn't good. Girl after girl ran giddily over to their respective teams, until all eyes were on me as I stood awkwardly next to another outcast. The captain picked the other outcast. As the song goes, "the cheese stands alone." I wanted to be accepted by my teammates, but I knew that wouldn't happen. They didn't expect much from me.

Religious leaders of Jesus's day didn't expect much of Him either. After all, He was just a quiet carpenter, Mary and Joseph's boy. The guy from Galilee. What they didn't know was that the quiet carpenter was the Messiah who was to come. Israel had waited with bated breath for the Savior who was to come. Then when He was finally revealed, many of the people turned away. Those leaders of the day would not accept this humble, unassuming carpenter as the Messiah that God promised. Jesus knew He wasn't wanted, but He persisted with the redeeming message of the cross. He did the will of His Father and triumphed over His detractors. I've continued to deal with rejection, but I've learned from Jesus to keep moving forward in faith. And that philosophy has made all the difference. —CAROL MACKEY

FAITH STEP: *Use Jesus as your perfect example to move forward in faith. Shake off the notion that you are not good enough. You are always more than enough in His eyes.*

THURSDAY, MAY 16

The LORD directs the steps of the godly. He delights in every detail of their lives. Psalm 37:23 (NLT)

ON A FORUM FOR PEOPLE with chronic illness, a patient mentioned how a specific type of doctor utilized a technique that had brought her relief. Since I hadn't tried any new approaches for a while and wanted to improve my own condition, I decided to look into it. A quick search found a practitioner only a mile or so from my home.

I made an appointment, filled out pages of forms, and kept my expectations low. In the days leading up to my appointment, I'd followed all the current research and knew that science was still years away from many treatment options. Still, I prayed that perhaps working with a new doctor could help me regain some daily function: perhaps muscle recovery, less pain, or better quality of sleep.

The doctor was knowledgeable and compassionate. As we talked, he asked if I'd read a certain research paper. I lit up. "Yes. Everyone believes it's the most groundbreaking paper in recent years."

He smiled. "A close friend of mine is one of the authors. I'll call him and get more advice on how to help you."

Coincidence? I call it a "God-incident." As my husband drove me home, happy tears filled my eyes. Jesus had guided me to a doctor with connections to one of the handful of knowledgeable researchers in the country. This reminder of His great compassion flooded me with encouragement. Jesus truly cares about every detail of our lives. Let's keep our eyes open for the divine God-incidences that our Savior arranges. —SHARON HINCK

FAITH STEP: *Next time you notice something that looks like a coincidence, look for the hand of Jesus in the situation.*

FRIDAY, MAY 17

"You have been faithful in handling this small amount, so now I will give you many more responsibilities." Matthew 25:23 (NLT)

IT WAS A CINDERELLA STORY. Austin Bibens-Dirkx threw pitch after pitch in the minors, always hoping for a chance in the majors. Twelve years passed, and at age thirty-two he received a call-up from the Texas Rangers. After two weeks as a bullpen reliever, on May 17, 2017, the new rookie took the place of a starter disabled by an injury. Austin Bibens-Dirkx was finally living his dream.

There were times when Bibens-Dirkx wondered if he would ever reach his dream, but he never gave up. He kept pitching faithfully in the minors, always hoping, always giving his best.

As a shepherd boy, David could have questioned his future too. Anointed as a king when only a teenager, David continued to tend sheep and play the harp. Time passed. One day, King Saul hired David to play for him, then made him his personal armor bearer (1 Samuel 16). David served faithfully, but the jealous king eventually turned against him. Had God forgotten David? Then one day, in God's own perfect timing, David was called up from the minors into God's major lineup: he was crowned the new king.

Writers? Teachers? Pastors? Parents? Whoever we are, most of us can identify with Bibens-Dirkx and David. A dream is born, but years pass, and nothing happens. Doubts arise. Has Jesus forgotten?

But Jesus has never forsaken His plans for us. While He never promises a *Cinderella* ending, He does guarantee that we will reap His kind of success if we don't give up (Galatians 6:9), if we trust Him, and if we are faithful in whatever we do. —REBECCA BARLOW JORDAN

FAITH STEP: *Ask Jesus to help you make faithfulness a habit.*

SATURDAY, MAY 18

Every high priest is a man chosen to represent other people in their dealings with God. . . . And he is able to deal gently with ignorant and wayward people because he himself is subject to the same weaknesses. Hebrews 5:1–2 (NLT)

ONE DICTIONARY DEFINES GENTLENESS AS "sensitivity of disposition and kindness of behavior, founded on strength and prompted by love." I see my son model that definition with his seven children.

Matthew is over six feet tall and towers over his little ones, but he stoops to listen when they talk. He hoists them onto his shoulders to take them for a walk. He cuddles them when they cry, and he patiently teaches them to persist when learning life skills.

Matt's gentle nature is especially obvious when the kids' tempers flare, when they cry because something seems unfair, and when they're cranky because they're overtired. His patience might run thin, but he controls his response because he knows they're imperfect people in process—just like him. Just like you and me.

Jesus is gentleness personified. He became human to show us that He understands humanity's foibles. He exercises grace toward us despite our imperfections. And He demonstrates faithfulness and compassion even when we don't deserve it.

Jesus knows that people can test our patience. That's why He sent the Holy Spirit to teach us to be gentle (Galatians 5:22). He helps us learn to listen and encourages patience so we are able and willing to wait for the right time to have a difficult conversation, and He gives us words that heal rather than hurt.

Jesus demonstrates gentleness with us every day. How can we do less with others? —GRACE FOX

FAITH STEP: *How have you demonstrated gentleness in the past week? Think of a situation in which you did not. How might you have reacted differently?*

SUNDAY, MAY 19

Therefore, confess your sins to one another and pray for one another, that you may be healed. The prayer of a righteous person has great power as it is working. James 5:16 (ESV)

I WAS RAISED IN A spiritual tradition that required that I confess my sins to clergy. It was usually a pretty formal process, punctuated by some "homework" to attain healing. This practice, however it was intended, always left me feeling ashamed.

James asserts confessing our sins is not meant to shame us but to free us and heal us! When I openly share my failings with another trusted person, I often find the person can relate and extend compassion. I feel the warm rush of God's grace come in to reassure me of His loving forgiveness. Talking to a trusted friend can help point the way to self-correcting.

Moreover, if the sin in question is an ongoing struggle, confession diffuses the danger and power of secrecy.

James's direction is not fluffy; it's practical and real.

Recently, I got an email that triggered a rush of guilty feelings about a mistake I'd made fueled by pride. The guilty feelings were so real they almost stopped me in my tracks. I called a friend to talk it through. She reminded me that I'd already confessed this sin and had already received forgiveness. Moments later, I got a follow-up email about my "mistake" that seemed to resolve the matter and my feelings of guilt. Coincidence? I don't think so, having experienced this pattern of confession and grace many times.

My heart is lighter and freer at the thought of confession as an instrument of loving grace. —ISABELLA YOSUICO

FAITH STEP: *Are you carrying the burden of unconfessed sin? Pray for Jesus to point you to His friendly emissary, a worthy confidante, and receive the healing power of confession.*

MONDAY, MAY 20

Yet to all who did receive him, to those who believed in his name, he gave the right to become children of God. John 1:12 (NIV)

As SOON AS I SAW the announcement for a local authors' event, my heart sank. *Why wasn't I invited to be part of it? I'm a local author!* The contact person was a friend of mine. Did she not want me there? Was I not important enough? Not a good enough speaker? Not cool enough? I spent the afternoon feeling like I was back in sixth grade, fighting back tears at my desk because the popular girls had rejected me.

An hour later, I found a week-old email invitation. I pretended to be surprised as I replied, "I would love to participate! Thanks so much for inviting me!" After I'd gotten over the embarrassment of my initial childish reaction, a thought came to me: *What if I really had* not *been invited? What would that mean?*

That my local author friends didn't like me?

That I truly wasn't cool enough?

That, perhaps, it had been an innocent oversight?

At some point, I would have had to accept that, though I felt overlooked, disappointed, and hurt, I still had value. When would I learn that my worth did not rest in whether I made the cut for an invitation?

As believers, we know that our worth lies in Christ, but life's disappointments have a way of overriding that truth. Even as we tend to our wounds, we can make the choice to believe that we are valuable, not because we are accepted by the right people, but because Jesus loved us enough to die for us and call us His. —JEANETTE HANSCOME

FAITH STEP: *Think of a time when you felt overlooked. How quickly did you recover from the hurt? Now think of someone who is often left out of activities and get-togethers. Consider ways to help this person feel more included.*

TUESDAY, MAY 21

Trust in the LORD with all your heart and lean not on your own understanding;
in all your ways submit to him, and he will make your paths straight.
Proverbs 3:5–6 (NIV)

THIS PAST FEBRUARY, WE WERE ready to move into our new rental, but we were told that because of some renovation holdups, our new rental wasn't ready for us yet. *Jesus, hold us close.* For two weeks, we stayed with some wonderfully hospitable friends. They were amazing, but I longed for home. For those of you who are homebodies like me, you understand that being without a home is unnerving. I told my friend Marty, who is a licensed therapist, "I thought I had dealt with all my control issues."

Nope. They were just in hiding. They were revealed on the day that I realized I couldn't find my underwear. My husband, Scott, had packed up our closet, and they vanished in the melee. My boys couldn't find theirs either. This had me calling out, "New underpants for everyone!" Because you can't be sleeping on the floor and not have underpants all at the same time. It is too much.

Life can be overwhelming when we're not in control. We get anxious because we like calling the shots...and we like to know where to find our underwear. But Jesus is the only one capable of calling the shots. He has all the grace and wisdom that we need. He knows our next steps, and He is not surprised by the twists and turns of life. If we can let go of our expectations and cling to Him, He will keep moving us forward in His grace, in His peace, and in His hope. —SUSANNA FOTH AUGHTMON

FAITH STEP: *What is an area of your life that you are longing to control? Are you willing to let go and ask Jesus to guide your next steps even if you can't see what is coming next?*

WEDNESDAY, MAY 22

Don't hide your light! Let it shine for all; let your good deeds glow for all to see, so that they will praise your heavenly Father. Matthew 5:16 (TLB)

LIVING A "FISHBOWL" LIFE AS both a pastor's daughter and a minister's wife may have contributed to my discomfort in the limelight. Or perhaps it was simply my temperament. Regardless, writing books ushered in new opportunities for speaking and new challenges.

When the university I attended presented me with a Distinguished Alumni Award a few years ago, I was so shocked I actually asked if they'd made a mistake. While recognizing that only Jesus can bring success and honors from our broken lives, I still struggled with "letting my light shine." After all, Jesus was the true Light of the World (John 8:12). Shining my light often felt confusing and prideful.

But over time, Jesus helped me understand that *my* light should simply be a reflection of *His* Light. When our focus is on Jesus and not ourselves, embarrassment flees. And letting our light shine by reflecting Him eliminates the kind of selfish pride and praise Jesus rebuked in the lives of hypocrite leaders (Matthew 6:2).

Every God-given gift or moment in the limelight should reflect our pride in the One who gave us good gifts and Who began the good work in us (Philippians 1:6). Whether it's accepting praise graciously, using our gifts creatively, or blessing others in caring, unseen ways, our goal and purpose are the same: to bring glory to Jesus. With that as our motive, it's always Jesus's greater Light that shines through our works. And people can see the difference.

Our Christ-like character will always speak louder than our works.
—REBECCA BARLOW JORDAN

FAITH STEP: *This week, ask Jesus to let His light shine through you.*

THURSDAY, MAY 23

You will know the truth, and the truth will set you free. John 8:32 (NLT)

ONE OF MY FRIENDS WHO had been depressed for seven years told his sister he was ready to commit suicide. The sister called the doctor, who had my friend committed to a psych hospital. He didn't want to go, but there was nothing else to do.

After a couple days, I visited him. The nurse who let me in—with a password—confiscated the Starbucks cup I'd brought him full of real coffee as well as the pack of Charmin. He led me to a room where a TV on mute seemed like a good metaphor for the rest of the people gathered there. Most were staring, not saying anything. My friend and I sat at a particleboard table in the corner on hard chairs.

At first, we just held hands and cried. Then my friend told me something astonishing. He said, "I didn't want to come here, but I'm glad I did. It's real. There's no hiding from the truth in a place like this—I have to face it. And in a weird way, that's given me hope."

I understood exactly what he meant. For seven years I'd been trying to help him figure out what to do to make his life better. We looked for new jobs, and we talked about relationship changes and changes in location. But the truth was that nothing could ever get better until *he* was better on the *inside*.

The truth can be a scary place to go. It can be ugly and inconvenient. But strangely enough, it always brings freedom. That's a promise from the One Who is truth, Who died to set us free. —GWEN FORD FAULKENBERRY

FAITH STEP: *Pray this prayer, filling in the blank as you feel led: Jesus, show me the truth about _____, even if it hurts, so that I can be free.*

FRIDAY, MAY 24

In the beginning was the Word, and the Word was with God, and the Word was God. He was in the beginning with God. All things were made through Him, and without Him nothing was made that was made. John 1:1–3 (NKJV)

TRAVELING IS ONE OF MY passions. Whenever I have the chance, I hop into the car or onto a plane for a new adventure. Last week, my husband, David, and I returned from my most recent journey—a trip to Rocky Mountain National Park.

Traveling the highway that courses those mountains is a one-of-a-kind experience. Three thousand Roosevelt elk roam the area. The high-elevation roads take visitors past meadows blanketed in wildflowers, through forests, and finally above the tree line.

The entire time we drove along that curving two-lane road, we watched Jesus's incredible creation in awe. From tiny, intricate blossoms to a magnificent bull elk, to the grandeur of the slopes they both call home, His creation amazed us. God thought of every detail and made everything uniquely beautiful. His creation renewed my outlook.

When we arrived home, I noticed with fresh eyes the everyday wonders He tucks into my world. Roses blooming, a cat asleep in a patch of afternoon sunlight, steam rising from a cup of herbal tea. A kiss from my husband. The blessing of knowing that both my spouse and I are part of this miracle and that Jesus sees beauty in us.

I glance out the window as a bird glides past, headed for our old wooden birdhouse, a twig clutched in her beak. How can I keep from smiling and bowing my head in thanks? He is life, and life is good—in so many different ways. —HEIDI GAUL

FAITH STEP: *Search your home and outdoor space for spots where life and beauty combine with the unmistakable touch of the Master's hand.*

SATURDAY, MAY 25

Can a mother forget the baby at her breast and have no compassion on the child she has borne? Though she may forget, I will not forget you! See, I have engraved you on the palms of my hands; your walls are ever before me. Isaiah 49:15–16 (NIV)

MY FRIEND TATUM JUST HAD her third baby. Having three children under the age of four is no small undertaking. Especially when the smallest one seems hungry all the time. I have all kinds of empathy for her. I remember those foggy days of early motherhood well. I told her, "It feels crazy when all of your days are chopped up into three-hour segments. That feeding schedule is relentless."

You feed the baby. Change the baby. Rock the baby. Try to meet the energetic demands of the four-year-old. Try to keep the two-year-old from ingesting something lethal. Put the baby down for a nap. Pick up the baby who won't stop crying. Separate the two-year-old's hands from the four-year-old's hair. Cry with the baby, the two-year-old, and the four-year-old. And then it is time to feed the baby again.

It doesn't stop. That schedule is emblazoned in my mind. It has to be when it is your job to keep someone alive. Jesus has that same kind of attentiveness to us and our needs.

There are times when the circumstances of life leave us feeling alone and forgotten. There are moments when we feel that we are the last thing on His mind. But He is near. He is meeting every need and wiping every tear, reminding us that He loves us. His job is keeping us alive with His mercy, His grace, and His unfailing love. We will never be forgotten. —SUSANNA FOTH AUGHTMON

FAITH STEP: *Remember a time that you felt forgotten by Jesus. Correct that lie in your mind. You are never forgotten. Jesus was with you then and will be with you always.*

SUNDAY, MAY 26

As Jesus passed on from there, He saw a man named Matthew sitting at the tax office. And He said to him, "Follow Me." So he arose and followed Him.
Matthew 9:9 (NKJV)

RECENTLY I HEARD A PASTOR on TV say that when you say yes to Jesus, you must say no to other things. That notion of sacrifice has been a part of my testimony. When I first became a Christian, I traded happy hours for evening church service. I traded shopping for the latest outfit for giving tithes and offerings. I gave what I had to the Lord and He gave back to me more than I could ever imagine. In order to be a true disciple of Christ, He must be our priority.

When Jesus dropped by the Sea of Galilee, He called brothers Peter and Andrew, two fishermen who were casting their nets into the sea. When Jesus told them to follow Him, Matthew 4:20 says they "immediately left *their* nets and followed Him" (emphasis mine). The very next line says He also recruited two other brothers, James and John, who were in a boat mending their nets. They, too, answered the Lord's call "and immediately they left the boat and their father, and followed Him" (v. 22). They responded without hesitation. They didn't argue or ask why or "Who are you?" They simply followed Him. Jesus asks the same of us.

He doesn't say "follow Christians" or "follow pastors." He says "follow Me." The disciples left everything—their livelihoods, their families and friends, and their cushy ways of life to follow Jesus, yet they lacked nothing. At times, you will too. All their needs were supplied, and yours will be too. Following Jesus isn't always easy, but it's always worth it. —CAROL MACKEY

FAITH STEP: *Say out loud, "I have decided to follow Jesus." Your reward will greatly outweigh your sacrifice.*

MONDAY, MAY 27

For the moment all discipline seems painful rather than pleasant, but later it yields the peaceful fruit of righteousness to those who have been trained by it.
Hebrews 12:11 (ESV)

DOES ANYONE REALLY LIKE DISCIPLINE? Sure, I don't mind gloating a bit when I'm able to exercise some *self*-discipline, but mostly I don't want anyone disciplining me.

Yet God says He disciplines those He loves and that discipline produces good results. My two boys are fine examples.

For a while, my ten-year-old son would argue and complain when asked to do something. I want to be a gracious parent, inspiring my kids to behave and excel out of love, not fear. Sometimes, though, it's firm discipline that produces the desired result: when my husband and I removed our son's coveted technology for a few days, peace and harmony once again reigned.

My goal in disciplining my son was not only about eliminating the very real annoyance of constant debate, but also about preparing him for a good future. I know my boys will be happiest and most successful if they can learn to, work with a positive, cooperative attitude.

Likewise, my heavenly Father disciplines me because He wants me (and others through me) to enjoy the harvest of righteousness.

I've, at times, confused discipline with punishment. If God sees me doing something harmful, or even something short of my best, He will allow me to suffer the consequences of my actions so I'll repent. In turning away from whatever it is, I can enjoy peace. This is not the heavy-handed punishment of an irate God, but the loving redirection of a good Father. —ISABELLA YOSUICO

FAITH STEP: *Do you sense you're bucking at some discipline right now? What is resistance costing you? Ask Jesus for guidance.*

TUESDAY, MAY 28

You are the light of the world—like a city on a hilltop that cannot be hidden. . . . a lamp is placed on a stand, where it gives light to everyone in the house. In the same way, let your good deeds shine out for all to see, so that everyone will praise your heavenly Father. Matthew 5:14–16 (NLT)

ONE OF MY FRIENDS VISITS a particular coffee shop every morning, gives a loaded gift card to the clerk with instructions to use it as payment for customers' orders, and asks to not be identified as the donor. Then he sits down to read and enjoy a cup of coffee.

The clerks generally respect his request for anonymity, but sometimes they send grateful customers his way. "Why do you do this?" they ask.

"Because Jesus has blessed me, and I want to bless others in return," he says. Then he engages them in conversation by asking questions: "What do you do for a living?" "What's the greatest challenge you're facing at this time?" He listens, offers a few encouraging words, and then asks, "Is it okay if I pray for you about that challenge?" So far, everyone has said yes.

My friend's actions shine as a light for everyone in the shop. More than once, the owner has told him that his generosity has made a huge positive impact on the employees. It's obviously making a difference in the lives of the customers with whom he talks too.

He doesn't do this for personal gain or glory. Love for Jesus and a desire to obey His command to shine as a light motivates him, and the joy he receives in return makes it all worthwhile. —GRACE FOX

FAITH STEP: *Darken your room and then either light a candle or turn on a flashlight. Note how the light illuminates the darkness. Ask Jesus to show you a creative way to shine for Him.*

WEDNESDAY, MAY 29

He rolled up the scroll, handed it back to the attendant, and sat down.
Luke 4:20 (NLT)

ONE OF OUR GRANDCHILDREN—who shall remain nameless—was in trouble again.

The situation called for some carefully constructed grandparent-talk. I started formulating my grandma version. Something to convince the child to make a better choice. Point A would lead logically to Point B and Point C, by which time said child would no doubt squirm and repent and perhaps volunteer to take care of us in our old age.

"Quit it," my husband, Bill, told the errant child. Then he left the room, enough said.

Jesus communicated a short message chock-full of power in the synagogue one day. "On the Sabbath," the Bible tells us, "he went to the synagogue as he normally did and stood up to read.... [Jesus] unrolled the scroll and found the place where it was written: The Spirit of the Lord is upon me, because the Lord has anointed me. He has sent me to preach good news to the poor, to proclaim release to the prisoners and recovery of sight to the blind, to liberate the oppressed, and to proclaim the year of the Lord's favor" (Luke 4:16–21).

What Jesus did next stunned the crowd. He rolled up the Isaiah scroll, gave it back to the assistant, and sat down. Enough said.

As the people stared, having expected the traditional several hours of reading from the ancient texts, Jesus said, "Today, this scripture has been fulfilled just as you heard it" (v. 21).

He was the fulfillment. He had their attention. He has mine.
—CYNTHIA RUCHTI

FAITH STEP: *In a journal, the margin of your Bible, or a note card, rehearse several two-to-four-word sentences that tell the story of Jesus: He died; He lives.*

THURSDAY, MAY 30

The LORD does not look at the things people look at. People look at the outward appearance, but the LORD looks at the heart. 1 Samuel 16:7 (NIV)

WHILE SHOPPING WITH MY TWELVE-YEAR-OLD granddaughter, Lacey, I showed her a white headband with the words *Hello Gorgeous* stitched in fancy script. "I might get this for washing my face and putting on makeup," I said. "But I would remove the embroidered words."

"Don't do that, Nana!" Lacey said. "It might be good motivation for you."

Bless her sweet, innocent heart. I didn't explain that seeing that greeting in my bathroom mirror in the mornings would motivate me, all right—to roll around on the floor laughing.

It's hard not to get fixated on physical beauty when we're bombarded with retouched, air-brushed images of perfect-looking women and men. Imagine how different it would be if our culture promoted inner beauty, the kind that truly matters and never fades away. The kind of beauty that we've all seen shine through someone who loves Jesus wholeheartedly.

Isaiah 53:2 tells us that Jesus had no special beauty to attract people's attention. Still, hymns about our "fairest Lord Jesus" and "beautiful Savior" remind us that real beauty can't necessarily be detected by human eyes. If we've trusted Jesus to be our Savior, then God already sees us as pure and unblemished. And the more we act like Jesus, the more gorgeous we become. —DIANNE NEAL MATTHEWS

FAITH STEP: *Which term for believers do you most need to hear right now: chosen, dearly loved child, beloved? Write it on a note to stick on your bathroom mirror. Imagine Jesus greeting you like that every morning.*

FRIDAY, MAY 31

First this: God created the Heavens and Earth—all you see, all you don't see. Earth was a soup of nothingness, a bottomless emptiness, an inky blackness. God's Spirit brooded like a bird above the watery abyss. Genesis 1:2 (MSG)

MY FRIEND MARY HAS CHICKENS, and she was just telling me that one of the hens has recently been determined to sit on her eggs after she lays them. No matter what Mary does, this hen is determined to sit. She wants to have chicks. And it is her brooding over the eggs that will allow them to come into being.

God's creation started with sitting around! God's Spirit hovered over the waters and was an essential precursor to . . . well, *everything.* We often think "Let there be light!" started it all, but sitting with the first few words of Genesis, we realize that the cosmos began with a generative stillness. A brooding.

As with God's Spirit and with hens, it's so with humans. Our creativity needs us to take a good deal of time just sitting around, brooding, for the creative spark to move from Spirit, to imagination, to action in the world. I think I avoid boredom because I'm afraid that the emptiness will feel truly bottomless—isn't it human nature to avoid an abyss? Can I trust that the miracle of creativity needs us all to sit with the nothingness long enough to bring new creation into being through us? —ELIZABETH BERNE DeGEAR

FAITH STEP: *Next time you catch yourself doing busywork in order to avoid being bored or "sitting around doing nothing," ask Jesus to sit with you and help you tolerate the emptiness. Trust that this is the path to new life.*

SATURDAY, JUNE 1

For we are God's handiwork, created in Christ Jesus to do good works, which God prepared in advance for us to do. Ephesians 2:10 (NIV)

DRAGON BOATS FOLLOWED THE COURSE, racing along the wide Willamette River. With brightly painted heads at the bow and curling and intricate tails at the stern, it appeared mythical creatures had come alive to float upon the water's surface. Inside each beautiful craft, two lines of rowers worked in tandem, every stroke of their oars in perfect harmony. As team members stretched their bodies to the limit to reach their objective, the hours they'd invested resulted in an excellent finish. I was impressed, knowing that if even one of the athletes had faltered, the entire crew would have suffered.

Seeing so many individuals working toward a common goal made me think of Christians. Whether we're singing in the choir, collecting items for the needy, or taking part in a mission trip, if we keep our eyes on Him, we remain part of something extraordinary.

But there are times I lose track of my mission. When I dwell on a thoughtless comment or some petty annoyance, I make myself and my feelings a priority—not Jesus. And my attitude threatens the group's effectiveness.

Stepping away for a few minutes alone with Jesus puts things back into perspective for me. His gentle ways are a reminder that He spent all His hours working toward harmony with others and not a moment thinking about Himself. With my eyes opened, I can get back on course, confident that, in this race, we're all winners. Because through Jesus we will have an excellent finish. —HEIDI GAUL

FAITH STEP: *Next time you attend church, scan the congregation. Think about the individuals making up different groups and committees and all the good they do working together for Jesus. If you haven't already, choose a "team" and start rowing!*

Sunday, June 2

Sing to the Lord a new song; sing to the Lord, all the earth. Sing to the Lord, praise his name; proclaim his salvation day after day. Declare his glory among the nations, his marvelous deeds among all peoples. Psalm 96:1–3 (NIV)

I love music. All kinds. Most mornings that I am driving in my car, you will find the music blaring and me singing along. Music has shaped my life. I have a special fondness for hymns. Growing up as a pastor's kid, I have memories of my mom playing the organ and my dad standing in the pulpit leading the congregation in hymn songs. "At Calvary." "All Hail the Power of Jesus' Name." "My Hope Is Built on Nothing Less." I always liked the anthems. I felt them in my soul. Standing shoulder to shoulder, singing out about the greatness of Jesus, was powerful. I wanted to sing the loudest of all.

All these years later, songs still play a big part in my relationship with Jesus. When I am happy? I sing. When I am discouraged? I put on worship music and let the lyrics wash over me. When I am struggling with dark thoughts, these old hymn songs rise in my mind like battle cries. When I have trouble recalling a certain Scripture, I have the uncanny ability to remember the words to songs. It seems that we were created that way.

Songs are linked to spirit. And our spirits were made to declare the amazing works of Jesus and how He moves in our lives. There is something powerful, in the face of fear or pain, when we sing about the goodness of the One Who loves us the most. It reshapes our thoughts and calms our fears. Today, I think we should try to sing the loudest of all. —Susanna Foth Aughtmon

Faith Step: *Put on your favorite hymns or worship music. Sing a new song to Jesus, declaring His goodness in your life.*

MONDAY, JUNE 3

Jerusalem, Jerusalem, you who kill the prophets and stone those sent to you, how often I have longed to gather your children together, as a hen gathers her chicks under her wings, and you were not willing. Matthew 23:37 (NIV)

A PAIR OF GEESE NESTED on the pond behind our house. I sat on our patio to watch the goslings toddle around. Tiny balls of fluff, the world must have seemed huge and new to them as they waddled about aimlessly. But when their parents led the way, the goslings followed them to the water's edge, and swam behind them in a neat line. If they refused to follow, they could become the target of a neighbor's dog or a nearby hawk.

Watching our local goose family reminds me of the comfort of nestling under the wings of our Savior. I cherish the way He nurtures me, and I long to stay close to Him, even when He leads me someplace unfamiliar and perhaps frightening.

I've learned something else by observing the geese. The mama and papa are very protective of their little family. If I tiptoe too near, they herd their little ones together and push them toward the pond. If I keep approaching, they can turn fierce. A tense goose with neck extended, hissing a warning, is nothing to mess with.

The image of being gathered under His wings makes me feel soft and warm. But I'm also comforted by the knowledge that Jesus is fiercely protective of us. He spoke about His love and longing for us as He looked over Jerusalem. But the poignant last phrase of the verse says, "you were not willing."

Are we willing? Are we willing to let Jesus draw us near and protect us? Are we willing to look to Him for guidance and follow Him? —SHARON HINCK

FAITH STEP: *Tell Jesus you are willing to be nurtured and protected by Him, and spend a few extra minutes today nestled in the shadow of His wings.*

TUESDAY, JUNE 4

Then they will see the Son of Man coming in clouds with great power and glory. Mark 13:26 (HCSB)

THE SUNCOAST OF FLORIDA HAS remarkable clouds. I've read it has something to do with the peninsular weather patterns, an appendage of land sandwiched between the Atlantic Ocean and the Gulf. Whatever the reason, the sky here is often breathtaking and dynamic, a rival to the endless, rolling green hills of our former mountain home.

I've had two dreams about Jesus's return, both miraculously consistent and vivid and involving clouds. Driving along well-traveled Florida roads, I routinely *see* real-life cloud formations that harken to my dreams. Puffy, churning, three-dimensional columns of clouds, infused with brilliant, ethereal light.

My ten-year-old asks me, "Will everyone see Him?"

I reply, "The Bible says yes."

"But how?" he asks, dissatisfied with my simple answer.

"I don't know, but God is God, and He can do anything!" I assert, suspending my own skepticism in the face of my life-changing experience of a mighty Messiah.

The God Who created heaven and earth will return in glory. Everyone will see Him. Every knee will bow in reverent awe or mournful fear.

Some days, when the headlines or my own life seem too much to take, I long for His return.

The beautiful skyscape is a heartening reminder of an unbroken future we Christians can anticipate with confidence and joy, no matter what's happening here and now. —ISABELLA YOSUICO

FAITH STEP: *Sometime soon, read Revelation 1 and look to the sky or Google paintings of the event. Spend a few minutes imagining Jesus's return.*

WEDNESDAY, JUNE 5

"[T]he ruler of this world approaches. He has no power over me, but I will do what the Father requires of me, so that the world will know that I love the Father." John 14:30–31 (NLT)

FEAR WAS A BIG DEAL for me when I began writing for publication. Would my words merit an editor's approval? If published, would they impact readers for good or bring criticism? Would they accurately teach truth or unintentionally misrepresent God's Word?

When I sensed Jesus telling me to write a book about overcoming fear, I resisted for a year. The fears of inadequacy and failure held me in bondage. Scriptures such as John 14:15—"If you love me, obey my commandments"—helped me understand that, because I am truly loved by Him, I should be willing to trust Him. And I'll be willing to do whatever He asks, even if it means doing it afraid.

Other Bible verses, including today's verse, helped me realize that Satan does anything possible to hinder or stop me from obeying Jesus, and his weapon of choice is often fear. By focusing on my fears rather than on Jesus, I'd given Satan power over me. I'd allowed him to padlock me in chains.

Grasping the truth that Jesus lives in me helped set me free (Galatians 2:20). Almighty God dwells in me; therefore, Satan has no power over me. Unless I give Satan my nod of approval, he cannot overcome me because Christ's power is at work within me.

Fear over God-given tasks still occasionally knocks at my door, but I refuse to let it linger. Instead, I focus on Jesus and His presence in me, and I'm empowered to do His will. —GRACE FOX

FAITH STEP: *Memorize the words "Jesus lives in me. The enemy has no power over me." When fear comes knocking, speak this truth aloud.*

THURSDAY, JUNE 6

Jesus replied, "The truth of the matter is that you want to be with me because I fed you, not because you believe in me." John 6:26 (TLB)

THE OLDER I GET, THE more I notice that many people fall into one of two categories: givers and takers. We all probably know at least one person who seems interested only in what he or she can get out of a relationship. In many ways, our culture promotes this self-centered behavior, especially with couples. If one side feels as though the relationship no longer meets their needs, they're often encouraged to move on and find a new partner.

Jesus felt the sting of being used after He miraculously fed a crowd of thousands with a few loaves and two fish. Some of the people followed after Him the next day. Jesus knew what was in their hearts. They sought Him because of the free food they'd received, not because they hungered for the truth. I can't imagine how sad Jesus must have felt at this response, after working so hard to open people's eyes to the gift of forgiveness and salvation He offered. All while knowing that He would soon lay down His life to pay for their sins.

Brother Lawrence, a seventeenth-century lay brother in a French monastery, learned to make the love of God his motivation for all of his actions. He found joy while performing even the most mundane chore, "seeking Him only and nothing else, not even His gifts" (from *The Practice of the Presence of God*). Those words made me evaluate my own attitudes: *Am I motivated to follow and serve Jesus for the blessings He can give me, or do I love Him simply for Who He is?* Like Brother Lawrence, I want to offer Jesus a love with no strings attached. —DIANNE NEAL MATTHEWS

FAITH STEP: *Evaluate your prayer life to make sure you include pure expressions of love for Jesus along with your requests and needs.*

FRIDAY, JUNE 7

The Spirit of the Lord GOD is upon me, Because the LORD has anointed me To bring good news to the afflicted . . . To comfort all who mourn . . . Giving them a garland instead of ashes, The oil of gladness instead of mourning, The mantle of praise instead of a spirit of fainting. Isaiah 61:1–3 (NASB)

WHEN WE WENT ON VACATION this past summer, we spent a lot of time in the desert. Being from the hills of Arkansas, with our house perched above the Arkansas River, my kids found this to be a completely new habitat. They collected different colors of sand in the Painted Desert, petrified wood in the Petrified Forest, and all kinds of weird rocks. But their greatest fascination was the cacti we saw everywhere, of every shape and size.

My daughter Adelaide dug up a tiny one she found on the side of the road and put it in a Solo cup, hoping to show her cousin Sophia when we got home. A native Arizonan told her not to water it, and she obeyed.

In the next few weeks of our journey, I noticed that the cactus looked dead. It got gray hairs all over it, so thick that no green showed through. One morning, I told Adelaide she needed to throw it out. "Look, Mommy!" she said, pointing to what looked like horns protruding from the top. "I think those might be blooms!"

Sure enough, the next day, that gray cloud of cactus burst into color with two gorgeous flowers. I could not believe my eyes. "Told ya it wasn't dead." The cactus made it home.

For me, this little plant is a reminder of what Jesus does in our lives. He brings good news when we're ready to give up and gives us beauty for ashes. —GWEN FORD FAULKENBERRY

FAITH STEP: *What in your life compares to that little cactus? Place it in Jesus's hands and leave it there. He has a way of resurrecting things.*

SATURDAY, JUNE 8

At midnight the cry rang out: "Here's the bridegroom!
Come out to meet him!" Matthew 25:6 (NIV)

IN JUNE, HALLMARK MOVIES USUALLY focus on brides and their wedding preparations, which can often run into thousands of dollars. With so much attention given to the perfect dress, flowers, food, and venue for the big event, the groom is often left behind.

In ancient Jewish weddings, the focus was different. The formal engagement would be sealed, binding a legal marriage agreement. Only the groom's father could set the actual date of the wedding ceremony. The groom immediately began adding onto his father's house to complete their home with a bridal chamber. But only the groom's father could make the final decision on when the room was ready.

The bride prepared mainly by keeping herself pure. In Jesus's parable of the ten virgins, every night the five wise virgins would keep oil available for their lamps in readiness to meet the groom. Not knowing when he would arrive, a virgin would let that light guide her if the bridegroom approached in the midnight hours. When they heard the shofar blow, the five foolish virgins scrambled to buy oil, but it was too late. The bridegroom arrived in their absence to capture his bride away, and only the five prepared, wise virgins entered the wedding banquet hall with them.

As part of the Church—the Bride of Christ—and as a follower of Jesus, I have no fear of being left behind. He is preparing a place for me, and when the time is right, He will return for His Bride. My lamp is filled with the oil of His Spirit, a gift He paid for with His life. —REBECCA BARLOW JORDAN

FAITH STEP: *If you know Christ, celebrate Jesus's soon-to-be return. If not, ask Jesus to "seal" your relationship with Him.*

SUNDAY, JUNE 9

But a Samaritan, as he traveled, came where the man was; and when he saw him, he took pity on him. Luke 10:33 (NIV)

ARRIVING FOR A LATE LUNCH at a favorite restaurant, my husband, David, and I watched a lone server struggling to serve all the tables. Her hands were full taking orders and busing tables. Near the entry, a boy hovered, a silver cross necklace glistening on his chest. Our waitress stole a moment to speak with him, and he moved out of sight.

Soon, we were the only diners left. I complimented our waitress on the way she'd raised her boy. She explained that he was her brother, not her son. She was starting life over and had been lonely, so he'd come to keep her company. She missed her home and country. I've visited it often, so we reminisced comfortably for a time. Then she opened up, telling us she'd come here to escape an abusive relationship.

I listened. I understood. She reminded me of the beaten roadside man in the Bible, the one so many people passed by, finally helped by a Samaritan. And of my younger self and the challenges I'd faced during my escape from hurtful relationships. As we talked, I told her aid was available and offered my help too. I left with her phone number and a hope for friendship—and for her future.

Jesus considered my broken soul worthy of rescue. When I needed it most, He placed me with caring people who helped me turn my life around. Now I can be there for others going through similar situations. —HEIDI GAUL

FAITH STEP: *From what sort of damage did Jesus lift you? How has He led you to help? Reach out to someone suffering that same type of pain. Be her Samaritan!*

MONDAY, JUNE 10

We wait in hope for the LORD; he is our help and our shield. In him our hearts rejoice, for we trust in his holy name. May your unfailing love be with us, LORD, even as we put our hope in you. Psalm 33:20–22 (NIV)

MY BOYS LOVE SUPERHERO MOVIES. I won't lie; so do I. They each have a favorite hero. And I love any story with a good ending. In the battle of good versus evil, we want to see the good guy win. During those treacherous movie moments, when all hope is lost, people break out cheering in the theater when the hero swoops in and saves the day.

There is something in all of us that longs for a hero in our world. We want someone to leap to our defense when we are in trouble. We want someone to find us and pull us from the dark. We want a savior. We wish we knew someone who had special powers and super strength. We forget, on a regular basis, that we do. Jesus.

He conquered death. He broke the power of sin over us. He breathes life into us. He sets captives free and cracks open the darkness with the light of His everlasting love. Jesus is the healer. He is the provider. He is the miracle worker. He is our righteousness. He is our deliverer. Jesus is our present help in times of trouble. There is no superpower that He does not possess.

How can we forget how He came into our lives and transformed us? How can we forget the power of His incomparable love that surrounds us? How can we forget that the entire reason He came to earth was to save us? His beloved. This is why we can rejoice and break out cheering. Jesus always wins. —SUSANNA FOTH AUGHTMON

FAITH STEP: *Jesus came to earth to save . . . you! Take a moment to cheer about that! Tell Him how you will always place your trust in Him.*

TUESDAY, JUNE 11

"Teach me to do Your will, For You are my God;
Let Your good Spirit lead me.'" Psalm 143:10 (AMP)

AFTER A MINOR MEDICAL PROCEDURE, for which my husband was required to fast, we immediately headed to a local restaurant.

While we waited for our meal, our conversation wandered from discussions about garden mulch to the latest antics of our grandkids to travel plans for the summer.

During a brief lull in the conversation, I heard a familiar voice coming from the booth behind me. That slow southern drawl with an edge of humor could only belong to one person. Desi had been a member of a church we'd attended years ago, a spitfire of a woman with a no-nonsense approach to life and all-nonsense comedic timing.

I wasn't sure she'd remember me. But I felt compelled to stop at her booth, reintroduce myself, and tell her how much I've always appreciated her. For some reason, I sensed I should lean in to give her a kiss on the check as I said good-bye.

Two weeks after that day, her niece posted on social media that Desi had been moved to hospice. That brief and unexpected encounter was our last. Jesus knew.

If we listen, Jesus will direct our steps so clearly that we'll know which restaurant to choose, which booth to sit in, and when the conversation should quiet long enough to hear Him say, "Go to the table behind you. Tell her you remember her fondly. Kiss her aging cheek, and wish her well on her journey." —CYNTHIA RUCHTI

FAITH STEP: *How comfortable is it for you to take direction when Jesus asks you to? Trust His leading. His direction is always purposeful.*

WEDNESDAY, JUNE 12

Jesus replied, "Foxes have dens and birds have nests, but the Son of Man has no place to lay his head." Matthew 8:20 (NIV)

"I'M OUTGROWING MY SPACE." I set a bag of donation items in the hallway. My youngest son, Nathan, and I had been living with my parents for almost five years. Originally, our belongings had been reduced to what fit in a ten-by-ten storage unit, my parents' garage, the area they'd turned into Nathan's bedroom and my bedroom/office. I'd emptied the storage unit three summers ago, keeping only what was most precious. Now my room needed attention. For a moment, I fought the same resentment that came whenever I had to part with some piece of my old life. It resurrected hurtful memories.

I reminded myself of the benefits I'd found in being reduced to so little: I'd learned to appreciate simplicity and the blessings of having a supportive family. They'd rearranged their house to create a special place for Nathan and a private room for me, and they'd come up with a financial arrangement that made it possible for me to continue writing and editing from home.

Jesus was homeless, I remembered. He always had food and companions, but never a home base. Many of His followers struggled to survive. And, of course, there are the many single moms who don't have families to take them in for as long as they need.

Jesus, help me be more grateful, I prayed. *Thank You that I have a room that is mine, extra to give away, and so much evidence of Your provision.* —JEANETTE HANSCOME

FAITH STEP: *Look around the room you are in right now. What do you have that someone else might appreciate? Fill at least one bag to donate to a local charity.*

THURSDAY, JUNE 13

Long before he laid down earth's foundations, he had us in mind, had settled on us as the focus of his love, to be made whole and holy by his love.
Ephesians 1:5 (MSG)

"DADDY, LOOK AT ME!" I remember those words tumbling out of my mouth as a child and then hearing them from my own children years ago and from my grandchildren not so long ago. From jumping ropes to balancing hula hoops, swimming laps to bouncing on trampolines, building sand castles to playing computer games. We all cry, "Watch me!" and crave affection from the ones we love—most certainly our fathers.

Jesus obtained His Father's approval and affection from day one. Centuries before Jesus's birth, Isaiah prophesied of Jesus who would be the "Wonderful Counselor," "Prince of Peace," "Mighty God," and "Everlasting Father." The angel Gabriel announced to Mary that she would give birth to Jesus, the "Son of the Most High." And when Jesus was born, the angels announced His arrival, calling Him "Savior," and "Messiah, the Lord." God made it clear at Jesus's baptism: "This is my dearly loved Son, who brings me great joy" (Matthew 3:17 NLT). How could Jesus ever question His importance to His Father?

Even at His death, Jesus never doubted or wavered. He wants us to know that His Father watches us (Psalm 121:8) and that He loves us just as His Father loved Him (John 15:9). Jesus's birth, life, death, and resurrection proved Jesus's love for us. While earthly fathers may fail us, Jesus never will. As His children, we bring Him pleasure and we are the focus of His love—a love that endures forever.
—REBECCA BARLOW JORDAN

FAITH STEP: *Write a love letter to Jesus today, telling Him how much you love Him and thanking Him for loving you.*

FRIDAY, JUNE 14

Above all, love each other deeply, because love covers over a multitude of sins.
1 Peter 4:8 (NIV)

MY FATHER WAS A GOOD MAN. He was a World War II vet who valued hard work, humor, and, above all, his family. But as he aged, a life filled with disappointment made him sour. He began drinking heavily, his temper raging against my mother and me. At the time, I didn't understand, and it changed the way I looked at my dad. But when I got older, I recognized my father was only human.

As a new Christian, I used to wonder how Jesus maintained His devotion to Father God. How did He feel, knowing He'd been sent to earth to die for us? Did God's forgiveness of our sins include Jesus's forgiveness of His Father? But as my understanding grew, I discovered the lie behind those thoughts. Jesus understood His purpose and never questioned it. He lived the commandment to honor His Father (Exodus 20:12) with perfect grace and selfless dignity. And His selfless act of love ultimately saved us all from the sourness of sin.

With Father's Day approaching, I'm meditating on how, during Dad's last days, Jesus opened eternity's door and welcomed him with open arms. He honored my flawed, mortal father and loved him beyond his faults.

Jesus is teaching me to love past the pain and look forward to a bright future reconnecting with loved ones in heaven. It's time for me to think on "whatever is admirable, whatever is noble" (Philippians 4:8). So, this Father's Day, I'm giving a gift wrapped in love. It's a heart filled with forgiveness, bowing in honor. One size fits all. —HEIDI GAUL

FAITH STEP: *Forgive the bad times and honor those memories from your past that were good. Post some photos of your parent (or parents) on your fridge to help you remember.*

SATURDAY, JUNE 15

The Father loves the Son. John 3:35 (NKJV)

I LOVED MY DAD. HE was a family man and a great provider with a tireless work ethic. The hardest thing I ever had to do was to tell him I was pregnant. I wasn't married at the time and was not a Christian. Although I was a twenty-two-year-old college graduate with a job, I felt like a pregnant teenager. I knew he loved me and would always love me, but I desperately wanted his approval. Still, I had disappointed him. He was so happy after I graduated from college and had high hopes for his ambitious baby girl. In the end, he adored and doted on my son. And later, when I married my child's father, my feelings evened out.

When I came to Christ and was still in the "toddler" stage of my Christian walk, I wanted God's approval, so I did everything in my power to please Him. I knew He loved me, but I wanted Him to *keep* loving me. Whenever I messed up, I assumed He was mad at me. If only I'd have looked at Jesus's relationship to the Father, I know I would have thought differently about my view of Him.

Our earthly fathers are good, and God placed them here as a proto-type of Him—protecting, providing, leading, guiding, and disciplin-ing when necessary. Jesus's first priority was pleasing His Father (John 5:30). He trusted Him and knew that everything God the Father told Him was right (John 3:33–34). He was even obedient to God when He took His last breath (John 18:11). Jesus's obedience to His Father should serve as a model for our obedience to Him. —CAROL MACKEY

FAITH STEP: *Don't beat up on yourself when you think you've "messed up." Consider John 3:16. Know that God loves you the way He loves Jesus—with an unfailing and unconditional love. He will never love you any more or less than He does right now.*

FATHER'S DAY, SUNDAY, JUNE 16

Because you are his sons, God sent the Spirit of his Son into our hearts, the Spirit who calls out, "Abba, Father." Galatians 4:6 (NIV)

WHEN MY KIDS HEAR MY husband walk through the door at the end of the day, they peal in delighted unison, "Daddy, Daddy!" rushing him with hugs and reports of the day.

"Daddy, Daddy!" sounds like joy, trust, and intimacy. My husband, Ray, is an awesome dad, more than worthy of that delightfully personal greeting. Yet, even as a fallible mortal who loses his temper, overindulges, or otherwise makes parenting mistakes, in discipline and reward, Ray is motivated by love, by the boys' best interests, and by the longing to bless them.

It makes me so happy to hear their greeting—for all of them and for me.

I've spent many years of my life, even as a Christian, talking to God the Father as a looming figure, remote and somewhat scary, even on good days.

But in Mark 14, Jesus called Him *Abba,* and in His name we can call God *the Father*, the same word that, translated, means *Daddy*. That simple moniker speaks volumes and changes, in an instant, my vision of Him.

I want to remember that. I want to be as confident as my children are with their father, to rush into His loving arms and call out, "Daddy, Daddy!" —ISABELLA YOSUICO

FAITH STEP: *List the attributes of your perfect Daddy.*

MONDAY, JUNE 17

When you pass through the waters, I will be with you; and when you pass through the rivers, they will not sweep over you. Isaiah 43:2 (NIV)

THE POND ON OUR PROPERTY is a memory-making setting. Our children and grandchildren learned how to fish there. We invite other families to experience their first fishing "outings" in this place that almost guarantees enough success to feed a fishing frenzy.

Initially protected by life jackets or other flotation devices and our watchful eyes, two generations of young people also learned to swim in our pond. Flotation devices held their heads above wind-generated or man-made waves, while they practiced skills they needed.

Did they get wet? Of course. But they were not pulled under by the splashing because of the protection that was provided, even before they knew how to tread water.

Do we get wet when we "pass through the waters and rivers" of life? Yes. It's the nature of living. But God provided a spiritual, emotional, and relational flotation "device" in His Son, Jesus. Through His Holy Spirit, Jesus doesn't merely encircle our arms or grip us around our torso when the storms of life threaten to pull us under. He lives within us, filling us with hope that floats.

Jesus knew this verse from Isaiah 43 didn't promise we would avoid waters that were threatening. But He also understood that He was the provision we needed—the buoyancy of divine hope.

Matthew 28:20 records Jesus assuring us of living flotation. He said, "And surely I am with you always, to the very end of the age," to the farthest reaches of the pond. —CYNTHIA RUCHTI

FAITH STEP: *Take a deep breath. Remarkable. You didn't drown when you took that breath, despite the waves and winds of your present circumstances. Thank Jesus for the hope that keeps your head above water.*

TUESDAY, JUNE 18

Be still in the presence of the LORD. Psalm 37:7 (NLT)

THREE WRITING DEADLINES WERE CLOSING IN—all at the same time. For a few weeks, I sat glued to my desktop computer from early morning until late at night, exiting my office only to prepare meals or sleep. During that time, my shoulders often grew tired, causing interrupted sleep at night.

One hot morning, I finally remembered to take a needed short break. I walked laps from one end of our home to the other. Each time I rounded the corner into my living room, I heard a sweet sound drifting through the closed back door. As it grew louder, I slowed down to listen more closely. The gentle *coos* drew me to the patio door, where I heard a friendly visitor talking—or singing—to me. The young dove rested on our fence, and I relished its personal greeting. I love how Jesus often speaks to us through His creation.

As I completed my walking circles and returned to my desk, I felt refreshed—but not necessarily because of the exercise. Somehow, taking the time to be still and listen that morning, I heard more than a bird's song. Each *coo* echoed in my heart as if Jesus had whispered to me: "Slow down. I love you, I love you, I love you."

And in that moment of realization, I bowed my head and breathed a thank-you to Jesus. My muscles relaxed, the writing flowed, and sweet sleep followed later that night. In the days following, until I finished my deadlines, I stopped more often. Once again, Jesus had reminded me to slow down, be still and listen, and take more time to enjoy His presence. —REBECCA BARLOW JORDAN

FAITH STEP: *Today, set a timer on your phone or one nearby to go off throughout the day, reminding you to stop and be still in the presence of Jesus.*

WEDNESDAY, JUNE 19

God can do anything, you know—far more than you could ever imagine or guess or request in your wildest dreams! Ephesians 3:20 (MSG)

SOMEONE RECENTLY MENTIONED WHAT A blessing my abundant imagination must be—and I had to think about that. It had made life more pleasant growing up, since I could entertain myself while working long, hot days in the cotton fields. It came in handy for writing assignments in school and, later, for a granddaughter always hungry for a story. But an overactive imagination can seem like a curse on a dark night in an empty house. Or when a loved one is late and not answering the phone. Or while watching the news.

What I don't fully understand is why it's so easy for my imagination to get carried away with dark, scary thoughts, but not so much when it comes to potentially joy-filled things to happen. Why is it harder to picture a relationship as healthy and thriving than as broken and hopeless? To envision myself succeeding at my God-given dreams instead of failing? To expect the best rather than brace for the worst-possible scenario? And the most important question: What does this tendency say to the One Who gave His life for me?

You don't have to be a full-fledged pessimist to struggle with moments of seeing the glass as half-empty. But the Bible teaches that Jesus made it possible to live a joy-filled, abundant life despite the pain that comes with this earthly life. So if my imagination runs wild, it should be focused on how God will work out everything in my life for good—which, according to Ephesians 3:20, is better than anything I could ever imagine. —DIANNE NEAL MATTHEWS

FAITH STEP: *What situation in your life tempts you to lapse into pessimistic thinking? Imagine yourself handing that circumstance, problem, or relationship over to Jesus and trusting Him to handle it.*

Thursday, June 20

They [our bodies] were made for the Lord, and the Lord cares about our bodies. 1 Corinthians 6:13 (NLT)

WRONG THINKING ABOUT MY PHYSICAL health landed me in dire straits. For too long, I allowed my schedule to override my body's need for exercise. *I don't have time to take a walk now,* I reasoned as I worked at my computer desk. *I'll walk later.* But later never came.

At the same time, I justified eating chocolate bars—big ones. *My brain's tired from thinking so hard, so I'll give it a little boost,* I thought. One bite led to another and then another. Before long, I'd eaten the entire bar. *Oh well, that's no big deal. I'll walk off the calories later.* But later never came.

Wrong thinking said I could eat whatever I wanted whenever I wished and exercise was only for athletes. The ever-increasing number on my bathroom scale, chronic pain, and the loss of mobility for three months convinced me to make a change.

I learned the hard way. But I learned a new way of thinking that transformed my life and restored my health.

Correct thinking about our physical health comes from understanding that we don't own our bodies. God does. He bought them with Jesus's bloodshed on the cross (1 Corinthians 6:19–20). Now we are Jesus's temple, His dwelling place, and we're responsible to be wise stewards of its care.

Since Jesus willingly paid for our bodies with His life, they must be worth a lot. Let's value them with proper nutrition and exercise. Don't learn the hard way like I did. —GRACE FOX

FAITH STEP: *Identify one wrong thought about your physical health and ponder its influence on your behavior. Now identify one step you can take to improve your health beginning today.*

FRIDAY, JUNE 21

Or which one of you, if his son asks him for bread, will give him a stone? Or if he asks for a fish, will give him a serpent? If you then, who are evil, know how to give good gifts to your children, how much more will your Father who is in heaven give good things to those who ask him! Matthew 7:9–11 (ESV)

THIS SUMMER, WE ARE PARTICIPATING in a farm share. Each week, a box arrives with vegetables harvested at the local farm. The selection depends on many things. If the spring was cold, we might get peas longer into the summer. If too much rain floods the fields, the potato crop may be thin. The farmer may be experimenting with plants that are new to us: garlic scapes, kohlrabi, or amaranth.

The element of surprise is part of the fun. After we pick up the box, we figure out how to make meals from what we're given. If I'm too set on making zucchini bread and, instead, get loads of green beans, I might feel disappointed. But if I'm open to whatever gift arrives, it's exciting and rewarding.

I need more of that attitude in my life. Sometimes, I get a goal stuck in my mind and then I'm disappointed if things don't go my way. I know Jesus won't send a stone when I ask for bread, but I forget that there are times when the thing I'm asking for is something He knows to be a stone or a serpent. Instead of demanding what I want, I can trust Him to fill my box with all the best.

When we welcome each day looking forward to unexpected blessings, our lives become an adventure. We can trust that whatever Jesus sends will be nourishing, strengthening, and exactly what we need. —SHARON HINCK

FAITH STEP: *Sign up for a farm share or visit a farmers' market. Open yourself up to unexpected options and thank Jesus for His unexpected blessings.*

SATURDAY, JUNE 22

Jacob went on his way, and the angels of God met him. And when Jacob saw them he said, "This is God's camp!" Genesis 32:1–2 (ESV)

LAST SUMMER, OUR FAMILY ACCEPTED an invitation to visit relatives by a lake. They have a beautiful home, and the setting is picture-perfect. But our host likes everything "just so" and has a habit of acting put-upon even as she insists on going out of her way for her guests. Our children weren't bothered by it, but it made my husband and me tense. The charming house is small, and there was only room for our children to stay, so my husband and I pitched a tent in a nearby state park and planned to spend the night there after spending the whole day with our hosts. By the time we said good night to our family and got back to the campsite, it had started to rain. We rushed into the tiny tent and spent the next twelve hours or so crowded inside until it was a "decent hour" and we could return to our host's home.

At the end of the weekend, I realized that those rainy hours stuck in the tent were the most relaxed and enjoyable of the whole trip! Limited physical space and bad weather can never crowd out Jesus's peace. It can find you anywhere. That weekend showed me how strongly a host's tone of hospitality affects the whole environment, even more than the physical setting, the food, or the conversation. Since then, when I'm getting ready to entertain, I spend a little less time fussing over the details and take a moment to ask God to help me welcome my guests and help them feel comfortable being themselves here. —ELIZABETH BERNE DEGEAR

FAITH STEP: *Imagine Jesus hosting you. What does He do that makes you feel most welcome? Can you bring that sense of welcome into your day?*

SUNDAY, JUNE 23

By this My Father is glorified, that you bear much fruit;
so you will be My disciples. John 15:8 (NKJV)

I LOVE HOW SCRIPTURE USES so many references to nature and vegetation in both the Old and New Testaments—trees, rivers, vines, branches, seeds, plants, and fruit. When I think of fruit, I think of a sweet and healthy treat. Sweet, ripe peaches are my favorite summer fruit, and I buy bushels of them during that season. I still smile, remembering an incident involving a "peach."

When I was growing up, my mom had a bowl of artificial fruit on the coffee table for decoration. One of my nieces, who was about four years old at the time, picked up a peach and bit into it. She frowned when she realized it wasn't real. We laughed and took it from her. The peach looked real—it had fake fuzz and everything. Though it was a good facsimile, it was a counterfeit.

Unlike that plastic peach, genuine spiritual fruit is what Jesus wants us to bear.

I believe the Lord wants us to "bear much fruit"—a full bushel of His love, grace, and mercy on this earth. Galatians 5:22–23 says, "But the fruit of the Spirit is love, joy, peace, longsuffering, kindness, goodness, faithfulness, gentleness, self-control." Fruit is sweet, good for you, and satisfying—just what this spiritually hungry society wants and needs. —CAROL MACKEY

FAITH STEP: *Which fruit of the Spirit do you exhibit in great quantities? Which fruit could use some bolstering? Pray and ask the Lord to help you bear more fruit in that area. He wants our spiritual fruit to grow and flourish so we can show the world that we are His fruit (John 15:5).*

MONDAY, JUNE 24

Therefore, if anyone is in Christ, he is a new creation; old things have passed away; behold, all things have become new. 2 Corinthians 5:17 (NKJV)

REMEMBERING THE SCENE FROM THE Netflix series *The Crown* still gives me chills. Princess Elizabeth's father has died, making her Queen of England. As she changes into a black mourning dress, she reads a letter from her grandmother, offering wisdom as she steps into her new role: who she used to be will always battle her new self, but in the end, "the crown must always win."

I've followed Jesus since childhood, but only recently have I grasped what it meant to become a new person in Him. When my husband left and my life changed overnight, I had to put away the person that easily gave in to hopelessness and fear, and call on Jesus to make me tougher than I felt. Almost six years later, on the other side of trauma and heartbreak, I was a stronger, healthier, more confident woman whose faith had become solid. The old me still tried to win occasionally, and at times my new life felt foreign. In those moments, Jesus sent friends to remind me that these changes were good. Unlike Elizabeth, whose new self was a result of royal lineage, I'd become—and continue to become—a new creation as a result of His kindness and grace.

"Therefore, if anyone *is* in Christ, *he is* a new creation…." Jesus makes us new the moment we accept Him, but transformation takes a lifetime, even when we are forgiven, saved, and longing to be different. When we begin to see His work change our lives for the better, we desire for His strength to rule. —JEANETTE HANSCOME

FAITH STEP: *How has Jesus made you new? Write a letter to your old before-Jesus self, offering words of wisdom and encouragement from the perspective of who you are now.*

TUESDAY, JUNE 25

You make known to me the path of life; you will fill me with joy in your presence, with eternal pleasures at your right hand. Psalm 16:11 (NIV)

DURING THE SUMMER, I SUBSTITUTE-TEACH at my boys' old preschool. This summer, I had the opportunity to work in the two-year-olds' class. From the time they were dropped off until the time they were picked up, they didn't stop moving. They were into everything. And they were excited to find out what was coming next. *Was it outside playtime? Was it snack time? Was it story time?* Whatever it was, they were ready with full-body joy. The only thing they could have done without was nap time. (I would have gladly taken their place.)

But the moment that got them most excited was when their person, either their mom or dad, came to pick them up. Their faces would light up! They would jump up and down. This was the person they loved and who loved them the most. They would run into those outstretched arms. Seeing them fling themselves at their parents always made me grin. The parents were just as excited to see their little ones.

This is what love looks like. A parent scooping up their own child and burying their face in that tiny neck, telling them that they love them and are so glad to see them. So good! It is the perfect picture of what it is like when we are in the presence of Jesus. He is our person. The One Who loves us the most. We can fling ourselves into His arms and know that He will always come for us. In His presence we find joy. He is leading us, protecting us, and guiding us. And we find that we are known for who we are and loved completely. —SUSANNA FOTH AUGHTMON

FAITH STEP: *Take a moment to bask in the joy of Jesus's presence. Tell Him how much you love Him. And know that you have found your Person who loves you most.*

WEDNESDAY, JUNE 26

Indeed, we felt we had received the sentence of death.
But this happened that we might not rely on ourselves but on God,
who raises the dead. 2 Corinthians 1:9 (NIV)

I SPEND AT LEAST A day a week in torment. No matter what's going on in reality, my mind seems to whirl with catastrophic scenarios or just stomach-churning anxiety. I've never been diagnosed with a mental health issue, and since many days I enjoy peace, I know these bouts of anxiety aren't altogether chemical.

When it happens, I'm compelled to launch all countermeasures. I stop and pray and praise Jesus many times per day. I read Bible verses I keep handy for just such times. I force myself to call or text a friend for a reality check. I divert myself by focusing on someone else in need, including my husband and two small kids.

Sometimes, all I can muster is, "Jesus, please help me."

A friend once said, "Your anxiety is the best thing you have going, because it keeps you on your knees."

Really? Pause. *Yes.*

When all is well, when I'm at peace, when the bank account is fat, and when things are going my way, I am not as earnest or as desperate and inclined to look to Jesus. I'm just not. Furthermore, I absolutely cannot muster sincere pursuit.

I cleave to Jesus most sincerely when I'm in pain. Anxiety and other trials are His gracious provision to keep me yoked to Him. Because that is where all power and security lies. —ISABELLA YOSUICO

FAITH STEP: *When have you been closest to God? Talk it over with Him.*

THURSDAY, JUNE 27

"If you love Me, you will keep My commandments." John 14:15 (NASB)

THE VAN DRIVER KEPT ME entertained the entire trip to the airport with stories of kayaking after quintuple bypass surgery, having been forbidden—by his grown children—to race motorcycles anymore, and experiencing the delightful antics of his grandchildren.

His precocious four-year-old granddaughter provided much material. One story held my attention long after I'd boarded the plane.

At a family reunion weekend, the little girl's dad hurriedly loaded the car for the trip home. He inadvertently slung one of the duffel bags onto his wife's favorite hat. Tensions escalated. The mother was disappointed that he'd been careless; the dad was sure it was the wife's fault for putting her now-crushed hat in that spot.

The four-year-old piped up. "Mom, do not yell at Daddy. Do not yell in the green house (their home in the city). Do not yell in the brown house (the cottage they'd shared for the reunion). Do not yell in the pink house (the condo rented for Mexican vacations)."

The "chastised" mom and dad laughed at the toddler's serious counsel. The argument ended, but escalated again on the ride home. "If you'd paid more attention . . ." the little girl's mom started.

Stifled laughter defused the argument again when their daughter said, "Mom, Dad, we've had this discussion before."

How many times has Jesus wanted to say to me, "Cynthia, we've had this talk before." He shouldn't have to advise me more than once.

What a great goal—respond to His wise counsel the first time around. —CYNTHIA RUCHTI

FAITH STEP: *Want to join me in creating a word-art card that says, "We've had this talk before"? I might stick one on my mirror, on the refrigerator, in my Bible, or on the television.*

FRIDAY, JUNE 28

Jesus, the One who says these things are true, says, "Yes, I am coming soon."
Amen. Come, Lord Jesus! Revelation 22:20 (NCV)

DURING LUNCH, I FOUND MYSELF wishing I had some duct tape to slap on my mouth—although that would have made it difficult to enjoy my salad. I sat and listened as my two friends went on and on about a particular television series. The previous night's episode had ended on a cliffhanger, as usual. Will the young prince be killed in the battle? Will his sweetheart's family really force her to marry that evil lord? Will the royal family discover the true identity of the blacksmith's son, who has no idea he is the rightful heir to the throne?

My friends were aware that I knew the answers to these questions. I had read the books that served as the basis for the series. Not only did I have to refrain from commenting, but I also had to keep a poker face. One friend kept stealing glances at me. I think a part of her wanted to know the outcome ahead of time, but another part of her did not.

I can appreciate surprise endings, but I often flip to the end of a novel to find out whether the main character survives, the villain gets his due, or the unlikely couple marry. For me, that eases the tension and lets me enjoy the story more. So I love that the last chapter in the Bible tells us how things turn out. The main character returns in triumph. (In chapter 22, Jesus says, "I am coming!" four times.) The villain (Satan) gets his due. And yes, there is a "wedding," between Christ and His followers. Although some days I struggle with doubts and anxieties, knowing the ultimate ending helps me enjoy the story of my life more. —DIANNE NEAL MATTHEWS

FAITH STEP: *Read the last chapter of Revelation. Think about how the uncertainties and troubles you're experiencing now pale in comparison to the glorious end of your story.*

SATURDAY, JUNE 29

And His disciples asked Him, saying, "Rabbi, who sinned, this man or his parents, that he was born blind?" John 9:2 (NKJV)

As THE MOTHER OF TWO adult sons, I believe I still am responsible for them in many ways. Their behaviors, belief systems, occupations, and other life choices—good or bad—are a result of how their father and I raised them. And some bad choices on their part translate into parental guilt that can be overwhelming.

In John 9, Jesus's disciples were sure *somebody* had sinned—why else would this man be born blind from birth? Jesus, in His infinite wisdom, assured them that neither this man nor his parents had sinned. His blindness would serve as a perfect example of God's healing power and grace (vv. 3–5). The disciples needed to see Jesus perform that miracle, on that man, on that day. God the Father knew this, and so did Jesus.

It's the same with us. We worry and fret over our adult children who may have abandoned the Christian faith and turned to drugs or alcohol or are leading ungodly, unhealthy lives. We may have raised them in church, instilled values, and taught them to be upright citizens. So we ask ourselves: *Where did we go wrong?*

Entering this new chapter of parenting, I knew I had to accept that, when they become adults, they make their own choices. I know I'm not my children's only influence. Jesus gave us His Word, His commandments, and His assurance that He'd be with us always. Our lives are in the Lord's mighty hand and so are our children's, and we should always trust in that. —CAROL MACKEY

FAITH STEP: *Write a letter to your children but don't mail it. Admit any shortcomings you may have had while they were growing up. Then give it to Jesus in prayer.*

SUNDAY, JUNE 30

Lo, I see four men loose, walking in the midst of the fire, and they have no hurt; and the form of the fourth is like the Son of God. Daniel 3:25 (KJV)

MY SON HARPER JUST FINISHED eighth grade. The newspaper can tell you he was quarterback of the football team. A school yearbook shows he's a leader and a heartthrob. Read his report card and you'll know he got an A in each of his classes, even Honors Algebra. So eighth grade was a banner year by all outward accounts. But as his mother, I can tell you it was a tough year for both of us.

Eighth grade was the first time his friends pressured him to drink. The first time they made fun of him for having high standards. The first time he shaved. The first time a girl broke his heart.

For me, his eighth-grade year was a ramping up of the feeling I quite often have as a parent. It was not the first time I'd felt inadequate, but it was a year I felt even more inadequate than usual. I can't tell you the late nights I spent up with that kid talking, praying over him in his bed.

One Sunday morning, my heart was so burdened. How would we make it through eighth grade—and the coming years—safely? I was sitting at the piano, teaching my church congregation a new song, when the answer came to me: *There is a name I call in times of trouble... Jesus.*

Eighth grade is just a snapshot of real life. It's beautiful and fun, and we win some. But how do we handle the fire when we're thrown into it, as we all are? Jesus. He stands beside us. That's the way we make it through. —GWEN FORD FAULKENBERRY

FAITH STEP: *Draw a picture of yourself in whatever current situation feels like the fiery furnace of Daniel 3. Then draw Jesus there beside you, holding your hand.*

MONDAY, JULY 1

And why do you worry about clothes? See how the flowers of the field grow. They do not labor or spin. Matthew 6:28 (NIV)

THREE YEARS AGO, MY HUSBAND, David, and I erected a backyard arbor, planting an heirloom climbing rose on either side—one deep red, the other golden yellow. We hoped they'd look stunning as they met and mingled atop the antiqued metal framework. We watered, prayed, and waited.

By the next summer, slender branches twined almost to the top. Last year, the plants met and began mixing just as we'd imagined, though the red rose seemed smaller, with fewer blooms.

Returning from a vacation, we found the arbor awash in roses. It was glorious—except for one thing. We counted only five red buds near the frame's base. Every other part sported yellow flowers.

We focused on the red climber, almost obliterated by the other bush. It was just as beautiful as the yellow, though not as sturdy; we needed to do something to save it. But what? Yesterday we made the decision and placed an order for a new metal arbor to shade our front walkway. Only one bush would grace its base. When transplanted, our lovely red rose could thrive unobstructed.

Jesus watches over all of us, making sure we're safe. When those of us who are weaker become endangered or overwhelmed by people smarter, wealthier, or more powerful, He replants us. Sometimes, He changes our circumstances; other times, He sends caring people. More often, He changes us from the inside out. In His care, we can grow and blossom anywhere. —HEIDI GAUL

FAITH STEP: *Go to the garden center and pick out a plant or flower that needs care. Take it home. As you nurse it back to health, remember Jesus does that for you.*

TUESDAY, JULY 2

"Come, follow me," Jesus said, "and I will send you out to fish for people."
At once they left their nets and followed him. Mark 1:17–18 (NIV)

MY HUSBAND AND I GREW up watching *Star Wars*. And so when *Star Wars: The Force Awakens* came out a few years ago, we were excited to share the experience with our children. On the first day it was released, we found ourselves at an early-morning screening at the biggest movie theater in town, 3-D glasses on our faces, and a container of popcorn to pass between us.

What I remember most was the last moment of the movie. The young heroine, Rey, found Luke Skywalker at the top of a mountain and presented him with his long-lost light saber. When Rey held out the weapon, it appeared to be floating in front of us. I looked over to my right, and watched as both my son and my husband reached out to take hold of the light saber. I was touched and amused that both father and son could be so wrapped up in the story of a Jedi knight that they would take his invitation as theirs. I wondered, *What was it that made each of them think they were a Jedi too?*

But now I realize that I have done a version of that same saber grab. When I read that story of Jesus inviting Simon and Andrew to fish for people, I swear I see *myself* dropping those nets and following Him! Certain stories are more than entertainment; they are inspiration. They connect us with our own life story and nudge us forward, giving us the vision and courage we need to take the next step in our journeys. —ELIZABETH BERNE DEGEAR

FAITH STEP: *Bring to mind one of your favorite scenes from the Gospels. Take some time imagining yourself in that scene and let Jesus inspire you.*

WEDNESDAY, JULY 3

"I've obeyed all these commandments," the young man replied. "What else must I do?" Matthew 19:20 (NLT)

I TRAVELED FOR MUCH OF June. Efficient for travel connections, but hard on my "there's no place like home" heart.

I missed strawberry season and making homemade freezer jam. When I arrived home, several small bouquets of lily of the valley and other massive bouquets of lilacs graced our table. But I had missed the major part of their short blooming seasons.

What I didn't miss was Jesus. All the travel was related to speaking for Him, about Him, or to Him.

In the Bible, one of the individuals with whom Jesus had a heartfelt conversation was a rich young man. His inquiries probed deep, but his motivation was self-serving, and Jesus knew it. "Which commandments do I really need to keep to enter heaven someday?" the young man asked. Jesus listed six key commandments.

"I've kept all you listed. What did I miss?"

The response Jesus gave showed what was rooted in the young man's heart—his grip on his earthly possessions, earnings, wealth. Jesus knew it would take more than the man could stomach to turn away from those relatively trivial things to make a commitment to follow Him. The man would have to be willing to miss everything else so he wouldn't miss Jesus.

"But when the young man heard this, he went away saddened, because he had many possessions" (Matthew 19:22).

The saddest part is that he didn't even own those possessions. They owned him. —CYNTHIA RUCHTI

FAITH STEP: *I'm taking a careful inventory today. Will you join me? What possessions, passions, or pleasures are we holding on to more tightly than Jesus?*

THURSDAY, JULY 4

Because of the sacrifice of the Messiah, his blood poured out on the altar of the Cross, we're a free people—free of penalties and punishments chalked up by all our misdeeds. And not just barely free, either. Abundantly free! Ephesians 1:7 (MSG)

I FELT LIKE A SALMON swimming upstream as I pushed my cart through the aisles of Walmart. My plans to dash in and out to pick up a one-hour photo, a prescription, and a few groceries faded. I had forgotten about the usual rush the day before a national holiday.

An hour later, when I finally reached the checkout line, I asked the woman behind me if she was buying things for her Fourth of July celebration. She pointed to her cart. "Yes, but I only came to buy hot dogs." We both commented about the long lines, but as we casually talked, we came to an agreement that the day wasn't about the food or fireworks; it was about our freedom.

On the Fourth of July, we do celebrate freedom, but our freedom was earned. It was paid for by those who fought for our independence as a nation and for the right to worship God as we wanted. In addition, freedom is not necessarily permanent. Throughout history, men and women have sacrificed a lot to keep freedom alive. Wars and fighting continue because people crave freedom from oppression and injustice.

The freedom that Jesus gives us was not free either. Paid for by His own blood and death by crucifixion, this spiritual freedom is universal and available to all. We can't earn it; we can only receive it by faith. One life—His—was enough to set us free. Unlike earthly independence, our spiritual liberty lasts forever.

Now, that's truly a reason to celebrate! —REBECCA BARLOW JORDAN

FAITH STEP: *Today, thank Jesus for our nation's freedom—and for your spiritual freedom.*

FRIDAY, JULY 5

---

*For you make me glad by your deeds, LORD; I sing for joy at what
your hands have done. Psalm 92:4 (NIV)*

WHEN A BEDBUG INFESTATION CAUSED us to relocate our long-awaited
family reunion to a rustic retreat center, I assumed we would cancel.
Most of Dad's twenty-plus cousins would have to sleep in bunk bed
dorms and run-down cabins. I assumed they wouldn't want to do
that. But halfway through the first full day, I became thankful that
"rustic" shared bathrooms and camp food hadn't scared away these
descendants of Dust Bowl survivors. Thanks to a narrow (and steep!)
winding gravel road, most of us stayed on the grounds for the entire
three-and-a-half days, taking long walks, playing games, and enjoying
our favorite family tradition of talking and laughing over coffee and
snacks. I met relatives who hadn't attended a reunion in decades,
bonded with others in deeper ways, and learned things about my
family that I'd never heard before. Dad's cousin Cheryl had brought
our family tree, a ton of old pictures, and a brief family history that
sparked amazing stories of resilience, strength, and our legacy of faith.

I didn't hear anyone express disappointment in the accommoda-
tions; they only said that they didn't want the time to end and were
grateful that we found out about the bedbugs before we brought them
home in our luggage. Our family tree had revealed a lot of hardship,
but it had produced loving people who would rather sacrifice some
comforts than miss out on being together. It reminded me to see
changes of plans as opportunities to experience Jesus's surprises and
reflect His character in my reaction, even if that means learning to
be thankful for bedbugs. —JEANETTE HANSCOME

FAITH STEP: *What do you appreciate most about your family? Send a
handwritten note to a relative whom you have special memories of.*

SATURDAY, JULY 6

God, who richly provides us with everything for our enjoyment.
1 Timothy 6:17 (NIV)

LIVING IN FLORIDA, WE HAVE many major theme parks nearby. My ten-year-old son is a big fan of big roller coasters. The steeper the drop, the faster the ride, the tighter the curves, the loopier the loops, the more unpredictable the path, the better.

I'm not a big fan, but wanting to be a good sport, I'm game to be my son's sidekick. I've learned to ride on an empty stomach and when we board, I always double-check that safety bar. It's much more fun when I feel confident that we're safe.

My former pastor used to say, "Life is a roller coaster, and God is the bar."

Yes!

It seems the more closely I walk with Jesus, the more I surrender to His unfolding plan. I experience a more thrilling, unexpected, and sometimes scary ride. Yet I'm also finding that as I double-check the bar of faith, by staying yoked to Jesus, I'm truly experiencing an abundant joy and peace that surpasses understanding (Philippians 4:7).

I've been experimenting with this notion by consciously choosing to trust God, relax, and enjoy the ride of life, even when threats seem to loom or the future's unclear.

Trusting God this way doesn't mean that the ride will take me where I planned to go, but that I can enjoy life in the process.
—ISABELLA YOSUICO

FAITH STEP: *Has God invited you on a thrilling, unpredictable ride? How can you check and trust the bar of faith that is Christ?*

SUNDAY, JULY 7

Jesus Christ is the same yesterday and today and forever. Hebrews 13:8 (ESV)

THANKS TO MY DIGITAL SOFTWARE, I have many different Bible translations at my disposal. Sometimes I gain new insight into a Scripture by reading it in different versions. But not always. Last week, I researched an Old Testament verse and grew more confused with each translation I compared. Not only had the translators used different words; some gave the line a positive connotation, while others translated it in a negative way.

Not so with Hebrews 13:8. The only difference between the ten translations I typically compare is whether they include two uses of *and*, or two commas and one *and*. How appropriate for such a clear declaration of our Lord's unchanging nature. In an ever-changing world, we can always count on what matters most. His holiness and sovereignty. His love and mercy toward us.

Jesus will never change His character or His plans—no matter what is happening, no matter what we see going on in the world, and regardless of our moments of doubt or unfaithfulness toward Him when circumstances tempt us to question His goodness.

Many things in life can make us feel unsettled. Sudden job loss, relocation to an area away from family and friends, serious illness, the loss of a loved one, broken relationships, coping with a permanent disability. We never know when life as we know it will be disrupted and we'll face another challenge. Thank goodness for the rock-solid promise in Hebrews 13:8 that our Savior and Lord will never change. —DIANNE NEAL MATTHEWS

FAITH STEP: *Are you facing changes or uncertainty in any area of your life? Meditate on the unchangeable nature of Jesus and your relationship with Him. Ask Him to help your faith stay steady and strong, unshaken by circumstances.*

MONDAY, JULY 8

Jesus answered, "Everyone who drinks this water will be thirsty again, but whoever drinks the water I give them will never thirst. Indeed, the water I give them will become in them a spring of water welling up to eternal life."
John 4:13–14 (NIV)

I LIVE IN CALIFORNIA, AND every decade or so we experience drought. The rain stops. The hills turn brown. Summer brush fires break out. And cities clamp down on water usage. Everyone is asked to let their front lawns suffer to save water. Instead of having lush green patches of grass lining the streets, everyone starts cultivating rock gardens and succulents to keep up appearances.

Water is precious. Water is life. And Jesus is the Living Water. We need a constant flow of His love and grace to nurture growth. We need His refreshing truth and life-altering forgiveness. The overflow of His goodness lets us flourish in every way.

There have been long seasons in my life when my faith has felt dry and dusty. Hope has hardened into doubt. Grief, financial difficulties, and the general stresses of life have drained me of His presence. I have felt like my spirit is one of those parched patches of California earth. But Jesus never looks at my hard heart and says, "Oh man, she will never grow again." Or, "I'm done with her. She has failed me one too many times." Instead, He says, "I am right here. Come find me…and never thirst again."

Jesus is all about new life, restoration, and new growth. Dry seasons are a part of this life. But He is always waiting to fill us up with His refreshing presence. —SUSANNA FOTH AUGHTMON

FAITH STEP: *Find a dry patch of dirt in your yard and water it. See how quickly it absorbs the water. Ask Jesus to bring new life to the hard places of your heart and fill you up.*

TUESDAY, JULY 9

O God, you are my God; I earnestly search for you. My soul thirsts for you; my whole body longs for you in this parched and weary land where there is no water. Psalm 63:1 (NLT)

TAP WATER IS UNFIT FOR consumption in many countries. When I travel overseas, I either run tap water through a portable filter I pack or buy bottled water.

We can run into serious problems when clean drinking water isn't readily available. I experienced this while riding a bus during a heat wave in Eastern Europe. Assuming I could buy water at stops along the way, I'd packed only one small bottle.

Imagine my chagrin when I discovered that the bus's air-conditioning was broken and its windows stuck shut. The vehicle's interior heated like an oven. Sweat trickled down my face, my chest, and my back. In order to avoid dehydration, I drank my water more quickly than I'd anticipated. As I recall, the bus stopped a couple of times so the driver and passengers could take cigarette breaks, but only once did we stop at a place where we could buy a drink.

The ride lasted about five hours. Relatively speaking, it's one of the shortest trips I've made in that country but by far the most difficult. It's the only time I've seriously questioned my survival. I grew so weary and discouraged on that journey, I could barely muster, "Jesus, help me!"

Desperation for water and a better understanding of its vital role for survival have helped me appreciate my need for Jesus, the Living Water. Without the salvation He offers and His ongoing presence in my life, I'd be spiritually parched or worse. He not only brings life—He is life. Clearly, I cannot live without Him. —GRACE FOX

FAITH STEP: *Read John 4:1–15. Drink a glass of water slowly, appreciating its role in your survival. Thank Jesus for providing you with living water.*

WEDNESDAY, JULY 10

Let no corrupt communication proceed out of your mouth,
but that which is good to the use of edifying, that it may minister
grace unto the hearers. Ephesians 4:29 (KJV)

ONE OF MY FAVORITE TV shows is *The Honeymooners.* The iconic lead character, Ralph Kramden, would say, "I've got a *big* mouth!" whenever he talked too much and got into trouble. It was a hilarious form of self-correcting on the show. But I can relate in real life those times I've said things I didn't think through.

Many of us have been in Ralph's shoes. David prayed for wisdom to keep his mouth shut, even "put a muzzle on my mouth" (Psalm 39:1 NIV)—smart man! It's only human to say things out of anger, frustration, sadness, or even fear. We've all done it. The Word of God says that no man can tame the tongue and calls it "an unruly evil" (James 3:8). But we are still responsible for what we say and need to be careful.

We misspeak or may retaliate when someone has hurt us. I have made that mistake (more than once), and I've always regretted it immediately afterward. The Lord wasn't pleased with me and I felt foolish. I know better now, so I make that mistake less and less. I understand now that when I'm tempted to respond to negativity with a snide remark, Jesus wants me to take the high road. There's nothing to prove by saying harsh words to someone. I know correcting those whose words hurt is sometimes necessary, but when we speak the truth, we should speak it in love (Ephesians 4:15). Jesus knew the power of words and used His wisely (Matthew 12:37), and we should too. —CAROL MACKEY

FAITH STEP: *Here's an exercise: When you're getting ready to say something out of fear, anger, or frustration, imagine Jesus is standing right next to you. Count to five and then respond. See what a difference it makes.*

THURSDAY, JULY 11

By this all people will know that you are My disciples,
if you have love for one another. John 13:35 (HCSB)

OUR HISTORIC PORTRAIT AS A nation is blotted with faces of hate. Each time it's revealed, I feel overwhelmed with sadness as well as somewhat paralyzed regarding what I can do to help. When I think about the men who marched with Nazi and KKK paraphernalia in Charlottesville or the image of the murderer behind the massacre in a church in Charleston or those who carried out the deadly blast at an Islamic center in Minnesota, I'm left to wonder, *How could this happen in America? Even today?*

Times like this, I'm reminded of a verse of the old hymn "Holy, Holy, Holy": "Though the darkness hide thee/Though the eye of sinful man thy glory may not see." The darkness seems so big, and I feel so small. I know Jesus is there. I know I have a part to play in spreading His light. But Virginia is far away from my house on the hill in Arkansas. I don't have a big public platform; my sphere of influence is about the size of a ping-pong ball. What can I do to make a difference?

Sometimes, I think I get paralyzed into doing nothing because I think I can't do anything big. So as I watch the news, I do what I can. I hug my babies. I talk to them about wrong and right, and standing up to bullies, and loving everybody. When I go to the grocery store, I buy a few items for the food pantry at our church. I read and educate myself, and I've even thought about how to broach this subject when my classes start. I also pray.

None of those things are big deals. But a lot of sparks can make a fire, and a lot of little efforts can show big love to a world that needs to see Jesus in us. —GWEN FORD FAULKENBERRY

FAITH STEP: *Do one tangible thing, no matter how small, to spread the love of Jesus today.*

FRIDAY, JULY 12

Again, the kingdom of heaven is like a merchant in search of fine pearls, who, on finding one pearl of great value, went and sold all that he had and bought it.
Matthew 13:45–46 *(ESV)*

OUR SON, DAUGHTER-IN-LAW, TWO GRANDCHILDREN, and their dog all moved in with us this week. We're thrilled to have this "close-up" time with them for a year while our son finishes his studies at a local seminary.

In our daily interactions, I've noticed what diligent parents they are. They are concerned with childproofing the house, with setting up crib sensors and monitors, with using nonchemical cleaners, with providing organic food. They have also studied various approaches to parenting and are incredibly patient with the children. All of this reflects that their children are precious pearls.

This morning, as I read about the pearl of great value, I thought about what it would look like if I viewed the Kingdom of Heaven as precious and valuable in a similar way. Would I take more thought and care in fostering a healthy environment for my faith? Would I diligently create protections against things that could endanger my walk with Jesus? Would I show patience in watching the Kingdom unfold in fullness, both in human history and my personal life?

In the parable, Jesus makes us consider the Kingdom of Heaven as something precious. He proclaims that we have found that which is most priceless and invites us to give our all to His Kingdom. We don't need to feel overwhelmed by this challenge, because Jesus doesn't leave us alone to care for and protect our faith. As He cherishes us, He teaches us how to value His Kingdom and changes our hearts to understand what is important. —SHARON HINCK

FAITH STEP: *List a few ways you care for what is most precious to you. Apply some of those to nurturing the Kingdom of Heaven in your heart today.*

SATURDAY, JULY 13

But blessed is the one who trusts in the LORD, whose confidence is in him.
Jeremiah 17:7 (NIV)

MY HUSBAND, DAVID, AND I love picnicking. Yesterday, we piled our basket and cooler into the car and headed for a beautiful spot we'd discovered, about an hour's drive from home. When we arrived there, everything seemed perfect. Almost everything. We moved from table to table but couldn't escape someone's loud music. Bass notes vibrated in my head, making it hard to appreciate our surroundings. Then a groundskeeper arrived. That would have been fine, but he kept his vehicle running as he worked.

David and I exchanged glances. There was nothing we could do. We'd driven so far, and the food was already on our plates. We thanked Jesus for our food. Then David whispered, "Lord, if it's your will, please quiet all this so we can eat in peace."

I turned my attention to our lunch. Sandwiches, fruit, cookies... all of it looked—and tasted—delicious. After a few minutes, he smiled, pointing out that the noise was gone.

Jesus had stopped the racket so fast, I hadn't noticed. I wondered, *How many times have I been blind to improvements He's placed in my life? Have I noticed all the good He's done?*

The park's peacefulness wasn't the only thing Jesus restored that afternoon. My confidence in Him—that He cares for all my needs—was too. Through this small prayer and much-appreciated response, we'd been transformed. Our eyes were opened to seek out more of the quiet blessings He'd sent our way, small kindnesses we'd missed in the past. And we weren't disappointed. —HEIDI GAUL

FAITH STEP: *For a week, log how Jesus responds to your prayer requests. Watch for blessings so subtle they almost slip past without notice.*

SUNDAY, JULY 14

He will wipe away every tear from their eyes, and death shall be no more, neither shall there be mourning, nor crying, nor pain anymore, for the former things have passed away. Revelation 21:4 (ESV)

I'M ALWAYS LOOKING FOR HEAVEN—IN people, places, and things.

We live on Florida's Suncoast, a tropical paradise. We used to live in the postcard-pretty mountain town of Berkeley Springs, West Virginia—a state John Denver dubbed "almost heaven." Yet neither place is actually "paradise" nor "heaven."

Here in Florida, along with lush landscapes, I'm discovering unfamiliar insects, including swarms of epidemic-carrying mosquitoes. With the warm, crystal Gulf and countless shimmering waterways comes a myriad of side effects of too much water—destructive storms, mold, and humidity. Beautiful and exotic wildlife includes invasive pythons, rats, and alligators.

West Virginia had its own assortment of sometimes harsh reminders that earth is definitely not heaven. Lush hillsides marred by aggressive mining. Hardworking families crushed by black lung and lost jobs. Quaint towns abandoned for more hopeful horizons.

I've looked for heaven in friendships that sour because of carelessness, injury, or no reason at all. I look for heaven in my human husband or hormonal preteen son, or my youngest, who has Down syndrome. Although I have to say, he comes closest to heaven.

Expecting heaven on earth overshadows my experience of all the heavenly glimpses this earth does deliver. Moreover, looking for heaven here takes our eyes off eternity and the only heaven God tells us will not disappoint. —ISABELLA YOSUICO

FAITH STEP: *Ask God to show you how looking for heaven here is preventing you from seeing and living for eternity.*

MONDAY, JULY 15

The LORD our God spoke to us at Horeb: "You have stayed at this mountain long enough." Deuteronomy 1:6 (HCSB)

I'VE EXPERIENCED SOME HEART-STIRRING MOMENTS through the years while on vacation. Many times, I didn't want to leave. To me those getaway spots represented Jesus's peaceful presence in amazing ways. Couldn't we stay a little longer? But whether it was Jesus's nudging or another warning, the reminder always came. "It's time to move on." Translation: *You've stayed at this mountain long enough.*

In Deuteronomy, Moses rehearsed the Israelites' forty-year journey in the wilderness. Only a year into their encampment, he reminded them of God's command to move forward. In the Horeb district of Mt. Sinai, an area rich with divine presence and power, God had given them the Ten Commandments. But they had "stayed at this mountain long enough." It was time to move forward and live free.

The children of Israel moved on, but they disobeyed, forgot what God had taught them, and wandered for years in the desert. Only their descendants would know the true freedom God had promised. Years later, those successors still encountered battles, but every time they trusted the Lord, they experienced victory.

Through the years, I've been trying to learn the lessons Jesus wants to teach me. Yes, leaving our comfortable spiritual retreats may plunge us back into conflict, like it did for the Israelites. But it doesn't mean we have to leave Jesus's presence behind. Living free means obeying the voice of Jesus, no matter where He takes us.
—REBECCA BARLOW JORDAN

FAITH STEP: *Think about the situations that challenge you the most. Ask Jesus to help you experience His presence—and His freedom—daily.*

TUESDAY, JULY 16

Let everything that has breath praise the LORD. Praise the LORD.
Psalm 150:6 (NIV)

I LIVE ON THE FORTY-FIFTH parallel, which means my town is located halfway between the equator and the North Pole. Because of this, summer days last longer than if we were farther south. During the hottest months, dawn occurs between 4:30 and 5:00 a.m.

Since I sometimes have trouble sleeping, I'm often awake before the first hint of light brightens the sky. I savor this time. It sets the course for the rest of my hours.

This morning, I prayed while surrounded by the semidarkness. The busyness of life hadn't intruded into my thoughts yet, and I spent quiet minutes with Jesus. Without distractions, I was able to bring Him my hopes and concerns and was better able to sense His will for the hours ahead.

Just past my window, as dawn progressed to sunrise, the natural world outside awakened, and the changes taking place were more dramatic. Minute by minute, the sun edged above the horizon, rousing all types of birds from their rest. As each variety woke up, they burst into song. By full light, doves, starlings, swifts, finches, and sparrows had joined together to greet the morning in a glorious cacophony of sound. It was as if they were all singing praises to our Lord, thanking Him for a brand-new day. I couldn't help smiling.

Today, like most days, Jesus graced me. And I'm praising Him for all He's given me. Light, joy, song, and always hope. —HEIDI GAUL

FAITH STEP: *Set your clock to wake you up before dawn. Watch and listen as the world around you comes alive. Thank Jesus for the chance at another day, filled anew with His blessings.*

WEDNESDAY, JULY 17

The apostles returned to Jesus from their ministry tour and told him all they had done and taught. Then Jesus said, "Let's go off by ourselves to a quiet place and rest awhile." Mark 6:30–31 (NLT)

A WIDOW FROM VANCOUVER, BRITISH COLUMBIA, attended a women's conference where I spoke. After the last session, she came to me and said, "My house has a large daylight basement with a room for people in career ministry. The beach is fifteen minutes away. You're welcome to stay there whenever you need a personal retreat."

After six months of traveling overseas and across North America for ministry purposes, I yearned for physical rest and spiritual renewal. A focused quiet time with Jesus, away from my home responsibilities, seemed just the right thing. I gratefully accepted her invitation.

The retreat lasted only two days, but it allowed time to read, reflect, and pray. I returned home refreshed, ready to write again, and feeling better prepared for an upcoming mission trip to Poland.

Jesus commends the discipline of withdrawing from busyness to sit in His presence. Luke 10:38–42 tells the story of sisters Mary and Martha. While Martha scurried about the kitchen, Mary "sat at the Lord's feet, listening to what he taught." When Martha expressed her frustration, Jesus gently told her that Mary had discovered the one thing that mattered most.

What's that one thing? Sitting in His presence. Jesus cares about our well-being. He created us with a need to rest and spend time with Him. When we withdraw from the noise and hustle, even if only for a few minutes, we experience renewal. —GRACE FOX

FAITH STEP: *Read Luke 10:38–42. Put yourself in Mary's place, sitting at Jesus's feet. Give yourself permission to sit at His feet for a few minutes today, guilt-free.*

THURSDAY, JULY 18

Now Deborah, a prophet, the wife of Lappidoth, was leading Israel at that time. She held court under the Palm of Deborah . . . , and the Israelites went up to her to have their disputes decided. Judges 4:4–5 (NIV)

MY HUSBAND AND I WERE hiking on a beautiful summer day after a heavy rainfall. On our way down the mountain, I mused aloud that I would need a walking stick to navigate through the thick mud, and I wandered off the trail to find one. A few moments later, my husband presented me with a stick. It wasn't as sturdy as the one I was working to free of its dead branches, but it was such a kind gesture, and I wanted to accept it. What's more, he had had a tough week at work and I knew it was good for him to be helpful and feel appreciated. The stick was helpful, until we got to a particularly steep section where the mud was deep. The stick sank and then snapped under my weight. So I chose another stick that I knew would work for me and we continued on.

The phrase that is translated in our Bible as "Deborah, the wife of Lappidoth" also means "Deborah, woman to the rescue." The Hebrew word for *woman* and *wife* is the same; *lappidoth* is a form of the word for redemption. As we mature and our spiritual life develops, we may come to understand that in our relationship with Jesus, He does not need us to stoke His ego. His powers as rescuer and redeemer are alive in our own instincts and in our ability to act in a given situation. Pretending we need help when we don't— especially when we are doing so because it seems like the "Christian thing to do"—may turn us away from the redemptive qualities in our personal connection to Christ. —ELIZABETH BERNE DEGEAR

FAITH STEP: *Begin your day with this prayerful question: "How is Christ the Redeemer alive within my own discernment and judgment today?"*

FRIDAY, JULY 19

For Satan disguises himself as an angel of light. 2 Corinthians 11:14 (HCSB)

ONE OF THE MOST BEAUTIFUL sights in Yellowstone is the Grand Prismatic Spring. It's the largest hot spring in the United States and the third largest in the world. Ferdinand Hayden, who led the first official expedition to the spring, said of it, "Nothing ever conceived by human art could equal the peculiar vividness and delicacy of color of these remarkable prismatic springs. Life becomes a privilege and a blessing after one has seen and thoroughly felt [them]."

To me, it looks like the giant wild eyeball of a unicorn or some other mythological creature. The deep blue middle fades into every color of the rainbow as it radiates away. Standing at the edge, you feel like you'd enter a magical world if you could jump into the spring for a swim.

Reality, however, is that if you jumped in, you'd boil. The center of the spring gets to 189 degrees, cooling by bits to the outermost ring, which is a mere 131 degrees. In other words, it's a beauty that burns.

The footsteps of Jesus lead us to deny ourselves, pick up our cross, and follow Him. It doesn't sound particularly alluring, but in His presence, we find protection, peace, and fullness of joy. Every time I am lured from this path, it's because something else appears more appealing. More exciting. More beautiful. And every time—every single time—I get burned. —GWEN FORD FAULKENBERRY

FAITH STEP: *Are you standing on the edge of a bad choice right now? Meditate on 2 Corinthians 11:14. Ask the Lord to help you see past the disguise and find truth in Jesus.*

SATURDAY, JULY 20

Then He lifted up His eyes toward His disciples, and said: "Blessed are you poor, For yours is the kingdom of God." Luke 6:20 (NKJV)

JAMAICA IS MY FAVORITE CARIBBEAN country. The pristine beaches, crystal blue water, scrumptious food, and friendly people draw me back time and time again. On my first trip, I was like a wide-eyed kid, marveling at the waterfalls and lush vegetation on the way to Negril, the northernmost part of the country. As our van crawled up the dirt roads, I also saw the abject poverty of many of the locals. Tin roofs covered houses no bigger than my basement. Goats and chickens roamed freely in the dirt outside their homes.

I met so many kind folks, most of whom were Christians and loved Jesus with their whole hearts. And I noticed that although they were poor as measured monetarily, their spirits were rich with joy. Their warm smiles and evident love for Jesus made them appear richly blessed. In the Bible, poor folks were drawn to Jesus like bees to honey. Why? He was never concerned with money and what people owned. Jesus didn't care if someone was dirt-poor or a wealthy tax collector. Matthew 5:3 says, "Blessed are the poor in spirit, for theirs is the kingdom of heaven." Jesus doesn't discriminate. He loves the poor, the homeless, the disenfranchised, the weak, and the hopeless. He is not only Lord of all; He is Lord *for* all.
—CAROL MACKEY

FAITH STEP: *Jesus says that when we help the "least of these," we help Him too (Matthew 25:40). Read to children in a library, volunteer at a food pantry, donate canned goods to food banks, and know it's a blessing to be a blessing!*

SUNDAY, JULY 21

No one is like you, LORD; you are great, and your name is mighty in power.
Jeremiah 10:6 (NIV)

THE OTHER DAY I TEXTED a friend who was not feeling well. Using *Jehovah Rapha (Healer)*, one of the names for Jesus/God, I told her I would pray that He would make her well. Unfortunately I typed the name wrong. Usually my iPhone's automatic spell-checker offers possible correct spellings. But this time, the words *No Replacement* appeared. So I retyped the name with the correct spelling and completed my message.

Later, I thought about that incident. Throughout the Bible, people consistently misunderstood the names and meaning of the one true God. In fact, they invented titles for their own gods. When God sent His Son to the earth, Jesus spoke of His Father often. Jesus taught that there was unity between His Father's name and His own, but people misinterpreted that and Jesus's claims (John 10:25–30).

Jesus spent three of His thirty-three years on earth in focused ministry: teaching, healing, loving, and reflecting the attributes of the God-Name He came to represent. Some followers "got" the truth of Matthew 12:21 (VOICE): "All the world will find its hope in His name." But others won't grasp that truth until the day when we see the power of His divinity clearly: "at the name of Jesus EVERY KNEE WILL BOW... every tongue will confess that Jesus Christ is Lord, to the glory of God the Father" (Philippians 2:10–11 NASB).

In the meantime, we can make His name known everywhere we go. There really is no replacement for the mighty name of Jesus. — REBECCA BARLOW JORDAN

FAITH STEP: *How has the name of Jesus impacted your life? Write down the names of three people with whom you could share the power of Jesus's name.*

MONDAY, JULY 22

Give thanks to him who made the heavens so skillfully. His faithful love endures forever. *Give thanks to him who placed the earth among the waters.* His faithful love endures forever. *Give thanks to him who made the heavenly lights*—His faithful love endures forever. *Psalm 136:5–7 (NLT)*

WE STAYED AT AN AMAZING rental house over the summer with my family. The house was on top of a hill overlooking a deep blue reservoir surrounded by windswept, brush-covered mountains. Over the hills, out to the west, was the vast Pacific Ocean. And to the east was the Anza-Borrego Desert.

One afternoon during our stay, a storm broke out over the house with the deep rumble of thunder, and the skies darkened with purple clouds. It was majestic. In the suburbs where I live, which are surrounded by strip malls and congested with traffic, I often forget about the amazing world that Jesus has created around us. But out in the mountains, surrounded by desert beauty, I can't ignore it. I find myself telling the Maker of heaven and earth, "Jesus! You are amazing. You are so creative. How in the world did you come up with all this? Thank you for your amazing work!"

In the day-to-day, we find it incredibly easy to focus on ourselves. It takes effort to turn our focus to Jesus. But when we do, it puts life in perspective.

What are our problems to the One who shaped the earth with His hands? How can we worry when the One who formed galaxies with a word is in control? How can we not throw up our hands and thank Jesus for His amazing creation and His ceaseless love? Let's focus on Him and shout His praises at the top of our lungs. —SUSANNA FOTH AUGHTMON

FAITH STEP: *Step outside. Look up at the blueness of the sky. Feel the brightness of the sun. Thank Jesus for His great work in creation and His amazing love.*

TUESDAY, JULY 23

Hear me, LORD, and answer me, for I am poor and needy. Psalm 86:1 (NIV)

NEEDY. I HATED THAT WORD. I used it in a self-deprecating "sorry to be a needy friend" type of way all the time. It resurrected memories of being labeled emotionally immature. I cried with someone who initially responded with, "Call if you need to talk" but then later avoided me. *"I know you're in a needy place, but I'm busy."* I associated my need for comfort with being a clingy pest. When years of unresolved pain drove me to counseling, I had to face the side of me that felt extremely needy, because I'd been hurt.

Knowing my feelings about *that word*, my counselor suggested that we replace it with something else. As much as I wanted to, I knew it was time to make peace with the word *needy*. How many times had David called himself "poor and needy" in his psalms? At least four. Not once did I see the Lord scold him for that. What was at the root of *needy*? Need. Aren't we all in need? Wasn't it normal to need comfort in our pain and someone to hear us? I wanted to be like David— able to tell Jesus, "I feel needy," and trust Him to send what I ached for, whether help came through a friend or through His presence.

Each of us came into the world as a bundle of need; that is exactly why we need Jesus, and why we need to stay constantly connected to the One Who knows what is going on in our hearts long before we cry, "Hear me, LORD...for I am poor and needy."
—JEANETTE HANSCOME

FAITH STEP: *Read Psalm 86. What are you feeling needy for today? Spend some time pouring out whatever is weighing you down, and ask Jesus to send the comfort and peace that only He can provide.*

WEDNESDAY, JULY 24

For anything that becomes visible is light. Therefore it says,
"Awake, O sleeper, and arise from the dead, and Christ will shine on you."
Ephesians 5:14 (ESV)

I WOKE UP IN THE middle of the night. My arm was under my pillow, and the weight of my head had squashed it and turned my arm into a numb lump. I touched it with my other fingers and even used my other hand to move it around. The arm felt nothing. Once I repositioned it so blood could flow into it, uncomfortable prickles started. Life returned. The limb that had fallen asleep worked again.

We were numb and dead in our sin until Jesus brought us back to life. But the call to "arise from the dead" isn't only for the time we enter heaven.

In a world that turns away from Jesus at every opportunity, it's easy for our hearts to become as lifeless as my squashed arm. Sometimes when we've been cut off from the supply of life blood (perhaps ignoring His Word, or prayer, or worship, or fellowship with others), we become numb to the needs around us and the rich grace that Jesus offers. I'm thankful that He is willing and able to resurrect us daily. The process isn't always comfortable at first. When we begin to spend time with Him, our hearts may feel prickles of conviction. Jesus may call us to change or to be His arms in service in a way that challenges us. But as He shines on us, the joy of coming back to life will fuel us in our walks with Jesus.

Let's heed the call to wake up and invite Christ to shine on us today. —SHARON HINCK

FAITH STEP: *Set an alarm clock and let it ring. Ask Jesus to wake you up to His presence and His life today.*

THURSDAY, JULY 25

A friend loves at all times. Proverbs 17:17 (NIV)

LAST NIGHT, I DREAMED ABOUT a close friend I knew as a teenager, someone I haven't seen for decades. For many years, we lost touch with each other, but both of us kept searching. At last, we made contact through social media. I had my dear companion back!

We live thousands of miles apart. The chances of us meeting again are very low, but we both daydream about it. Yet if I have to wait until heaven for one of her hugs, I can. It'll be worth it. For now, I'm happy with our steady interactions, both online and during phone conversations.

I occasionally attended church as a child, but didn't give my life to Jesus until my twenties. After I made that commitment, I could see how much His presence had been missed in my young life. *How could I miss someone I barely knew?* Yet I did. I needed Him—always had—more than I realized. Like the reunion with my long-lost bestie, this was a reunion with my Maker, and it was at this point when Jesus's tenderness poured into me like oxygen as I lay gasping. He brought me to abundant life.

Christ and I stay in touch day and night, through prayer, Bible study, and the countless blessings He shares with me. When I'm down, He lifts my spirits, and He builds me up when my strength is flagging. Sometimes, I can almost feel His hug, as real as any other loved one's.

My dream of an actual embrace from Jesus will come true the day He'll wrap both arms around me, welcoming me to heaven. For now, His magnificent love is enough. —HEIDI GAUL

FAITH STEP: *Look up someone you've fallen out of contact with. Get in touch via computer or phone. Pick up where you left off and start blessing each other in friendship again.*

FRIDAY, JULY 26

Then Jesus said, "Come to me, all of you who are weary and carry heavy burdens, and I will give you rest." Matthew 11:28 (NLT)

AS A FRIEND AND I spoke on the phone, she poured out the impossibilities of a family relationship crisis that seemed unending. They would make significant progress, then retreat into old habits, old bitterness, old regrets that fueled old arguments.

"I don't know what to do anymore but pray," she said.

The brief silence between us marked the moment we both realized how quick we are with a reply like that, although we both knew the power of prayer and the comfort of knowing Jesus calls us to come to Him when we're facing the impossible.

"It's not as if He says, 'Here I am in a corner of the basement,'" I reminded both of us. "He doesn't say, 'It's dark here in the cellar and full of cobwebs. Damp. Kind of disgusting. But come to Me. We'll sit here on the cold concrete floor together.'"

She agreed that would not be like Jesus.

"Instead," I added, "He calls us to where He sits beside waters He stilled for us, in green pastures He 'greened' for us. 'Come here,' He says, 'to where I wait on the balcony with a great view. I'll comfort you here.'"

When you think of calling out to Jesus in a desperate situation, is it a basement or a balcony mental picture?

He calls us to live in the light as He is in the light (1 John 1:7). When we have nowhere to turn but to Him, we're not relegated to the basement of our faith, but the balcony. —CYNTHIA RUCHTI

FAITH STEP: *Do you keep a prayer list of desperate people and impossible situations? Find a picture of a light-drenched balcony and add it to the page or file as a reminder of the Source of Hope to which you're turning.*

SATURDAY, JULY 27

Then I saw heaven opened, and behold, a white horse! The one sitting on it is called Faithful and True, and in righteousness he judges. Revelation 19:11 (ESV)

OLD FAITHFUL, THE FIRST GEYSER to get a name in Yellowstone National Park, is called a "highly predictable geothermal feature" in that "since 2000 it has erupted every forty-four to one hundred and twenty-five minutes." As scientists have gotten smarter, and instruments of measurement more accurate, you can now go there with your family and see at the visitor center a calculated prediction of when it is expected to erupt. You can get an ice-cream cone, take a seat, get your camera ready, and plan on yelling, "Thar she blows!" to embarrass your teenagers with precision. Because now, there's only a ten-minute margin of error as to when Old Faithful will shoot boiling water out of the ground. It's like clockwork.

A ten-minute margin of error is pretty good for geyser-watching. But what if the situation is a bit more dire? What if you are by the bedside of a loved one and leave just before that person takes a turn for the worse? What if you are trying to make it to the hospital as you are ready to give birth?

There are plenty of scenarios in which a ten-minute margin of error is not acceptable at all. When we need to know—right now—someone is there to bear witness, to help us, to see us, to hear us, to fight for us.

There's only one whose faithfulness has no margin of error. In fact, he is called Faithful and True. We can always count on Jesus to be there. Always. —GWEN FORD FAULKENBERRY

FAITH STEP: *Is there someone who needs to see the faithfulness of Jesus demonstrated in you today? Find a place where your presence is needed to listen, pray, help, or serve. Then step out in faith and faithfulness.*

SUNDAY, JULY 28

And my God will fully satisfy every need of yours according to his riches in glory in Christ Jesus. Philippians 4:19 (NRSV)

EARLIER THIS YEAR, OUR PASTOR made a statement that nagged at my mind: "The greatest need we have as a church is to see our need." I couldn't help wondering how that applied to me as an individual. How well do I see and understand my own needs? If you had asked me a couple of months ago what I needed, I would have ticked off a list: I need to lose weight and get fit, land a new book contract, get painting and repairs done on our house, work on our landscaping...and more. But if I'm being honest, I have to admit that while these represent reasonable goals, they are not truly needs.

The Bible promises that God will meet all our needs through Jesus. In Luke 10:42, Jesus clarified what that means. He explained that only one thing is needed or necessary; Mary had demonstrated it by sitting at His feet and soaking up His words. The most important part of our day is time spent alone with Jesus in worship, prayer, and the Word. If we make Him our highest priority, we don't have to worry about being without.

I no longer use the word *need* loosely. If I notice that my shoes are scuffed, I may be tempted to say I need a new pair. But then I consider how many people in the world don't own any shoes, so I say that I "would like" new ones. Although I still begin my day with a to-do list, I think of the items as things I hope to accomplish. Because if I focus on spending time with Jesus first, then I can trust Him to take care of everything else. —DIANNE NEAL MATTHEWS

FAITH STEP: *List what you consider the top five needs in your life right now. How do you think spending time with Jesus might change your attitude toward these issues?*

MONDAY, JULY 29

Who then will condemn us? No one—for Christ Jesus died for us and was raised to life for us, and he is sitting in the place of honor at God's right hand, pleading for us. Romans 8:34 (NLT)

MY DOCTOR ORDERED AN ULTRASOUND for me at a clinic thirty miles away. I arrived at the facility with a half hour to spare.

I'll grab a cup of coffee, I thought upon seeing a teeny café in the building's foyer. The woman behind the counter greeted me warmly. Her accent told me she was Eastern European, so I asked her about her country of origin.

"Poland," she said.

"Really? I visit Poland every year," I said. The moment she realized my personal interest in her homeland, she began talking to me as though we were best friends.

"My husband and I immigrated to Canada in 1994," she said. "We came with only one suitcase of belongings and had to start life over." She told me that they've reached retirement age and are unsure whether they should stay in Canada or return to Poland. "Finances are the issue," she said. "We don't know what to do."

"May I pray for you about that?" I asked. She nodded. I thanked Jesus for loving this woman and for having good plans for her. I asked Him to give wisdom and guidance for this decision, and then I asked Him to reveal Himself to her in a tangible way. The prayer lasted fifteen seconds, but I trust the impact lasts for eternity.

I'm growing more courageous about praying for strangers who share their concerns with me. Why not? Knowing that Jesus prays for me brings me great encouragement. Seeing others' responses when I pray for them tells me they're encouraged too. —GRACE FOX

FAITH STEP: *Ask Jesus to give you opportunity to pray for a stranger.*

TUESDAY, JULY 30

The LORD will give strength to His people; the LORD will bless His people with peace. Psalm 29:11 (NKJV)

MY MARRIAGE HAD BEEN ON life support for several years before I decided to pull the plug. The early years were good—lots of hope and dreams. The latter years were not—full of treachery and heartbreak. And although I had a relationship with Jesus, I had no peace in the marriage. I prayed, I fasted, I cried, and I waited to hear from God. Then God literally sent an angel who counseled me and comforted me. I made an appointment to see a lawyer. Although Jesus gave me peace about my decision, it was still the most heartbreaking decision I'd ever made. After almost four years of tough litigation, the final judgment arrived in the mail: we were officially uncoupled. I felt relieved and remorseful. This wasn't the way Christian marriages were supposed to end. But circumstances drove me to this decision, and I found peace—finally.

The Lord held my hand through the worst emotional ordeal of my life, and He refused to let go. Jesus offers His help and assurance. John 14:27 says, "Peace I leave with you, My peace I give to you; not as the world gives do I give to you. Let not your heart be troubled, neither let it be afraid." This verse tells us He *left us* His Peace (the Holy Spirit), He *gives us* His Peace (His Word), and He doesn't want us to be sad or afraid. I've learned to trust in that promise. From one life storm to another. —CAROL MACKEY

FAITH STEP: *The Lord is with you during the most stressful times of your life. He will hold you up when your legs wobble and your tears won't stop. Lean into Him. He wants to take that load off. Allow Him to give you His peace.*

WEDNESDAY, JULY 31

For God has not given us a spirit of fear, but of power and of love and of a sound mind. 2 Timothy 1:7 (NKJV)

THE RULES FOR THE DOLPHIN pool were clear: *Let them come to you; only touch them if they swim alongside the edge in a way that allows you to stroke their side or back.* I prayed that one would swim close enough for me to touch it, even if my fingertips only brushed its skin. As I waited, I prayed that fear would not hold me back from seizing the opportunity when it finally came.

I have battled fear my entire life. My phobias of water used to drive my poor mom and dad crazy. In the past, I would not have dipped my hand into any pool containing large sea creatures. But I had come a long way in my fight against fear, and today, I was determined to touch a dolphin. Just when I was about to tell my family, "We can go. I guess it isn't meant to be," I heard my mom gasp, "Jeanette!" as a dolphin sailed through the water toward me. I plunged my hand in and felt the firm silk of its back all the way down to its tail. I could hardly breathe.

"That was the coolest thing ever!"

Thank You, Jesus.

Fear had caused me to miss out on a lot in my life, but not that day.

If we belong to Jesus, we live under the protection of the One Who can help us overcome our fears, Who can celebrate with us as we do, and Who can provide the freedom that comes from refusing to be afraid. —JEANETTE HANSCOME

FAITH STEP: *What have you missed out on because you were afraid? Write down one thing you would like to do that requires overcoming a fear. Ask Jesus for the courage and opportunity to do it.*

Thursday, August 1

And he said to them all, If anyone will come after me, let them deny themself and take up their cross daily and follow me. Luke 9:23 (JUB)

This summer, while my husband and I were enjoying a short getaway together, we met a mature couple we liked immediately. They had just climbed to the top of a Vermont mountain. There was something about the woman that impressed me and made me want to get to know her better. She seemed very grounded and wise, comfortable in her skin, and like she really knew how to live. I thought, *It must be her work that has given her this fountain of life wisdom she draws from.* So I asked her what she did for a living. But I was wrong to think that her profession was the source.

Seven years ago, the couple's younger son had committed suicide at age thirty. This was a cross they had picked up daily since then. Living in the world without him was a forced renunciation, and one that they clearly were never free from. But as I listened to them talk about their lives—about the residential treatment center they had started in their son's name, about the husband's work as a grief counselor with other families, about their other son and their adorable two-year-old granddaughter—I realized that by fully entering into mourning and loss, they had not let their tragedy deprive them of a full and meaningful life. As we parted ways, the woman laughed and bestowed a blessing on me and my husband: "I hope you're still kissing on the trail like we are—forty-five years in!" This couple wasn't Christian, but Christ spoke to me through them. Their example helped me understand that carrying your cross and following wherever it leads is a life path worth taking. —Elizabeth Berne DeGear

---

Faith Step: *In the spiritual presence of Jesus, revisit a painful loss in your past. Ask Jesus to give you the strength you need to pick up this cross and follow Him.*

FRIDAY, AUGUST 2

---

*Trust in the LORD with all your heart and lean not on your own understanding;
in all your ways submit to him, and he will make your paths straight.*
Proverbs 3:5–6 (NIV)

TEMPERATURES CONTINUED TO RISE AS I raced to complete a series of errands. I sighed, stepping into the car. Two more stops and I could head home.

As I turned the key in the ignition, a light shone on the dashboard, accompanied by incessant ringing. The needle on the temperature gauge flipped over to red, telling me the engine had overheated.

My day was crazy busy as it was, and I didn't have a minute to spare. Calling for a tow would eat up at least an hour. Fighting panic, I called my husband David's cell. No answer. I tried again with the same result.

I was on my own. Panicky, I lowered the window and stared at my hands, open and empty in my lap—empty, but not useless. I decided to pray. *Why had it taken so long?* I'd put it off as a last resort, something to fall back on when everything else failed. I bowed my head and asked for Jesus's help. I didn't know what was wrong with the car or how to fix it. But I knew what was wrong with me. I'd trusted Jesus with my forever, but not my today. If my soul came equipped with a warning light, it would have lit up the car's interior. As I prayed for forgiveness, His peace filled my soul.

Minutes ticked by, then an hour. Enough time passed for the engine to cool. My mood improved, and I drove straight home. Jesus had rescued me, for today and forever. —HEIDI GAUL

FAITH STEP: *Next time you face an upsetting experience, take a deep breath and pray. Ask Jesus for direction. He'll clear your head—and straighten your path.*

SATURDAY, AUGUST 3

Don't be afraid, for I am with you. Don't be discouraged, for I am your God. I will strengthen you and help you. I will hold you up with my victorious right hand. Isaiah 41:10 (NLT)

MY EIGHT-YEAR-OLD GRANDSON, LUKE, WATCHED several older cousins ride the giant swing at a Christian campsite. "That looks like fun," he said. "I want a turn." He stepped onto the platform and asked the swing operator to buckle him into the harness.

As the operator began, Luke changed his mind. "I'm not so sure this is a good idea after all," he said. Cheering onlookers assured him that he'd be safe. He visibly relaxed and remained on the ride.

The operator raised the swing until Luke's back was parallel to the ground, and then he released it. Luke soared through the air, hooting and laughing. When his ride ended, the operator lowered him and unbuckled the harness.

"Wow—that was fun!" said Luke. "I wasn't even scared."

"Why weren't you scared?" I asked.

Luke's answer was simple but profound: "Because I prayed, 'Jesus, help me to not be afraid,' and He answered."

Are you riding a giant swing today? Maybe you're dealing with a crisis into which you've suddenly been buckled—an illness, an accident, a financial setback, a relationship issue. The future looks uncertain, and fear is rattling your nerves. If so, recall today's key verse and the truths it contains: Jesus is with you. He'll strengthen and help you. He's holding you with His victorious right hand.

Pray Luke's simple but profound prayer—"Jesus, help me to not be afraid"—and trust Him to answer. —GRACE FOX

FAITH STEP: *Doodle a child's swing set. Draw one seat flying high with a stick figure representing you. Write Luke's prayer, and claim it as your own.*

SUNDAY, AUGUST 4

Turning around, Jesus saw them following and asked, "What do you want?"
They said, "Rabbi" (which means "Teacher"), "where are you staying?"
"Come," he replied, "and you will see." So they went and saw where he was
staying, and they spent that day with him. It was about four in the afternoon.
John 1:38–39 (NIV)

As I READ THE FIRST chapter of John today, I was challenged by Jesus's words to the disciples who approached Him. I spend a lot of time asking Jesus to come into my life, my day, my activities. I tell Him about my goals and ask Him to bless them. In effect, I'm saying, "Come see what I'm up to and join me."

But I often have things backward. These disciples asked Jesus where *He* was staying. Although they were speaking of a physical location, their question reminded me to ask this of Jesus in a metaphorical way. I can ask Him what He is focusing on that day, where He is "staying." Is there a ministry at my church that is being prompted forward in a new way, where I could contribute? Is there a theme regarding character or Christian discipleship among my circle of friends that He is stirring up to encourage us to grow a new direction? Instead of setting my own course, I can acknowledge Jesus as my Teacher and follow Him.

Let's take our cue from the disciples who first met Jesus by the shores of the Jordan River. We can ask Him to open our eyes so we can see where He is staying. We can drop our own agendas and stick close to Him. As those early followers did, we can spend the day with Jesus. Our day will glow with a new richness as we watch Him at work in our world. —SHARON HINCK

FAITH STEP: *Read a church newsletter, a daily paper, or a few emails from friends. Where do you see Jesus at work? Ask Him how you can join Him in that work.*

MONDAY, AUGUST 5

Jesus traveled throughout the region of Galilee, teaching in the synagogues and announcing the Good News about the Kingdom. And he healed every kind of disease and illness. Matthew 4:23 (NLT)

IN FEWER THAN FOUR WEEKS, I will officially be a middle school teacher. I accepted a position as a lit and writing teacher at my boys' school. This makes me laugh that high, hysterical hyena laughter of nervousness. I haven't faced a life change this big since having kids. I have been scribbling ideas for books and projects. Reading young adult lit. Poring over lesson plans. Reading teaching books. And I have been meeting with my former fifth grade teacher who has been a mentor and teacher for the last twenty years. She is the best teacher ever! I loved her when I was ten. I love her more now. She is setting my feet firmly on the path of teacher wisdom with thoughts like: *Be firm. Explain everything. Set boundaries. Have routines. Share procedures. But be ready to improvise because teaching is fluid.*

Last meeting I told her, "I have a lot to learn."

She said, "Keep thinking that. The teacher who thinks they know it all is finished."

I am far from finished. It is that way with Jesus too. His disciples called Him "Teacher" and so can we. He is the best teacher ever. He teaches us how to live, how to believe, and how to trust. He guides us with grace and mercy. He mentors us in the ways of love. He has answers for our questions and heavenly wisdom to draw from. There is so much to learn from the Teacher, we will continue to learn until we see Him face-to-face. —SUSANNA FOTH AUGHTMON

FAITH STEP: *Write down the lessons that Jesus has been teaching you in this season. What has He been showing you? How have you asked for His guidance?*

TUESDAY, AUGUST 6

Is this not the carpenter's son? Is not His mother called Mary? And His brothers James, Joses, Simon, and Judas? Matthew 13:55 (NKJV)

ONE DAY WHEN I HAD an appointment in New York City, I decided to walk to the commuter train from the suburb I live in. I typically drive, but it was a balmy summer day and I needed the exercise. As I hurried through the large parking lot, I passed dozens of cars and I noticed something: almost all of them had vanity license plates—you know, the ones with personalized messages. In addition, there were license plate frames touting colleges, sports teams, sororities and fraternities, occupations, even Jesus! It was a mass showing of people wanting to be identified with something that they are proud of.

I thought about Jesus. When the folks in the synagogue heard Him teaching with authority and conviction, they couldn't believe He was Who He claimed to be—the coming Messiah. They identified Him as being Mary and Joseph's son; He identified Himself as being God's only begotten Son. They saw Him as the quiet carpenter from Galilee; He saw Himself as the Lamb of God who came to save the world. They resented that He, a mere man, could put Himself on par with God. "'Who does he think he is?' They got their noses all out of joint" (Matthew 13:57 MSG). As followers of Christ, we may find our identity in Him questioned, ridiculed, or even mocked. Don't fret. His name is written on our hearts, and our names are written in heaven. That's better than any message on a license plate! —CAROL MACKEY

FAITH STEP: *Who do you identify with most? What are you most proud of? Think about your relationship to Jesus. You are and will always be His number one (John 6:37).*

WEDNESDAY, AUGUST 7

"So I say to you, keep asking, and it will be given to you. Keep searching, and you will find. Keep knocking, and the door will be opened to you."
Luke 11:9 (HCSB)

WHEN MY HUSBAND, RICHARD, AND I visited our daughter's family last summer, seven-year-old Roman wanted to take up fishing. The week included three trips to the sporting goods store, stops for bait and licenses, and jaunts to local lakes. All of which netted one tiny fish. Not what Roman had imagined. Six weeks later, we visited again and learned that Roman had been researching fishing tips online. At his request, I helped him locate library books on fishing, and Richard bought him a much nicer rod and reel along with the lure that "guaranteed" a good catch.

During that second visit, Richard, Roman, and my son-in-law returned from their trips empty-handed, talking about broken lines and lost lures. Roman was completely discouraged; after returning from one fishing trip, he went to his room and cried. I wondered if he might give up and move on to another interest. A couple of weeks later, we received a text from our son-in-law showing Roman holding a sizable fish, with a sizable grin on his face.

I felt proud of my grandson, but I wondered, *When it comes to my prayer life, do I push through even when I don't see results?* All too often, I feel tempted to give up when my prayer seems to go unanswered. But Jesus urged His followers to keep on asking, searching, and knocking. And since He called His disciples fishers of men, He may have urged them to keep on fishing as well. —DIANNE NEAL MATTHEWS

FAITH STEP: *Are you on the verge of giving up on something—a prayer request, a God-given dream, a relationship? Fill in the blank "Keep on _____."*

THURSDAY, AUGUST 8

Let my teaching fall like rain and my word settle like dew, like gentle rain on new grass and showers on tender plants. Deuteronomy 32:2 (HCSB)

AN UNUSUAL AUGUST RAINSTORM HAD pushed through our area, causing power outages overnight. The next morning calm returned, along with cooler temperatures. I moved to the back patio, coffee and Bible in hand, to enjoy the change of weather. I relished my time alone with Jesus.

A few days later, another cool morning arrived, so I headed out again to my beloved spot, opened my Bible, and smiled at the words from Deuteronomy 32. Preparing for his death, Moses took time to instruct the assembly of Israelites, making sure they understood what God expected of them in the coming days. He devoted an entire chapter to a song that he recited to them. One of the things Moses emphasized was the importance of God's teaching, using a metaphor of rain. I remembered my experience earlier on the patio and thanked Jesus for the living illustration He had shown me along with an instant understanding of the passage.

I thought about how we sometimes approach God's Word—desperate for restoration from a "power outage" in our lives—then after the storm has passed, we forget about its light-giving properties. Like the Israelites, sometimes we may ignore God completely, choosing to remain in the dark (Nehemiah 9:34 MSG). But Jesus wants us to let His Words fall on our spirits like a gentle rain soaking our roots. We are nourished by the constant drops of living refreshment from His Word. And when His teaching seeps into our souls, we will grow spiritually. —REBECCA BARLOW JORDAN

FAITH STEP: *The next time you experience a gentle rain, extend your hand or step into it for a moment. Use this as an opportunity—and reminder—to soak yourself in God's Word daily.*

FRIDAY, AUGUST 9

In the last days, God says, I will pour out my Spirit on all people.
Your sons and daughters will prophesy, your young men will see visions,
your old men will dream dreams. Acts 2:17 (NIV)

THE BIBLE IS FULL OF prominent old folks God recruited for vital kingdom missions. Abraham and Noah, Elizabeth, mother of John, and assorted mature apostles. God is definitely not ageist.

One of the things I most enjoy about living in the Sunshine State is the median age. At fifty, I'm not always the oldest person in the room. Everywhere, I see seniors who are living meaningful and fun-filled lives of purpose, many with second or third careers and ministries, new romances, dynamic leisure activities, and revived dreams.

American culture favors youth more than any other on the globe. Having recently hit the mid-century mark, I'm amazed that I'm enjoying one of my best decades yet. I've fulfilled some lifelong desires—including living near the beach—and find new, deeply satisfying friendships and exciting opportunities emerging at a time when I might have been in the twilight of my career. Here, just in case I wanted something more concrete than God's Word, I'm surrounded by many supportive examples of people finding new purpose and joy in their second halves of life.

God used a very old Noah to build an ark and blessed menopausal Elizabeth with John the Baptist, who paved the way for Jesus, so He can still use us as we grow in our maturity. The ageless God is not hindered by age! —ISABELLA YOSUICO

FAITH STEP: *In Christ, it is never too late. Jot down some of the unfulfilled dreams you fear you're too old to fulfill. Talk to God about whether and how He may help you realize them now.*

SATURDAY, AUGUST 10

He commanded our ancestors to teach them to their children, so the next generation might know them—even the children not yet born—and they in turn will teach their own children. Psalm 78:5–6 (NLT)

MY DAD'S FAMILY BUILT A vacation cabin in the Sierras when I was in kindergarten. It's full of memories of snow trips, hot days at the lake, and playing house under an old oak tree with my sisters and cousins using a nearby stump as our kitchen. Some things haven't been updated since the seventies, like the rosewood paneling and Formica countertops, and storing sleds in an unfinished room known as the dungeon. Other things have changed: the TV now gets more than three fuzzy channels, and we finally remodeled the bathrooms. Now, a new generation is collecting memories of the cabin.

This summer, I lugged my suitcase to the bedroom I'd claimed, and spotted Grandma's copy of *Streams in the Desert* and her father's Bible sitting on top of the Cabin Journal—a fake-leather diary that I'd left so anyone who wanted to could write in it. I picked up the devotional. For me, that and the Bible represented a legacy far sweeter than the journal, or even the place where I'd spent so much of my childhood. They reflected the foundation of faith that began when Grandma became the first family member to accept Jesus as her Savior. I hoped that I would continue to pass down what she started. When my sons visit the cabin, I want them to find memories of fun and reminders of Jesus.

As a follower of Christ, each of us has someone to thank for our faith in Him—a parent, a grandparent, a close friend. Our gratitude for their enormous gift can motivate us to do everything in our power to pass it on to the next generation. —JEANETTE HANSCOME

FAITH STEP: *Who do you have to thank for your faith? Who are you trying to pass the legacy on to? Take a moment to thank Jesus for what you have received.*

SUNDAY, AUGUST 11

Jesus was in the stern (of the boat), sleeping on a cushion. Mark 4:38 (NIV)

I WOKE FROM A DREAM with a heavy heart. I'd been dreaming about a young woman dear to me and my family. In the dream, she was bombarded by lies and untruths. They pelted her like hail. I wanted to place myself between her and the hailstorm but couldn't.

Or could I?

I didn't need sleep as much as I needed peace. So I prayed for the young woman, asking Jesus to protect her from every thought that wasn't from Him, to steer her thinking, to woo her away from lies.

The dream may have been a product of my imagination. But the time I spent in prayer wasn't wasted. Within days, I heard she'd been wrestling with her faith.

We know Jesus slept, but do we know what filled His dreams?

What was He dreaming about, if anything, when the storm raged around the small boat in which He and His disciples traveled across the lake? He slept through much of the storm. Were His dream thoughts of His Father, of the heaven He'd left for our sake, of the Calvary road ahead of Him?

Or, somewhere in the depths of His mind, was He aware of danger, but still sleeping because of His rock-solid faith?

The Bible tells us Jesus now ever lives to intercede for us (Hebrews 7:25). He no longer needs to rest. But He still sits bolt upright to pray about the things that put us and our spiritual health in danger.

What a gift to know He's praying for us, no matter the hour of the day or night. —CYNTHIA RUCHTI

FAITH STEP: *Don't wait for a disturbing dream to wake you. Spend some time today praying for young lives susceptible to lies and spiritual untruth. Jesus is.*

MONDAY, AUGUST 12

And he said: "Truly I tell you, unless you change and become like little children, you will never enter the kingdom of heaven." Matthew 18:3 (NIV)

As MY FAMILY AND I were driving along the interstate, I glanced down just as two dashboard lights came on. My stomach tightened, sinking like a stone. I pulled off the freeway to park under a shade tree. With no buildings in sight, we'd broken down in the middle of nowhere. I felt as helpless and alone as a lost child.

Ninety-degree air wafted through the open windows as we each searched for our own solutions. My daughter called a mechanic to seek advice. My son-in-law surfed the internet searching out repair videos. My husband, David, pored over the car's manual. I stayed quiet, waiting. But none of us considered the obvious solution—calling for help.

Fifteen minutes later, the car remained disabled. The situation was beyond our control. I pulled out my automobile club card and dialed the number. The relief we felt when we saw the tow truck was as strong as a lost toddler's upon first spotting a parent. As strong as when we reach for Jesus in faith.

All believers face challenges we approach in different ways, according to our nature and skill sets. Some problems are easy to tackle. In other instances, we cry out in need for Jesus, as dependent as babies. But without His help, we can't solve anything. When we come to Him as children, He lifts us from the muck and mire that fills our lives and cleans up the mess. He repairs the things we've broken. We need only hang on to our faith like a child. —HEIDI GAUL

FAITH STEP: *Think back on how you felt as a child, wrapped up safely in a loved one's embrace. Close your eyes and climb onto Jesus's lap to tell Him your problems. He's listening—and He knows the solution.*

TUESDAY, AUGUST 13

But you say, "If anyone tells his father or his mother, 'What you would
have gained from me is given to God,' he need not honor his father."
So for the sake of your tradition you have made void the word of God.
You hypocrites! Matthew 15:5–7 (ESV)

WHEN THE CHILDREN WERE YOUNG, exhaustion sometimes pushed me past the point of reason. "I worked hard for hours to make this nice dinner. Now sit here and enjoy it!" or "We saved all year for this outing, so we aren't leaving until you stop whining and have fun." I ruefully shake my head at those memories.

When Jesus challenges the Pharisees' twisted logic, He also challenges me. They felt rather smug in their choices. Why should their parents complain about not being cared for? The Pharisees had self-righteously given huge amounts to God instead. The problem was, that wasn't what God was asking of them.

What might family life have been like if I'd focused less on making sacrifices for the kids that left me cranky and, instead, focused more on being a loving and present mom? The seeds of the martyr complex still germinate in me these days. When my husband gets home from work, I rattle off all I've accomplished, while slumping in exhaustion. He'd rather I do less and have a little joy for him.

Sometimes, I do tasks to honor Jesus and help others that I think are altruistic, but they aren't what Jesus is actually asking of me. When I hear Pharisee-type defensiveness in my voice, it's time to ask Jesus for help. He can sort out which activities are truly reflective of His love and which ones are my own ill-conceived priorities. —SHARON HINCK

FAITH STEP: *Are you feeling resentful about any sacrifices you've made? Ask Jesus to show you if you need to make new choices.*

WEDNESDAY, AUGUST 14

*I have redeemed you; I have summoned you by name; you are
mine. . . . When you walk through the fire, you will not be burned;
the flames will not set you ablaze. Isaiah 43:1–2 (NIV)*

WE TOOK OUR KIDS ON an epic adventure this summer, from Arkansas to the West Coast, exploring as much of the country as we could before heading on up to the giant coastal redwoods of California.

Every little town up there has its own "drive-through tree" where people literally drive their cars through a giant redwood. We stopped at one of these tourist traps and stood in the man-made space. What kind of living thing sustains that much damage and keeps on standing?

We camped somewhere off the grid, near the Avenue of the Giants. When the sun came up, we felt like the first humans in a prehistoric world. The ferns were as tall as we were. And the trees—such trees—could only be called majestic. We walked around under them like ants.

The most interesting ones to me were those that had been hollowed out by wildfires. They had these massive rooms within them called goose pens, because the first settlers used them to house livestock. Fire had not stopped those trees. Their scars became useful to others as they kept on growing, straight up to the sky.

I realized that, in Jesus, I am like those trees. I've gone through fire that hurt and scarred—but it did not consume me, and no fire ever will. I'll keep standing, even growing and thriving. Because He is the One Who sustains my life. —GWEN FORD FAULKENBERRY

FAITH STEP: *Plant something today that you can watch and nurture. Let it be a reminder to you of Jesus's faithfulness to keep bringing you new life and growth, even out of painful circumstances.*

Thursday, August 15

He will not let your foot slip—he who watches over you will not slumber;
indeed, he who watches over Israel will neither slumber nor sleep.
Psalm 121:3–4 (NIV)

Yesterday, we were at the beach near San Diego. The sky was clear, the sand was hot, and the waves were big. My sister, Erica, sister-in-law, Traci, and niece, Aly, were with me, staked out on a blanket. A myriad of teenage cousins were going boogie boarding. My brother-in-law, Brett, an avid surfer, warned the kids about the riptides. He instructed them not to go out above their waists, in case they lost their boogie boards in the waves and needed to swim to shore. They headed out into the surf with shouts of joy.

But while the kids had fun careening through the surf, the blanket brigade spent the afternoon doing head counts. We were making sure no one was getting pulled under. We weren't the only ones being vigilant. Lifeguard stations on stilts were positioned down the length of the beach. They were ready to act if anyone was in distress. One lifeguard constantly rode the break line on a jet ski, scanning the waves, making sure everyone was safe. We were thankful for them.

In the same way, we can be thankful that Jesus is keeping watch over us. He guards our lives, constantly directing us to a place of peace, looking out for moments of distress so that He can guide us and keep us safe. He has an excellent view of our lives. He is relentlessly guarding our hearts and our minds. He is watching over our spirits, ready to act on our behalves when we are floundering. There is never a chance that He will let us go down. —Susanna Foth Aughtmon

Faith Step: *Jesus is keeping watch over you, day and night. What does it mean to you knowing that your life is being guarded and protected at every turn?*

FRIDAY, AUGUST 16

The Voice took on flesh and became human *and chose to live alongside us. We have seen Him, enveloped in undeniable splendor—the one* true *Son of the Father—*evidenced in *the perfect balance of grace and truth. John 1:14* (VOICE)

DAREDEVIL NIK WALLENDA HAS ALWAYS fascinated me with his death-defying feats. He's a high-wire artist and holds nine Guinness World Records.

A few years ago, I watched a televised event of Wallenda completing one of his greatest accomplishments: crossing a tightrope directly over Niagara Falls. I'd read that Nik had repeatedly dreamed of that moment since he was a small child. His great-grandfather, Karl Wallenda, had also been a daredevil and circus performer. He was the one who'd inspired Nik's dreams and ambitions, but Karl was killed in an acrobatic attempt in 1978. I thought about that as I watched Nik. *What if he fell?*

In several interviews, Wallenda has talked about his tightrope walk in life, always seeking to maintain a good balance between his faith, family, and work. Like Nik, we all walk our own tightropes, trying to sustain balance, though our efforts may not seem as dramatic as the acrobatic stunts of Nik Wallenda: ambition versus contentment, worry versus rest, fear versus faith. We need balance in our interactions with others—and especially in our relationship with Jesus.

We also share Wallenda's "secret" for keeping our balance: Jesus, Who "took on flesh and became human" and Who walks beside us. His perfect grace is our "balancing pole" to keep us from falling, and His presence gives us "patience, steadiness, and encouragement" to help us "live in complete harmony with each other" (Romans 15:5 TLB). —REBECCA BARLOW JORDAN

FAITH STEP: *List the areas in which you struggle most with balance. Beside each one, write Jesus's name and thank Him that He walks beside you.*

SATURDAY, AUGUST 17

*For the gate is narrow and the way is hard, that leads to life,
and those who find it are few. Matthew 7:14 (RSV)*

MY FRIEND ELICIA HAS A favorite Hebrew song, and it was sung at her son's bar mitzvah. The lyrics are "The whole world is a very narrow bridge, and the most important thing is not to be afraid." The Hebrew word for narrow, *tzar*, is also the word for trouble, adversity, and distress. In Psalm 107, when the refrain says, "They cried to the LORD in their trouble, and he delivered them from their distress," this "distress" that makes people cry out to the Lord is *tzar*. So, if the "narrow bridge" of life is a distressing ordeal we all must cross, how can we *not* be afraid?

Life is anxiety-provoking. So much of what our culture offers us is meant to numb that anxiety—food, entertainment, consumerism. But this is the wide path, the easy way.

I believe the song my friend Elicia loves singing and the image that Jesus gave us about the narrow gate both distinguish between two kinds of fear: distress and anxiety. Distress is what we experience when we face the troubles of life, and these troubles threaten to overwhelm us. Anxiety is what we experience when our fears keep us from facing what needs to be faced and doing what needs to be done. It takes more courage to choose the difficult path of distress than to let our anxiety dictate our choices, encouraging us to cling to an illusion of safety. Perhaps that is why so few seem to be able to find that narrow path through life that—while harrowing at times—is not bogged down by anxiety. —ELIZABETH BERNE DEGEAR

FAITH STEP: *Real courage does not mean a fear-free existence. It means saying yes to the life we are given and crying out to God in the scary moments so that we can make it through. Today, let Jesus be with you in your fear.*

SUNDAY, AUGUST 18

Rejoice always, pray without ceasing, in everything give thanks; for this is the will of God in Christ Jesus for you. 1 Thessalonians 5:16–18 (NKJV)

WHAT DOES IT REALLY MEAN to pray without ceasing? Does it mean we chant at the wailing wall in Jerusalem? Or is it more like the meditative murmurs of a cloistered nun? I used to think that was the picture of devoted prayer. Today, it looks like constant, humble reliance on Jesus.

I confess, I'm not much for humble dependence. I much prefer confident self-reliance. But when I consider my place as a daughter of the Almighty, I recognize the luxury of this privilege. I can consult the God of the universe as I go about my day. To gain strength at the weak point, solutions to problems, or just the grace to wait. Why wouldn't I pray without ceasing?

Over time, I've gotten better at praying throughout the day, consulting my epic Life Coach, praying and praising at milestone moments. But truly praying without ceasing has seemed utterly unattainable, some ideal truly reserved for only the most holy.

Lately, though, I've realized that praying without ceasing is attainable with a few hard-for-me but not impossible guidelines. I can apply some principles captured in the seminal Christian book *Practicing the Presence of God*. Bottom line: Slow down. Slow way down, and see and seek Jesus in everyone and everything.

If I take my day task by task, moment by moment, it is far easier to consult Him continually. Jesus is, paradoxically, most accessible in the small moments of the day, speaking into the silence of deliberate practice. —ISABELLA YOSUICO

FAITH STEP: *Just for today, slow down enough to consciously seek Jesus in the unfolding of every task. Whether changing a diaper, balancing a budget, or running, consider practicing being in the presence of God.*

MONDAY, AUGUST 19

I am leaving you with a gift—peace of mind and heart. And the peace I give is a gift the world cannot give. So don't be troubled or afraid. John 14:27 (NLT)

ONE OF MY SUMMER HIGHLIGHTS was attending a weeklong Bible camp in Washington State with my two daughters and their husbands. Each morning, there was a program that included a chapel service that began with a half hour of singing.

One morning, we sang "It Is Well with My Soul:" "When peace, like a river, attendeth my way, When sorrows like sea billows roll; Whatever my lot, Thou has taught me to say, It is well, it is well, with my soul."

The songwriter, Horatio G. Spafford, was a successful lawyer and real estate investor. In 1871, the Great Chicago Fire destroyed his downtown properties. Two years later, his four young daughters drowned at sea. In the midst of unimaginable pain, Spafford—a follower of Jesus—penned these lyrics as his testimony. His words have blessed millions, reminding us that we, too, can know peace in the midst of life's storms, because Jesus is with us.

The guitars and keyboard fell silent as the camp worship leader led us into the final chorus. Four-part harmony filled the auditorium. When the song ended, no one moved. No one spoke a word. Christ's presence hung over the room like the glory of God filled the Temple in Old Testament days. I wish I could have bottled the moment.

I reflect often on that morning, and my heart breaks into song. Thanks be to Jesus for the gift of *shalom* peace. Wholeness, completeness, harmony, and tranquility of soul is ours because of Who He is and what He's done for us. —GRACE FOX

FAITH STEP: *Play a favorite worship song. Either sing along with it or meditate silently on the lyrics. Whichever you choose to do, let its truth address your heart's deepest needs.*

TUESDAY, AUGUST 20

Always be prepared to give an answer to everyone who asks you to give the reason for the hope that you have. But do this with gentleness and respect.
1 Peter 3:15 (NIV)

IT'S SAD HOW EASILY A simple question on social media can ignite a firestorm of argument. Most everyone seems ready to present their opinions as the only plausible one, regardless of whether they have the correct facts or any experience with the issue. Often, the discussion quickly veers from the original topic down some rabbit trail. And sadly, the comments sometimes contain such hostility and offensive language that the person who started the whole thing feels the need to unfriend some commenters.

As followers of Christ, we're expected to be ready at any moment to respond to a question or comment about our faith. Not for the purpose of showing off our knowledge or making another person look like a fool. Our goal is to help others understand that Jesus offers them love and forgiveness. That's why we need to be ready to respond in a gentle, respectful manner as to why we hope and trust in Him.

Our answer may vary depending on the person initiating the conversation. Some will be interested in historical references or Bible passages; others will be affected more by our personal testimony. We don't need to worry about having all the answers either. When the Jewish leaders questioned the blind man about who had healed him, he said, "One thing I do know. I was blind but now I see!" (John 9:25). If we share what we know about Jesus in a winsome way, maybe someone else will want to know Him too. —DIANNE NEAL MATTHEWS

FAITH STEP: *Imagine that someone has asked you why you believe in Jesus. Write out your answer and keep it to revise as you continue to ponder and pray about the best way to answer.*

WEDNESDAY, AUGUST 21

The generous will prosper; those who refresh others will themselves be refreshed. Proverbs 11:25 (NLT)

MY STACK OF MAIL INCLUDED a bill, a letter informing me that I qualified for a car loan (I don't even have a driver's license), a piece of junk mail addressed to my ex-husband, and a fat envelope with my name written in bubble letters. As soon as I saw the lettering, I knew I'd received something fun from my friend Lisa. The envelope contained an encouraging note, a handmade coloring sheet that she'd created, and a pocket-sized card with an inspirational quote on it. I'd been feeling discouraged, and Jesus clearly knew what would help. Lisa's note reminded me, *You are valuable and loved.* It provided the lift I needed to go on with my day. I wanted to hug Lisa, but she lived three thousand miles away. I sent her a card and one of my hand-crocheted coasters that I enjoy making for friends, praying that it would arrive exactly when she needed it.

Sometimes, we just need a reminder that we matter—that someone besides a billing office is thinking about us—that our unspoken prayer needs, and our concerns, have reached someone's ears. When we feel the refreshment of a handwritten card, a surprise gift, or even an email, text, or phone call "because you've been on my heart," we tend to want to do the same for others, including the person whom Jesus used to refresh our spirits. They remind us that even when we don't communicate our needs, He sees them, He cares about them, and He knows exactly how to meet them. —JEANETTE HANSCOME

FAITH STEP: *Who comes to mind as one who could use a little "just because" refreshment? Take a few minutes to pray for this friend or loved one and think of a fun way to reach out to him or her.*

THURSDAY, AUGUST 22

But if you do not forgive men their trespasses, neither will your Father forgive your trespasses. Matthew 6:15 (NKJV)

IT'S BEEN SAID THAT UNFORGIVENESS is like taking poison and waiting for the other person to die. So, basically, not forgiving someone hurts us more than it hurts the other person. Forgiveness is vital to our growth in Christ, and the Lord commands we offer it up freely to those who have offended us. Yet it's the hardest thing for us to do. A spouse commits adultery. A friend betrays a confidence. An unjust judge rules against you. All of these things can knock the wind out of our sails and make it hard to trust—and in some cases, to love—again.

It seems impossible. I know it felt impossible for me at times. But the Bible has often given me reminders that it is an important practice of my faith. Jesus did it. He forgave His tormentors while still suffering, dying on the cross. "Father, forgive them, for they do not know what they do" (Luke 23:34). God wiped my slate clean because of Jesus's sacrifice. So I've had to learn to do the same with others, even when it hurt. It's the ultimate test of our faith and commitment to the Lord. I believe that's why He commands us to do it. On our own, we are powerless to forgive. We must depend on Him for the strength, the presence of mind, and the heart-change necessary to utter those three little words, "I forgive you."—CAROL MACKEY

FAITH STEP: *Think of the person you've found it hard to forgive. Now ask the Lord to soften your heart and give you the courage to forgive. He wants you to be free!*

FRIDAY, AUGUST 23

Call to me and I will answer you, and will tell you great and hidden things that you have not known. Jeremiah 33:3 (ESV)

MY HUSBAND, MY FRIEND JOYCE, and I recently attended a special exhibit at our local museum. As we entered the first room and started looking at the relics and art, we heard a man speaking with authority from the side of the room. We made our way closer and listened in as he spoke to a small group. He talked about being part of the team that made the discoveries during an archaeological dig, about the selection of items for the exhibit, and about the history it all represented. One of the docents nearby told us that the speaker was the curator for the whole exhibit and was taking an elite group of patrons on a tour.

We took our time studying the items in the first room, and when the curator moved to each next room, we followed at a distance and were able to hear all his specialized information. It made the museum visit even more interesting.

Glancing around, I noticed that many of the museum guests were wearing rented headsets that provided audio explanations as they browsed. However, because they had the headsets on, they didn't hear the curator.

I'm quite sure we had the better museum experience.

Our world is full of human wisdom to which we can listen. Radio shows, podcasts, audiobooks friends, experts, and internet voices all have things to tell us. Some may be valuable. But I prefer advice from our personal Guide, the Maker and Keeper of our souls. Jesus is willing to speak to us throughout our exploration of this world, if we will just edge close enough to listen. —SHARON HINCK

FAITH STEP: *Set aside an hour of silence today. Turn off computers, phones, and televisions. Ask Jesus to speak to you through His Word.*

SATURDAY, AUGUST 24

Don't worry about anything; instead, pray about everything. Tell God what you need, and thank him for all he has done. Then you will experience God's peace, which exceeds anything we can understand. His peace will guard your hearts and minds as you live in Christ Jesus. Philippians 4:6–7 (NLT)

OUR DOG, FLASH, IS A cross between a Jack Russell terrier and a Chihuahua. He is cute and fast and loves to play. He loves it when you throw him the ball. He just has one problem. Once he brings the ball back to you, he won't let it go. You can tell he wants to give it to you as he nudges it toward you. But as soon as you try and pick it up, he snatches it and growls. Then he looks at you, as if to say, "Why aren't you playing with me?"

The dog has issues. So do I. That is probably why I like him so much. I am just like Flash, who worries over his toy, constantly moving it around, never taking his eyes off it. This is what I do with my problems. I cannot let them go. I keep thinking about them, feeling sick to my stomach. All the while, my eyes are on Jesus and I am saying, "Why aren't You doing anything about this? I keep bringing it to You." I bring my problem to Him. But I forget to let it go. I forget to say, "I would like You to take care of this, so I am placing it in Your hands."

When we pray, we are "tossing the ball." Laying our worries, our cares, our dreams at the feet of Jesus. But it is only when we have emptied our hearts and minds of our worries that He can fill us up with His overwhelming peace that passes all understanding.
—SUSANNA FOTH AUGHTMON

FAITH STEP: *Picture yourself throwing your "ball" of worries into the sky. Release them to Jesus's care and ask Him to fill you with His overwhelming peace.*

SUNDAY, AUGUST 25

He is the image of the invisible God, the firstborn of all creation; for in him all things in heaven and on earth were created, things visible and invisible, whether thrones or dominions or rulers or powers—all things have been created through him and for him. Colossians 1:15–16 (NRSV)

THERE ARE TIMES WHEN I think I have Jesus somewhat figured out. I sing about Him at church, tell stories about His miracles to my five-year-old, and write devotions that make people feel good. I understand His mercy. His kindness and compassion are things I crave, and I know being a Christian means I imitate Him and show His love to others.

But then there are these moments when I see through a new lens— moments like reading Colossians 1—and I am painfully aware of my ignorance, my inability to comprehend Who this "person" is. I've made Him my friend. I know this is real, and I'm thankful for our relationship. Yet He's so much more. And if I don't see that, don't live with awareness and respect and awe, then I'm missing a lot of the picture.

It's like standing up to your knees in the ocean and saying you've plumbed its depths.

We haven't. We don't understand the image of the invisible God— can't even begin to. We can only stand in awe.

My brother is the superintendent of the school district where my kids attend. To them, he's Uncle Jim, a big teddy bear who takes them on rides and throws them in the pool. The first time one of them saw him on campus with his suit and tie, however, they saw him through a new lens. He was Mr. Ford. The one in charge.

Jesus is our friend, but He's also God. The one in charge.
—GWEN FORD FAULKENBERRY

FAITH STEP: *Do a word study on the different names of Jesus. Write down all the ones you find and keep it close to remind you of all He is.*

MONDAY, AUGUST 26

I know what it is to be in need, and I know what it is to have plenty. I have learned the secret of being content in any and every situation, whether well fed or hungry, whether living in plenty or in want. I can do all this through him who gives me strength. Philippians 4:12–13 (NIV)

A FRIEND AND I WERE talking through our ongoing struggle with balancing family life, personal ambition, calling, and the need to help provide for our families' needs and a few wants.

I have worked from home for more than a decade since my first son was born. Like most other work-at-home moms I know, I've struggled with feast-or-famine income, feelings of isolation versus the freedom to be an integral part of my kids' daily lives and to manage the household.

Listening to my fresh round of laments about the financial and professional sacrifices I'd made by forgoing a nine-to-five job, my friend asked, "Well, what would make you happy?"

I had a clear answer. "What would make me happy is to not feel the need to ask myself what would make me happy."

I realized Jesus is the answer to every longing, whether it's a longing we have the means to fulfill or not.

In Philippians 4, Paul urges us to be content wherever God has us, to trust Him day by day. Now that my boys are both in school, the time may soon come that I'll be led to do something more in support of my financial and professional goals. But just for today, I want to choose contentment, and I know that more of Jesus is the only lasting way. —ISABELLA YOSUICO

FAITH STEP: *In your journal, make a list. Title it "What would make me happy?" Ask God to help you where you are as He continues to move you where you will be.*

TUESDAY, AUGUST 27

The LORD is good to those whose hope is in him, to the one who seeks him.
Lamentations 3:25 (NIV)

WHAT'S WRONG WITH ME? WHY can't I get it right with her? No matter how I framed comments, I managed to offend my friend repeatedly. I was frustrated and wondered who would listen, pray for me, offer wise counsel, and help me figure out what was going on. Then I remembered times when I'd confided in someone after a conflict and resorted to gossip.

Lord, who can I talk to that I won't cross that line with?

Another time, I took advice that only made a problem worse.

How about if you talk to Me?

Jesus already knew every detail of this complicated situation and the best way to resolve it.

As I poured out my confusion and allowed Him to speak, I began to see when I'd blown it and when I'd done what I thought was right. He prompted me to pray for my friend, but also to consider whether we were a good match as friends. In the end, I received answers that the wisest sister in Christ couldn't have provided.

When we experience conflict, we need guidance. Though there are times for sharing our burdens with trusted friends and prayer partners, Jesus is the only One we can count on completely for sound advice. We don't have to worry about naming names or being careful with details. We can trust His guidance and His grace as we wait for the right timing. As answers come, we see that He truly is good to those who seek Him. —JEANETTE HANSCOME

FAITH STEP: *Who do you run to when you need help untangling a relational mess? What mess are you trying to untangle right now? Spend time with the One Who knows every detail and the best solution.*

WEDNESDAY, AUGUST 28

Now the tax collectors and sinners were all gathering around to hear Jesus.
Luke 15:1 (NIV)

IN THE SUMMER AND FALL, my favorite place to collect my thoughts—but more important, to listen to Jesus's whispers—is on my screened-in front porch. White wicker chairs that'll have to be replaced someday soon. Flowers in window boxes that match the colors of the chair cushions. A morning breeze, tree-filtered sun, a cup of strong tea, and my Bible.

One morning, I settled in for an extended time of reading. Highlighter at the ready, I prepared to dive in to see what I needed to glean from Jesus's life and teaching that day. My highlighter and my thoughts planted themselves on the first word I read: *All.*

Luke 15:1 says that "*all* the tax collectors and sinners were gathering around Jesus to listen to him" (emphasis mine). All of them? And their purpose? To listen to Jesus. Not to defend their actions or criticize Jesus. They didn't gather around Jesus to dispute His teachings or prove Him wrong. They listened.

By comparison, verse 2 of that chapter says the Pharisees and legal experts were grumbling. None of them were listening. They were too busy condemning Him for the company He kept.

How often do I miss the mark, grumbling instead of listening? How often have I been guilty of frowning over how generously Jesus loved when I should have been doing the same? —CYNTHIA RUCHTI

FAITH STEP: *Who do you know who is far from where they need to be spiritually? I have an appointment for coffee with a "far from" friend tomorrow. I intend to love as He did.*

Thursday, August 29

But blessed are those who trust in the LORD and have made the LORD their hope and confidence. They are like trees planted along a riverbank, with roots that reach deep into the water. Such trees are not bothered by the heat or worried by long months of drought. Their leaves stay green, and they never stop producing fruit. Jeremiah 17:7–8 (NLT)

MY ELDEST DAUGHTER LIVES IN eastern Washington State, and we make the five-hour drive to visit her a couple of times each year. The scenery changes dramatically when we cross the mountains east of Seattle. Forest greenery and lakes behind us, we enter a parched landscape complete with tumbleweeds. It resembles a scene from an old Western movie with one exception—fruit orchards.

The region's heat and soil provide ideal conditions for growing apples, peaches, apricots, and grapes. But success also depends on irrigation. Without that moisture, the orchards would shrivel and die.

Every time we travel this road, I marvel at the contrast between the fruit-producing irrigated land and the brown, scorched hills. It reminds me of my relationship with Jesus. Apart from Him, my life would resemble those sunbaked hills. But because He's drawn me into relationship with Him, I'm like a well-watered tree that flourishes with hope, peace, and joy no matter what adverse conditions I face. The more I get to know Him, the more I grow in every aspect of my life and the more fruit I produce.

Jesus is the well that never runs dry. Blessed are we when we make Him our hope and confidence. —GRACE FOX

FAITH STEP: *Eat some fresh fruit today—a handful of grapes, an apple, a peach, or an apricot. As you munch, read Jeremiah 17:5–9 and note the contrast between people who follow Jesus and those who don't.*

FRIDAY, AUGUST 30

Blessed are you when people insult you, persecute you and falsely say all kinds of evil against you because of me. Rejoice and be glad, because great is your reward in heaven, for in the same way they persecuted the prophets who were before you. Matthew 5:11–12 (NIV)

AS A LIFELONG PEOPLE PLEASER, I really don't like it when people don't like me. I avoid conflict and confrontation. And while I'm not one to flaunt my faith or factions on Facebook, I know my faith is evident. Apart from the obvious, like writing for *Guideposts*, my convictions just seep out of me unbidden in everyday conversation.

I've been persecuted for it.

I used to think of persecution as imprisonment or banned books. Coptic Christians, Middle Eastern missionaries, and Communist Bloc Bible runners were persecuted. That's not me or anyone I know.

But Christians are persecuted. We're persecuted in the silent eye-roll of our cubicle mate. We're persecuted by the neighborhood party to which we're not invited. We're persecuted by the clenched-mouth greeting of our intellectual brother-in-law. We're persecuted by the niggling feeling that we're an outsider at our book club. Jesus's name may never be uttered with scorn, but it feels like persecution all the same.

I have to wonder, *How might I process these nearly daily slights differently by trusting what Jesus said as true? Dare I thank and praise God for the blessing of persecution? Dare I bless those who persecute me?* (Romans 12:14). Today, I choose not to personalize persecution in any form, recalling Jesus's own words and loving example. —ISABELLA YOSUICO

FAITH STEP: *In light of this reading, prayerfully list recent persecutions. Thank God for them and bless the perpetrators, knowing it's not about you but about Jesus. Praise Him!*

SATURDAY, AUGUST 31

And this is love: that we walk in obedience to his commands. As you have heard from the beginning, his command is that you walk in love. 2 John 1:6 (NIV)

UNTIL RECENTLY, I KNEW LITTLE of prayer labyrinths. Unlike mazes, they don't offer choices along the trail. The only decision you make is to enter, trusting the path will lead you closer to God. The footpath represents the complexities of faith as we face life's trials. It should be walked slowly, praying with every step. Walkers might leave with a sense of God's will, or a word or phrase clear in their minds.

At first, I questioned the spirituality of this practice, but worshipping Christ is a good thing. Because I have mild attention deficit disorder, it's hard for me to focus on one thing at a time. Doing something to keep my body busy as I reached out to Jesus would help with concentration, so when I discovered a labyrinth at a nearby garden, the idea appealed to me.

Stepping into the labyrinth, I had no idea the intensity of the experience that lay ahead. Navigating the twists and turns, I grew impatient but felt I had no choice but to continue forward, praying. The trail—and Jesus—waited. When I reached the center, triumph filled my soul. I'd obediently followed the path set before me and felt eager to continue back out, to complete the entire walk.

Now, when life offers challenges and I can't find my way, I look back on that labyrinth. The more obedient I am to Jesus, the closer my walk with Him will be. I know where my life started and where it will end. I can trust Jesus to direct me through the zigzags and curves along the way. —HEIDI GAUL

FAITH STEP: *Invite a friend to join you as you walk an unfamiliar path or trail. Talk about ways Jesus has guided you through the unexpected curves life has handed you.*

SUNDAY, SEPTEMBER 1

The former priests were many in number, because they were prevented by death from continuing in office, but he holds his priesthood permanently, because he continues forever. Hebrews 7:23–24 *(ESV)*

MY FRIEND ORDERED A BUNCH of ceramic mugs that said, "God of All Comfort," and gave me one as a gift. I've used it for years, thinking of her whenever I drink my tea from that cup. But after years of use, most of the words have worn off. All that remain are the big gold letters "God."

Last weekend, another friend was visiting, and I set out teabags and that mug for her. She stared at it and said, "I'd feel a little presumptuous using that cup." We both laughed, and I explained what had happened to the lettering. Later, as I washed the dishes, I smiled at the tangible reminder that so many things are temporary in this life, but God remains.

Throughout Scripture, the children of Israel had a series of priests. Some served faithfully, while others were selfish or corrupt. Regardless of their legacy, their role was temporary. They served to point to the One who would offer the enduring sacrifice on our behalf. Our one true Priest, Who reconciles us with God forever, is Jesus.

All our human efforts here on earth will eventually pass away like the letters fading from my cup. But Jesus's love, redemption, and role in our lives will never fade. He is emblazoned like gold on our hearts for eternity. —SHARON HINCK

FAITH STEP: *Look for an object that has faded—a photo, a cover of a book, a design on a plate or cup. Thank Jesus that, in the midst of impermanence, He is eternal and unchanging.*

Monday, September 2

Every good and perfect gift is from above, coming down from the Father of the heavenly lights, who does not change like shifting shadows. James 1:17 (NIV)

When a writers' conference speaker encouraged us to start a Blessings Folder, I knew it would be a good idea. My life was falling apart, making it difficult to see anything positive. The speaker passed out copies of her favorite Bible verse and a funny story to get us started. As soon as I got home, I put them in a folder, along with a story that my oldest son had published. My Blessings Folder became one of my lifelines during a dark time, as I filled it with encouraging cards that arrived right when I needed them, notes about miraculous provisions, and other mementos. Every treasure that I added to the folder felt like a present from Jesus, saying, *I'm still here, and you still have a lot of good in your life.*

One day, I discovered that I'd run out of room in my folder. I moved my collection to a pretty box. My Blessings Box now sits on a shelf in my closest, stuffed beyond capacity—a sweet reminder of the many gifts that came from Jesus at a time when it seemed like life would never be good again.

"Every good and perfect gift is from above...." We don't need to be overwhelmed or grieving to have a reason to collect blessings. In fact, it is often when everything is going well that we miss out on them. When we make a practice of paying attention to how Jesus takes care of us and shows us *I am with you; I know what you need; I know what will make you smile,* we gain the ability to see the littlest things as gifts. —Jeanette Hanscome

Faith Step: *Start a Blessings Box or put a few items in the one you have that felt like gifts from Jesus when you received them.*

TUESDAY, SEPTEMBER 3

Be patient until the Lord's coming. See how the farmer waits for the precious fruit of the earth and is patient with it until it receives the early and the late rains. You also must be patient. Strengthen your hearts, because the Lord's coming is near. James 5:7–8 (HCSB)

SINCE I GREW UP AS a farmer's daughter, I can easily relate to agricultural illustrations in the Bible. I remember my dad watching the weather, hoping our dusty cotton fields would get enough rain to keep the plants healthy and lead to a good harvest. Those few cotton bales represented our main source of income—some years, the only source. My dad sowed the crops in spring; we had to wait until after we chopped weeds all summer and then picked the cotton in autumn to see if the money would be enough to cover us for a year.

Waiting is just plain hard, but Jesus calls us to exercise spiritual patience. That's the kind we need as we go through life's daily temptations, disappointments, and troubles that shake us to the core. As we struggle to think and respond in a godly way. As we watch the news and feel like the world has gone mad. As we wait year after year for answers to the prayer that represents our deepest longing.

A farmer doesn't know for sure that the rains will come; drought is always a possibility. But thanks to God's Word, we can know some things with certainty. Our trials and sufferings—and waiting—will produce a harvest of righteousness in our hearts and lives. And one day, Jesus will return to the earth to eradicate evil and put things right. These promises are what help us persevere, no matter what field we work in. —DIANNE NEAL MATTHEWS

FAITH STEP: *What are you waiting for today? Ask Jesus to strengthen your heart and help you wait patiently, trusting that the harvest will come.*

WEDNESDAY, SEPTEMBER 4

But when the goodness and loving kindness of God our Savior appeared, he saved us. Titus 3:4–5 (ESV)

THERE'S A SONG I LOVE by contemporary Christian band Big Daddy Weave called "My Story." My favorite lyric talks about the kindness of Jesus and how it draws us in. There are a lot of other concepts like grace, hope, life, etc., in the song, but it's this particular line that gets me every time.

I think the reason may be that those other qualities are things I focus on more. But kindness is smaller. Quieter. In some ways more personal.

When my daughter Stella was nervous about starting kindergarten, I talked to her about how smart she is, and pretty, and how she is loads of fun. "But you know what is most important? The thing I want you to remember most?"

Her eyes were as shiny as diamonds.

"Be kind to everyone. This is the most important thing. Jesus is with you, and He will help you."

When she got home that first day, she showed me her papers, which were all stellar. We talked about the new friends she met. Then she said, "I did what you said, Mommy. There was a girl in my class who can't walk. I held her hand. And when some kids got stung by wasps on the playground, I helped them be calm."

There it is. That thing so small that no one else may ever see. But when Jesus walks with us—in all the ways His kindness appears—He saves us. —GWEN FORD FAULKENBERRY

FAITH STEP: *Since Jesus's heart toward you is kind, don't you think it's time to be kind to yourself? Ask Him to help you see yourself through His lens.*

THURSDAY, SEPTEMBER 5

For I am convinced that neither death nor life, neither angels nor demons, neither the present nor the future, nor any powers, neither height nor depth, nor anything else in all creation, will be able to separate us from the love of God that is in Christ Jesus our Lord. Romans 8:38–39 (NIV)

WE KEEP SEVERAL BIRDHOUSES IN our yard because we enjoy providing a place for birds to raise their young. In every corner of my garden you'll find one, nestled among the branches or hanging from a shepherd's hook. Large, small, and everything in between—they bring whimsy and joy to the space.

Two of the tiny homes are occupied almost every year. My favorite hangs just above the hose bib. Every time I turn on the water to sprinkle the garden, I try to sneak a peek inside.

That's where the connection lies. Before the eggs are laid, even as the male and female gather material for their nest, the flying parents-to-be perform their gallant show of courage. They dive-bomb me as I hand-water any plants or flowers near their future babies' abode. These little creatures, not yet born, are loved with a fierceness so rare most can only imagine it.

Because I know Jesus, I'm blessed to understand that depth of caring, the protective devotion He has for all believers. Nothing can separate me from His love. As I live each day, I'm secure in the knowledge that He's constantly watching over me, fighting on my behalf whenever necessary. He's dedicated to growing my faith to full maturity. He feeds me all I need in order to become a sound reflection of Him in the world. Jesus's nurturing gives me wings to fly. —HEIDI GAUL

FAITH STEP: *Go to a bird sanctuary if you don't have access to nesting birds near home. Watch the intense caring the parents show toward their young. Knowing Jesus loves you so much more, take wing and fly!*

Friday, September 6

And we know that in all things God works for the good of those who love him, who have been called according to his purpose. Romans 8:28 (NIV)

THIS PAST SPRING, WE PURCHASED a bunk bed. We thought we would put it together in a few hours. Not possible. We could not get the screw holes to line up on the frame. My husband, Scott, and I worked on it. My oldest son, Will, worked for hours trying to adjust the frame with an Allen wrench. And then a screwdriver. And then the Allen wrench again. At one point, the *entire* family was working on it. We gave up after two days.

My younger son, Jack, was reading Dante's *Inferno* at the time. He was convinced that trying to build furniture surely occupied one of the rings Dante wrote about. Finally, our friend Juan came over. He showed us that we had screwed the screws in too tight. We were supposed to keep them loose and then tighten all of them once the final piece was added. He came in with a power drill and made all the pieces fit. We nearly cried with relief.

Jesus does the same for our lives. We have an odd assemblage of experiences, joy, pain, new dreams, old wounds, and relationships that we are trying to fasten together into a good life. No matter how closely we try to follow the rules, we can't seem to make sense of it. But Jesus can take our failures and successes, our dreams and our brokenness, and bring beauty from them all. He is the Master Builder, bringing order from chaos and healing to our bodies, minds, and spirits. When we let Him have control, He fashions us a life worth living, full of grace and truth. —SUSANNA FOTH AUGHTMON

FAITH STEP: *Are the pieces of your life not fitting together right now? Where are you getting stuck? Ask Jesus to take over and, in His timing, make it beautiful.*

SATURDAY, SEPTEMBER 7

"My grace is all you need. My power works best in weakness."
2 Corinthians 12:9 (NLT)

RECENTLY MY HUSBAND, LARRY, WAS returning from a men's weekend fishing trip. Shortly after leaving the lake, several miles outside the small town, he called to let me know his truck had broken down. After trying repeatedly to restart it, he had finally phoned for help. The roadside assistance service, however, was unavailable. Larry was out of range of their area, and it was on a busy weekend.

Fortunately, he had a marine battery in his boat. So he tried to jump-start the engine using that battery. The engine revved to life, but with each attempt, the truck died as soon as he disconnected the battery. He wasn't sure what to do, but as we said good-bye, I agreed to pray with him for a solution.

A half hour later, Larry called again. A crazy idea had hit him to place the marine battery in the front seat floorboard with the jumper cables connecting it to the truck battery under the hood. He would need to keep the motor running all the way home.

I prayed harder, visualizing an angel holding one finger on the battery to keep it powered.

Jesus's grace prevailed. Two hours later, Larry arrived home.

So many times I feel like that truck, powerless and too weak to go any distance. Then out of nowhere comes a remedy for my situation. Hesitant to try but desperate for a solution, I go for it. And suddenly, my body and spirit feel energized again. That's when I recognize the perfect Power Source in my life. Jesus's grace and strength always meet my need. —REBECCA BARLOW JORDAN

FAITH STEP: *When have you felt powerless? Take time today to "jump-start" your life, thanking Jesus for the times He has strengthened you in your weakness.*

SUNDAY, SEPTEMBER 8

For now we see through a glass, darkly; but then face to face: now I know in part; but then shall I know even as also I am known. 1 Corinthians 13:12 (KJV)

THIS MORNING I NESTLED IN bed, too ill to attend Sunday worship. But I booted up my laptop, grateful that our church live-streams its services.

Halfway into a worship song, the feed froze. I clicked a few buttons, and the service resumed playing, but soon froze again with a "buffering" message. Eventually, the connection couldn't be rebooted at all.

Many of us encounter the frustration of glitches when we use technology. A link that dissolves into static reminds me of the difficulty I sometimes have tuning in to get a clear connection with Jesus. He is truly beyond our understanding, so the image of Jesus can be unclear. He may lead us in directions that feel overwhelming—such as calling us to love our enemies. Or, perhaps, we find Jesus's timing difficult to understand. Sometimes our prayers seem to hit a message like "Buffering; connection will resume shortly." Through the distorted reflection of our limited experience, we feel disconnected from the Savior.

I'm grateful for a video-streamed church service or a long-distance FaceTime call with family—even when the connection is of poor quality. But nothing can replace the joy of truly being in the presence and fellowship of those we love. Jesus gives us the promise that we will one day meet Him face-to-face. All the questions that torment us and fracture our connection with Him will fall away.

Today, if we feel disconnected, let's thank Jesus for coming to give us a clearer reflection of God's love and for promising that, one day, we will know that love more completely. —SHARON HINCK

FAITH STEP: *Next time you experience a bad connection while using technology, pause and thank Jesus for how He has connected us to our heavenly Father.*

MONDAY, SEPTEMBER 9

Peace I leave with you; my peace I give you. I do not give to you as the world gives. Do not let your hearts be troubled and do not be afraid. John 14:27 (NIV)

THE FORECAST WAS GRIM AND getting grimmer by the minute. Hurricane Irma was an epic storm of historical proportions, her exact path completely unpredictable. All of Florida was in her crosshairs.

Having recently moved to the state's beautiful Suncoast, we'd never been through a hurricane and didn't know what to expect. Even some jaded native Floridians were packing up and evacuating.

We were peaceful. Conspicuously peaceful.

We'd assembled our preparedness kit, but from the sounds of it, there was no preparing for the potential devastation ahead. Yet, we trusted God would care for us one way or another. As a family, we prayerfully made the decision to stay close to home and be available to help in the aftermath. At someone's suggestion, I used my cell phone to film the contents of our house for an eventual insurance claim and found that I wasn't as attached to my belongings as I'd once been.

I calmly purchased life jackets for all of us, eerily marking names and phone numbers on them.

Still, being reasonably prepared—emotionally, spiritually, and practically—couldn't account for the deep peace we all felt. I *know* this peace was not of me. *Only Jesus.*

We took shelter in a neighboring church, praying, praising, and worshipping the One Who promises and delivers peace that surpasses understanding (Philippians 4:7).

We weathered Irma, virtually untouched except for a few days without power or internet. Jesus promises enduring peace, and I am grateful. —ISABELLA YOSUICO

FAITH STEP: *Are you troubled? Pray John 14:27.*

Tuesday, September 10

"Assuredly, I say to you, unless you are converted and become as little children, you will by no means enter the kingdom of heaven."
Matthew 18:3 (NKJV)

JESUS LOVED KIDS. THE BIBLE doesn't speak much about His interactions with them except in a few verses, but it's enough to recognize His kind and loving nature and understand He treasured children. He urges us to do the same. I believe Jesus's admonition went well beyond our posterity. He clearly wants us *to become childlike* in our faith in Him. Young children are innocent and pure. In much the same way, God sees us as "innocent" and "pure" once we have accepted Christ, Who forgives our sins. Jesus wants us to become childlike in our faith, pure and trusting. Young children don't question what Mom or Dad tell them to do; Jesus wants us to have that kind of obedience.

Think about the qualities of young children. They are honest, some brutally so. They believe what they see and hear and even read. They also trust their caregivers to provide everything they need. Aren't all those the qualities the Lord wants us to have? Jesus wants us to be like "little children" when it comes to following Him and obeying His Word. That's why He calls us His "children" and loves us like His own. —CAROL MACKEY

FAITH STEP: *Jesus wants us to have childlike faith—to depend on Him to provide for us, to protect us, and to trust Him. Today, do something that makes you feel like a kid again!*

WEDNESDAY, SEPTEMBER 11

For the word of God is alive and active. Sharper than any double-edged swords, it penetrates even to dividing soul and spirit, joints and marrow; it judges the thoughts and attitudes of the heart. Hebrews 4:12 (NIV)

I HAVE A ROW OF books that I call the Books That Changed My Life. It includes the first book I learned to read (*Ann Likes Red*), the book that made me fall in love with reading (*A Little Princess*), and the book that inspired me to want to be a writer (*The Diary of Anne Frank*). I've set apart poetry, memoirs, Christian classics, and novels that ministered to me through grief, inspired me as a writer, and took me to a deeper place with Jesus. For a short time, I included a book that brought back painful memories, until Jesus healed that wound and I decided it was time to put it on another shelf.

So, why didn't I have a Bible with the Books That Changed My Life? I guess it just seemed strange to shelve God's Word next to *Ann Likes Red*. Today, as I considered what a monumental part of my life it has been, I couldn't *not* add it. It contains some of the first stories I heard as a child, not to mention the message that moved me to accept Jesus as Savior at age five and get baptized at thirteen; its words have ministered to me in ways that no Christian classic could. It's inspired my writing and continues to draw me closer to Christ. Some verses have convicted me in ways that felt like wounding, but in the end, Jesus used them for my healing, and I learned to treasure them.

In a world filled with great books, I pray that I will never overlook the one that changes me in the most lasting ways.
—JEANETTE HANSCOME

FAITH STEP: *List five of your favorite books and why they are special to you. Which stories from the Bible have changed your life? Commit to spending more of your free time reading it.*

THURSDAY, SEPTEMBER 12

He heals the brokenhearted and binds up their wounds. Psalm 147:3 (NIV)

ONE OF MY MANY JOBS as a mom is chief nurse. With my boys, I have seen countless scrapes and bruises, cuts that need cleaning, and, sometimes, stitches. And then there have been the races to the hospital with broken bones. Pain is never fun, but there are times in all our lives when it is a part of our journeys. This past week, I have spent time talking to two different friends who are both mourning the loss of a loved one. Their heartbreak is so real it is palpable.

When we lose the people we love, there are yawning gaps in our hearts. Broken places. Wounds that will not easily be fixed. And I wish I could nurse people in their broken places, offering bandages and hugs and words of comfort. Sometimes, there are no words that can bring comfort. And a hug just isn't enough. There is just that winding road of grief that has to be walked out and endured. We wonder where Jesus is when we hurt.

How can He just stand there when our world is falling apart? How can He not move and take the pain away?

The truth is, even when we don't feel Him close, even when we are in a place of pain, Jesus is at work. He is always close to the brokenhearted. It is where His heart is moved most for us. He is bringing healing to the deepest wounds of our hearts, gently binding the jagged edges of our grief and comforting our broken spirits. His love always moves us toward wholeness. —SUSANNA FOTH AUGHTMON

FAITH STEP: *Is there a place of brokenness in your life right now? Tear a piece of paper in half. Refit the edges together and know that in every painful area of your life, Jesus is moving you toward wholeness with His love.*

FRIDAY, SEPTEMBER 13

Jesus called the crowd to him and said, "Listen and understand."
Matthew 15:10 (NIV)

RESPECT FOR A BLIND FRIEND soared the day we sat together in a banquet hall prior to the keynote address. As the speaker adjusted his microphone, my friend pointed into space she could not see and asked me, "Is he there? This direction?"

At first, I wasn't sure what she meant. Then I realized the sound system made it difficult for her to determine where he was standing.

I took my friend's extended arm and aligned it with the person preparing to address the audience. "There."

My friend adjusted herself to face that spot on the platform. She wanted the speaker to know he had her full attention.

Recently, I watched a short video segment of a speech President Harry Truman gave decades ago. Two men behind him chatted with each other through the entire speech. Though I didn't yell at the television screen, the words "How rude!" felt appropriate.

When Jesus spoke to His audiences, He expected their full attention, the kind my friend would give Him, even though she can't see. Jesus didn't chitchat. Whenever He spoke, His words deserved the full focus of those within earshot.

Even if we don't yet understand or can't "see" what He's saying, our responsibility is to offer our complete attention.

Jesus, I want to face You when You speak to me. When my mind drifts, pull my attention back to You. —CYNTHIA RUCHTI

FAITH STEP: *If that's a prayer from your heart too, consider returning to this page often throughout the day to remind yourself of your commitment.*

SATURDAY, SEPTEMBER 14

"Let anyone who is thirsty come to me and drink. Whoever believes in me, as Scripture has said, rivers of living water will flow from within them."
John 7:37–38 (NIV)

I LOVE BEING NEAR WATER. Whether I'm at the coast, a creek, or a lakeside, it settles me. But my favorite place is along the banks of the river running through my town. The Willamette is wide, with beautiful old trees and countless birds calling it home.

As I watch this river, I sense Jesus's peace and power while the massive flow moves past with barely a ripple. Picking up stones to toss in, I feel my transformation as He smooths away my rough edges. When I spot fish struggling upstream, I understand the challenges they face. Jesus teaches me to push forward, to never give up.

Yesterday evening, I walked the bank. The heat of the day was gone, replaced by a coolness hinting at autumn's glory. A gentle breeze carried the welcome scents of dust and falling leaves. As I rounded a bend, sunset lit the water's surface with a soft white glow, resembling molten silver. The image was emblazoned in my mind, depicting the way my soul is being refined.

But the picture I hold close is of the living water that flows within me. Like a stone in that river, I'm following the course He's set for me through my obedience, rejoicing within the freedom of His boundaries. I trust His guidance around every bend, secure in the knowledge He knows the way. I'm willing and ready to guide others I meet along the curves of my life, leading them to Jesus and praying they never need thirst again. —HEIDI GAUL

FAITH STEP: *Visit a body of water near you. Listen and watch as Jesus speaks to you in the stillness of a lake, the rush of crashing waves, or the babbling of a brook. Offer a prayer of thanks.*

SUNDAY, SEPTEMBER 15

Anyone who can be trusted in little matters can also be trusted in important matters. Luke 16:10 (CEV)

SOMEONE HAS APTLY SAID, "IT's the little things that matter." That truth materialized a few years ago when a television camera caught Dallas Cowboys' quarterback Dac Prescott sitting on the bench, chugging a cup of water, and then tossing the cup over his shoulder toward a nearby garbage container. Only he missed it and the cup landed on the ground. To my amazement, the entire clip—especially what happened next—went viral on social media.

Dac, unaware he was being filmed, had walked calmly over to the cup, picked it up, and placed it in the trash can. What was the big deal? The big deal is that little things really do matter. They often point out deeper issues like character or integrity—and the ability to be trusted in more important matters, as the faithful steward in Luke 16:10 demonstrated.

Years ago, we sold a puppy to a single young lady. I was attached to the dog and wiped away a tear when she walked away with it. My husband wrapped his arm around me to offer some comfort. Apparently, the girl noticed. She returned the puppy the next day because of an apartment restriction. But she offered these words: "When I marry, I want a marriage like yours." What was the big deal?

We discovered that small hug had equaled an intimate marriage relationship to this woman. Before she left, we shared with her our intimate relationship with Jesus, and she expressed the desire to know Him.

Little things matter. They may open the door for us to influence someone for eternity. —REBECCA BARLOW JORDAN

FAITH STEP: *Ask Jesus to help you pay attention to the little things in your own life.*

MONDAY, SEPTEMBER 16

For I long to visit you so I can bring you some spiritual gift that will help you grow strong in the Lord. When we get together, I want to encourage you in your faith, but I also want to be encouraged by yours. Romans 1:11–12 (NLT)

HOPING TO DELAY SPINAL SURGERY, my doctor connected me with a physical therapist who recommended modified exercises to strengthen my core muscles. Since I had planned to leave town for two weeks, I put off starting the program. Then I needed a week to unpack when I returned. I kept thinking of other reasons to procrastinate. Suddenly, it was time for an appointment with the physical therapist—to measure how much progress I had made.

I also procrastinate when it comes to spiritual exercises, like Bible reading, prayer, and personal worship. God has provided tools and resources to help us strengthen our faith, grow in godliness, and prepare ourselves to serve Him faithfully. Inconsistency or neglect in these areas can leave us weak and stunt our spiritual growth. But until I read Romans 1, I hadn't thought about how my failure to stay spiritually fit affects others as well as myself.

We were created to "do life" together with other Christ followers, helping each other stay strong and grow deeper in the faith. We don't have to be a pastor or leader to do that. Words of encouragement at just the right time. Spurring someone on to fully use their spiritual gifts. Sharing words from the Bible that speak to someone's struggle. Extending practical help during difficult times. Or, maybe offering a listening ear and a warm hug. Basically, just sharing Jesus.

To think that I might help someone else grow stronger in their faith—what a sacred privilege! —DIANNE NEAL MATTHEWS

FAITH STEP: *Ask Jesus to show you someone whose faith could be strengthened by connecting with you.*

TUESDAY, SEPTEMBER 17

The gatekeeper opens the gate for him, and the sheep listen to his voice.
He calls his own sheep by name and leads them out. John 10:3 (NIV)

I DID A LOT OF praying and research before we moved to Florida. Based on a few key criteria, we focused on a particular area where there seemed to be more jobs and services for my special-needs son. We had some misgivings about the housing costs and the local culture's fit for our family, but since my husband had been offered a job, we pushed through them. Then, when we couldn't sell our house and the job offer expired, we suspended our move indefinitely, content to stay put.

Time passed and eventually we started to think about moving again. This time, we decided to take a mission vacation to explore the state. We visited five areas, including our original destination. It was immediately obvious we wanted to be someplace else entirely. Trusting God, I flew down again to look at houses over a long weekend.

The realtor insisted I see a house in a town that had not made my short list. Had Jesus opened this gate? Was it His voice calling us here? I prayed continuously. The house stood out as the best value. I sent the listing to my husband, and we prayed and made an offer, which was promptly accepted.

In short order, we could see that this community, this home, and most especially this town, were absolutely perfect for us. The town that hadn't made my well-researched short list turned out to be home sweet home. When it was God's time, everything came together perfectly. —ISABELLA YOSUICO

FAITH STEP: *Recall a time when Jesus opened a gate or led you in an unexpected direction. Can you apply that lesson to a circumstance you face today?*

WEDNESDAY, SEPTEMBER 18

Then the Lord said to him, "You Pharisees are so careful to clean the outside of the cup and the dish, but inside you are filthy—full of greed and wickedness! Fools! Didn't God make the inside as well as the outside? So clean the inside by giving gifts to the poor, and you will be clean all over."
Luke 11:39–41 (NLT)

MY DISHWASHER HAS A PLACE on the bottom rack where cups and jars don't come clean. More than once, I've run the cycle and then emptied it, stacking the contents in the cupboard only to later find a mug that's still coffee-stained on the inside. That's a bit annoying, especially if guests find a dirty cup before I do.

Dirty cups serve little use. Perhaps that's why Jesus compared them to the Pharisees. These leaders fixated on looking good on the outside by obeying religious rules, but they cared less about their hearts' condition. Their public behavior garnered man's praise, but their hidden thoughts and motives received Christ's rebuke. In the context of today's verses, they were theologically clean, but lacked an understanding of practical Christianity demonstrated by love. They were of little use in building Christ's kingdom on earth.

I fear that sometimes I bear a striking resemblance to the Pharisees. Maybe you can relate. We look clean on the outside because we read the Bible, attend prayer meetings and Bible studies, and even assume leadership roles. But we remain dirty on the inside as reflected by actions that are motivated by a desire for man's approval rather than a love for Jesus. Jealousy, anger, greed, and unforgiveness stain us.

Allowing Jesus to cleanse us from hidden grime is humbling but necessary, for then He can use us for His highest purposes. —GRACE FOX

FAITH STEP: *As you wash a dirty cup or dish today, invite Jesus to cleanse you from anything that might hinder Him from using you to accomplish His purposes.*

THURSDAY, SEPTEMBER 19

And I will pray the Father, and he shall give you another Comforter, that he may abide with you for ever. John 14:16 (KJV)

KINDERGARTEN WAS QUITE AN ADJUSTMENT for our youngest, Stella. The first day, she got stung by a yellow jacket on the playground. The second day, she came home and declared, "I hate kindergarten. I cannot be just me. I have to be a different me at school. It rained all day, and I couldn't run, jump, whistle, sing, or laugh. I have to sit crisscross applesauce for six hours while the teacher talks, and we don't get anything to eat that whole time. Plus, I hardly get to see Jim at all."

Jim, her uncle, is the superintendent of the school district. Stella assumed since he worked at school, she would have constant access to him. She must have imagined he'd be there to hug her, play with her, and help her navigate her new world. Superintendents don't have anything else to do at school, after all.

The third morning, she cried and begged to stay with Granny and PaPa, who have been her caregivers her entire life. Being the mean mother I am, I made her go to school, but I sent out a family text for prayer. At the end of the day, Stella reported: "Today was the best day ever of kindergarten. We got to go outside for all three recesses, and Jim came at lunch, and I runned and hugged him. That was the best of all that I got to see Jim."

What comfort it is when we know we're not alone; when someone strong and wise is there to help us. Like Stella says, it's the best of all. Jesus knew we needed someone to abide with us—always there to help us navigate our world. That's why He sent the Comforter, His Spirit. So we never have to go it alone. —GWEN FORD FAULKENBERRY

FAITH STEP: *Volunteer at your local kindergarten. For the love of Jesus, give out all the hugs you can.*

FRIDAY, SEPTEMBER 20

Make me to know your ways, O LORD; teach me your paths. Lead me in your truth, and teach me. Psalm 25:4—5 (NRSV)

ONE OF MY FAVORITE PRAYER practices is hiking. Well, I call it hiking, but what it really is is just walking in nature. After a walk, I feel much more connected. God's ways seem much clearer to me.

This is particularly true if the hike is on uneven and changing terrain. Spending a morning or an afternoon concentrating on where to place my feet, one step after another, does something to my brain. Letting the soles of my feet find their way securely over rocks, tree roots, fallen leaves, mud, and moss takes a certain level of concentration that I just don't use in my urban daily life. The level of concentration needed increases as I get older, even as the paths I choose are less strenuous.

And because what I am concentrating on is my physical movement through and with God's creation, I experience a level of peace and clarity after a hike that seems sacred to me. It is as if by traveling nature's path, I get to experience the path's simple truth. Through my footsteps and my concentration, I have internalized what the wisdom of nature had to offer in that particular moment, along that particular trail.

To me, this is what Jesus may have meant when He said, "I am the Truth, the Light, and the Way (John 14:6)." I wonder if, in response to followers desperate for answers, He was suggesting that the best way to find the truth, the light, and the way is to walk the paths God offers, bask in the light God shines, and let the reality in those experiences become who we are. —ELIZABETH BERNE DEGEAR

FAITH STEP: *Trust that there is a connection between the soles of your feet and your soul. Spend a few minutes walking on a path through nature and lose yourself in the activity. Then notice if your way in the world seems easier afterward.*

SATURDAY, SEPTEMBER 21

For we walk by faith, not by sight. 2 Corinthians 5:7 *(ESV)*

AS A CONFERENCE SESSION ENDED, a friend leaned close and clutched her white cane. "I have to meet my driver in a few minutes on the lower level. Could you direct me?"

She laid her hand on my forearm as we walked miles of corridors to get to the correct escalator to the lower level. As we approached, I confessed that I can barely get myself on a downward escalator without looking clumsy. "I'm not sure how to get us both on without one of us tumbling face-first."

She squeezed my arm. "My dear, I travel alone all over the world. I've managed escalators and people movers in more countries than you'd realize. It's not hard. Close your eyes."

Close my eyes? How would that help?

"Can you feel the vibrations in your feet?" she said. "We're getting close. Now step forward. Feel the incline changing?"

I kept one eye open, but marveled that even without her sight, she managed better than I did.

"And now the escalator's coming to an end, isn't it? Wait. And . . . step off."

We can learn so much when we stop using the senses we usually depend on. When the road shrouded with uncertainty or fear makes us wonder how we'll navigate the impossible challenges we see in front of us, Jesus leans close. It's as if He's saying, "Close your eyes. Stop using your sight. Feel by faith. You can travel far without ever seeing what's at your feet. Faith in me removes the fear factor."

I can almost feel His hand on my forearm now as we take the next step forward. —CYNTHIA RUCHTI

FAITH STEP: *Perform one small task today with your eyes closed to demonstrate that faith remembers what we forget. Practice walking by faith. It'll come in handy.*

SUNDAY, SEPTEMBER 22

I say this for your own benefit, not to lay any restraint upon you, but to promote good order and to secure your undivided devotion to the Lord. 1 Corinthians 7:35 (ESV)

MY HUSBAND, RAY, AND I wake up most mornings in the dark. I often roll out of bed and onto my knees, asking God to frame the day, to make me useful in His hands. We both retreat to our metaphorical prayer closets, before the children wake, for carefully guarded quiet time. I grab a hot cup of coffee and my supply of Bible, books, and journal, and settle down for reading, prayer, journaling, and meditation.

Sounds really holy, doesn't it?

It's not.

A few minutes into it, my iPad chirps and I check Messenger. That inevitably leads to a few minutes scrolling my Facebook news feed. *Like, like, like.* Time for more coffee. *Gosh, the counter has a sticky film on it, let me just wipe that down. Wait, let me get back to my devotional.* I jot some notes of remembered prayers.

My husband is leaving for a run and asks if I could I walk the dog. "Why me?" I ask with a nasty tone.

Back to my sacred reading space, an email appears, that might be irritating or troubling. I hear one of my kids stirring.

Heavy sigh.

In the end, I usually do carve out a chunk of time that's for God. Or better, for me. What I read, what I write...it does filter through all the clutter to help me start the day. But it's always, *always* a discipline of choice for me and remains so throughout the clutter-filled day. I've learned to accept this as I accept that God loves me anyway and appreciates my erratic devotion. —ISABELLA YOSUICO

FAITH STEP: *Just for today, smile at the many distractions that compete for your time with God and ask Him to redirect your thoughts as you seek Him.*

MONDAY, SEPTEMBER 23

And Jesus said to them, "I am the bread of life. He who comes to Me shall never hunger." John 6:35 (NKJV)

I'M GENERALLY CHEERFUL AND DON'T get cranky very often. When I do, it's usually because I'm hungry. I get impatient and snippy at loved ones over the simplest things. All I know is when my stomach is growling, I growl with it. And I will eat just about anything that's edible. Most of the time, I reach for potato chips. (I guess that's why experts warn to never go food shopping when you're hungry.)

Jesus was human, too, and knew exactly how uncomfortable hunger could be. That's why He felt compassion for the crowd that followed Him into the hills to hear Him preach (Matthew 14:14). They'd been with Him all day and were hungry—all five thousand of them! When the disciples thought He should just send them on their way, Jesus refused. You know the rest of the story: He fed them all "as much as they wanted" (John 6:11) with only two small fish and five barley loaves given to him by a young boy in the crowd.

Empty stomachs aren't the only things Jesus fills in our time of need. He sees our spiritual hunger too. When we forget to feast on God's Word, our spirits begin to crave the "bread from heaven" (John 6:31), nourishment that only Jesus can provide—His healing touch, comfort, provision, or protection. Anything else is junk food—a poor substitute. —CAROL MACKEY

FAITH STEP: *Jesus is the Bread of Life and our Sustenance. Ask Him to fill you up daily and you will never go hungry.*

TUESDAY, SEPTEMBER 24

*Blessed are those who hunger and thirst for righteousness,
for they shall be satisfied. Matthew 5:6 (ESV)*

YESTERDAY, I SNACKED ON SOME cheese and nuts right before dinner. When it was time for supper, I didn't eat much. Since I was no longer hungry, the food didn't taste great. Years ago, I did a three-day fast. The first thing I ate afterward was a banana. I've never before or since tasted a banana that delicious. Hunger can make anything taste amazing.

In much the same way, some days I read a section of Scripture and the words taste dull. That's because I'm full of self: self-confidence, self-indulgence, self-assurance. I don't come to the Bible with an awareness of my need and emptiness. I don't come to Jesus hungry.

Then there are other days I'm starving for the comfort food Jesus supplies. My heart is breaking while I'm watching a loved one approach the end of life. Or, despite my best intentions, I've spent time complaining and whining and now feel ashamed. Or I'm confronted by loneliness and ache for connection. Or fear has me in an icy grip because of a new job that seems too big for me to handle. As difficult as those days are, they stir a new hunger in me. They remind me that Jesus invites those who are in need to come to Him. In the beautiful upside-down descriptions of the Beatitudes, He reminds me that a place of inner poverty and need is a place of blessing.

Today, as we approach the Word, let's acknowledge our deep need so that we have a new appetite for the truth. As we hunger and thirst for the Righteous One, we will find Him in the Scriptures, be filled with His presence, and be truly satisfied. —SHARON HINCK

FAITH STEP: *Consider fasting from a meal or two, and ask Jesus to increase your hunger for knowing Him.*

WEDNESDAY, SEPTEMBER 25

Even youths grow tired and weary, and young men stumble and fall; but those who hope in the LORD will renew their strength. They will soar on wings like eagles; they will run and not grow weary, they will walk and not be faint. Isaiah 40:30–31 (NIV)

THE OTHER NIGHT, MY SON, Jack, woke me up an hour after I had gone to bed. His dad had warned him against it, but Jack wanted to remind me to order his summer reading books. I greeted him with great anger. I was delirious and had to apologize to him the next morning.

I said, "Jack, I can't remember what I said to you last night, but I know it wasn't very nice."

He told me. "You said, 'What is wrong with you?' and 'Why in the world would you wake me up?' You were pretty mad."

Harsh words for a son who is trying to be responsible about his schoolwork. "I am so sorry, Jack! I was tired, but I shouldn't have gotten upset at you."

He forgave me, but he probably won't ever wake me up again. Life can drain us of all energy and goodwill. We get worn out spiritually, emotionally, and physically. We require full-body refreshment and renewal on a regular basis. We forget that our bodies and spirits are attached. Weariness in the body can cause weariness in the spirit and vice versa. We need to remember our true strength comes from Jesus. He can heal our bodies and minds. He can restore our souls and give us the rest we need. Time spent with Jesus brings renewed strength to every part of our beings. —SUSANNA FOTH AUGHTMON

FAITH STEP: *Take a walk. Recognize the connection between your mind, spirit, and body. Ask Jesus to restore your emotions, body, and thoughts with His strength.*

Thursday, September 26

Am I now trying to win the approval of human beings, or of God?
Or am I trying to please people? If I were still trying to please people,
I would not be a servant of Christ. Galatians 1:10 (NIV)

MY GRANDDAUGHTER LILAH WAS A good eater for the first couple of years. But after turning two, she became more finicky. Sometimes she rejected foods, saying, "Oooo, gwoss" or "S'gusting" in imitation of her older siblings. One evening my daughter, Holly, prepared pork chops, roasted baby potatoes, and steamed broccoli. She glanced up when she heard Lilah declare, "Yum, delishush!" Holly smiled, feeling appreciated. Then my son-in-law informed her that Lilah had just eaten a big forkful of ketchup.

Wouldn't it be nice if everyone showed appreciation for everything we do for them? Unfortunately, our work at home, on the job, at church, and in the community isn't always acknowledged or valued. There's no guarantee that we'll receive even a simple thank-you for our efforts, regardless of how we knock ourselves out. Whether it's a lack of gratitude or someone being impossible to please, we may end up disappointed if pleasing people is our goal.

As followers of Jesus, we already have God's approval; now our objective is to live a life pleasing to Him. Serving Christ means doing the best we can for others in every relationship and every environment. If we receive recognition for our work, that's nice. And if we don't, that's okay too. Because the One we really want to please promises to bless and reward us. —DIANNE NEAL MATTHEWS

FAITH STEP: *Is there someone you wish would show you a little appreciation? Read Colossians 3:24–25, then think of a special way to serve that person. Tell Jesus that you're doing it for Him.*

FRIDAY, SEPTEMBER 27

"And why do you, by your traditions, violate the direct commandments of God?" Matthew 15:3 (NLT)

THE NEXT OWNERS OF OUR house will have more than one head-scratching moment.

"Why did they wallpaper this portion of the hallway with three-inch strips?" *Because it was cheaper than buying a new roll of wallpaper to finish off that small section.*

"Why would they not have planted flowers or shrubs in that wide stretch between the flower beds near the deck?" *Well, the septic tank is under there, and when it needs emptying, we didn't want to uproot plants to uncover the access lid.*

"Is there a reason they didn't cut down that scraggly-looking crab apple tree?" *Yes. The deer are crazy fans of what falls from its branches.*

Our traditions may not be appreciated by the new owners. And that's okay.

Jesus confronted those who accused Him of breaking traditions handed down to God's people. He asked, "Why do you break the command of God by keeping the rules handed down to you?" (Matthew 15:3). In other words, Jesus asked, "Why do you let your traditions overrule what my Father and I have taught you?"

Of the tradition-steeped, Jesus, quoting from Isaiah 29:13, said, "Their worship of me is empty since they teach instructions that are human rules" (Matthew 15:9).

How much of what I do is tradition I inherited rather than compliance with what Jesus really said? —CYNTHIA RUCHTI

FAITH STEP: *If a question like that rattles you too, find a small piece of wallpaper to use as a bookmark and slip it into either Matthew 15 or Isaiah 29.*

SATURDAY, SEPTEMBER 28

Be devoted to one another in love. Honor one another above yourselves.
Romans 12:10 (NIV)

YESTERDAY, I MET WITH A diverse group of Christian authors over lunch. It started out as a job-related gathering, a time to brainstorm and critique each other's pieces. An inspirational writer's life can be isolated, so receiving feedback from others in the field seemed to be a good idea. Our personal differences spanned politics, income, writing styles, and personalities, making for lively conversation.

Over time, our talks spread into other areas of our lives. Illness, unemployment, rejections from editors; we covered them all in tea and sympathy. Prayers over challenges were matched by praises over weddings, births, and writing contracts. Sharing our joys and sorrows wove a tapestry of deep friendship.

Bringing together Christians of diversity delights Jesus. He spots goodness in others that we might otherwise miss. He enjoys seeing compatibility in the midst of contrast. He knows all of us inside and out, and pieces us together like a colorful mosaic, each bit unique but of equal value.

When Jesus set the gears in motion for my joining this group, I wondered what the takeaway would be. A meal out? Better writing? Stronger connections in publishing? Each of those benefits came to pass, but the true treasure I received is richer, a cherished gift. With nothing more in common than a talent for writing and unfailing love for Jesus, my friends and I had more than enough. Now we delight in both our differences and similarities. Whether we join together in laughter or comfort, I see Jesus's love in their eyes and feel His warmth in their embraces. —HEIDI GAUL

FAITH STEP: *Are you part of a group so dissimilar, only Jesus could have assembled it? He's also a member. Give your heart to them as you do to Him.*

SUNDAY, SEPTEMBER 29

Sensible people control their temper; they earn respect by overlooking wrongs. Proverbs 19:11 (NLT)

SOMETIMES, I WONDER WHY GOD places certain, unique individuals in my life. One such woman I know has no verbal filter. She says whatever comes to mind regardless of its impact on others.

She and I used to attend the same church and occasionally spent time together. One day, she and I went clothes shopping together. Things went surprisingly well until we paid for our purchases. As we left the store, she looked at me and said, "You're overweight. Shed twenty or thirty pounds, and then I'll go shopping with you again." I didn't know whether to laugh or cry.

For several years, I allowed her words to offend me. I wrestled with hurt and anger. I even held make-believe conversations with her in my head. I defended myself with imaginary retorts that left her in stunned silence. Thank goodness that's no longer the case.

She comes from a family that regards others with suspicion, often misinterprets their words and actions, and severs relationships when they feel offended. That's not the way I want to live, so I've chosen a different response: I will be unoffendable.

"Help me see this woman through Your eyes," I pray when I feel negative emotions surface. Then I follow Jesus's example when He prayed for those who nailed Him to the cross, saying, "Father, forgive them, for they don't know what they are doing" (Luke 23:34).

Maybe this woman does know what she's doing; maybe not. That's not my concern—it's Jesus's issue. My concern is to live as He lived, extending grace and forgiveness. —GRACE FOX

FAITH STEP: *Who's that unique individual in your life? Ask Jesus to help you see him or her through His eyes.*

MONDAY, SEPTEMBER 30

I will be with you always. Matthew 28:20 (NCV)

MY SON HARPER HAS A group of friends he's been close with since third grade. They all play sports together, and they love hunting and fishing and having a good time. I love them all. My husband, Stone, and I enjoy having them at our house for campouts and cooking big pancake breakfasts in the morning.

As they've gotten older, however, I've had some concerns about how my son might navigate the differences he has with many of his friends. Teenage years bring decisions about girls, parties, and other things that can be challenging. Harper had his first "real" girlfriend this year, and when they broke up, it broke his heart.

One evening, we were talking about everything, and he told me one of the worst things about breaking up with his girlfriend was that he was counting on her to help him make good decisions about his friends. Because she and he shared similar ideas about peer pressure, he thought they could figure that out together. Without her company, it was going to be a lot harder, he said.

It's hard to tell a teenage kid he might have to stand alone. Harder still, as I remember, to be a teenager and actually do it. What I told Harper is that doing what he feels is right may be really hard. But he can do hard things. And he is never alone. He may not have a girlfriend, and other friends may choose things he refuses. But Jesus is with him always. —GWEN FORD FAULKENBERRY

FAITH STEP: *Is there something difficult you're facing, and you feel like you're doing it alone? Write Matthew 28:20 on a card you can keep in your pocket to remind you that you're never alone. Jesus promises.*

TUESDAY, OCTOBER 1

[Jesus said], When evening comes, you say, "It will be fair weather, for the sky is red," and in the morning, "Today it will be stormy, for the sky is red and overcast." You know how to interpret the appearance of the sky, but you cannot interpret the signs of the times. Matthew 16:2–3 (NIV)

WHEN I AM IN NATURE, I often hear Jesus reminding me: "The answers to your questions are right here. Open your eyes to the truth and beauty unfolding all around you. I'm communicating with you through all creation!" Just the other day, I was on a hike up a mountain, and I brought my troubles with me. In my mind, I was replaying an argument I had had with my husband and was feeling frustrated. The trail was surrounded by dense woods until, somewhere near the top of the mountain, I came to a clearing. Looking out, I could see a mountain range extending far into the distance, mountain after mountain, green, then blue, then smoky gray. The points of the farthest mountaintops faded into the horizon. White clouds floated rapidly in the sky, casting moving shadows over the landscape, which seemed to dance. As beautiful as the mountains were, it was the moving shadows animating the whole spectacular scene that made my heart leap.

I got what Jesus was telling me! The small arguments and ongoing frustrations are the clouds of our marriage, casting their shadows as they pass through. If I could take this time to find a clearing, and gaze upon my marriage at a distance instead of replaying a particular moment in my head to feed my annoyance, I would see that the bickering comes and goes, and the shadows it casts are part of the beauty that animates our marriage. —ELIZABETH BERNE DEGEAR

FAITH STEP: *Take a problem you've been thinking a lot about with you as you spend an hour or two in a natural setting. Let nature tell its story and see if it speaks directly to your situation.*

WEDNESDAY, OCTOBER 2

Just as a body, though one, has many parts, but all its many parts form one body, so it is with Christ. 1 Corinthians 12:12 (NIV)

MY TWO SONS ARE ELEVEN-and-a-half years apart, so I had an energetic preschooler and a moody teenager at the same time. Both are tall and lanky, extremely smart, have beautiful, big, brown eyes, and inherited my quick sense of humor—that's where the similarities end. They may have come from the same parents, but they couldn't be more opposite.

Christian, my oldest, has a mass of tight curls and a gentle, quiet spirit. He grew up watching me sing at church but had no desire to be in the spotlight. Instead, he worked in the sound booth and became an amazing cook. He now works in an art museum that's as peaceful as he is.

Nathan didn't even have curls as a baby. What he did have was a lot to say, a contagious laugh, a strong will, and a knack for making friends. Nathan loves sports and had the confidence to try out for Jazz Band in seventh grade (he made it). I have no idea what he will do with his life, but whatever it is, it will be exciting.

I love my opposite boys! I hope that they will always know that, though they are different, they are equally valuable to me and to Jesus. He has a unique use for each of these young men who entrusted their hearts to Him at a young age. His kingdom needs men like Christian and guys like Nathan.

How amazing it is to know that He values and uses each of us, in all our uniqueness, to accomplish His purposes. —JEANETTE HANSCOME

FAITH STEP: *Write a note or text to all the members of your family and name at least one thing that you appreciate about their personalities. Ask Jesus to also help you appreciate your own uniqueness.*

THURSDAY, OCTOBER 3

Do not remember the rebellious sins of my youth. Remember me in the light of your unfailing love, for you are merciful, O LORD. Psalm 25:7 (NLT)

TWO WOMEN IN THEIR LATE twenties or early thirties approached me where I stood at the back of the room after a speaking engagement.

"Hi," said one. "You probably don't remember us." They grinned self-consciously and waited for my response.

A momentary search of my memory bank found their file. They'd been my students at the Christian high school where I'd worked in the dean's department nearly three decades prior. Their names came to mind, and so did their history. How could I forget sitting in the principal's office with them and their parents on the morning of graduation day, discussing whether their antics the night before would deny them the privilege of participating in the ceremony?

I smiled. "Of course I remember you."

"That's too bad," said the other. "We were hoping you'd forget. We're sorry for being such stinkers back then."

I smiled again. "That was then, and this is now. No doubt you're not the same today as you were back in high school."

Like these two gals, I'm sorry, too, for being a stinker in my youth and into my young adulthood. I did more than a few things that I regret. I still remember them, but Jesus does not. His ability to blot them from His memory is beyond my comprehension, but then again, so is the scope of His love. And it's through the lens of that love that He sees me—not as the stinker I once was but as the woman I'm becoming in Him. —GRACE FOX

FAITH STEP: *Jeremiah 31:34 says, "I will never again remember their sins." Make a list of past sins that you can't forget. Tear the paper into little bits, thanking Jesus that He's blotted them from His memory.*

FRIDAY, OCTOBER 4

And there we saw the Nephilim (the sons of Anak, who come from the Nephilim), and we seemed to ourselves like grasshoppers, and so we seemed to them. Numbers 13:33 (ESV)

AFTER A RESTLESS NIGHT, I approached my desk with dread. I'd prayerfully accepted a writing project, but right after I'd made the decision, the deadline loomed large. Instead of getting started on the work, I was paralyzed by my fear, much like the children of Israel on the threshold of the Promised Land.

When the twelve spies went ahead into Canaan, they returned with a report of amazing blessings. But ten of the men could only focus on the giants in the way. I relate to that strange combination of longing and panic. We want to go forward, but the way seems impossible.

Jesus has given us today a friend to comfort, a family member to support, a story to write, a garden to weed, children to feed, a business to run. Whatever the task, when we first set eyes on it, we are likely to spot a few giants in our way.

We can quickly feel like grasshoppers in the face of a stack of work too massive for any human to complete or a family schedule so full of commitments it requires superhuman energy. Perhaps we are advocating for a sick child against a mountain of bureaucracy. We may face an unjust boss who takes credit for our work or office politics that threaten an unstable job. We may contend with physical pain that makes each task feel like we're grasshoppers facing the Nephilim.

But Jesus calls us to pull our gaze away from the giants and look at Him. He is the Warrior who will fight on our behalf and help us take the "land" today. —SHARON HINCK

FAITH STEP: *Sketch the "land" you want to conquer today and mark a few of the giants in your path. Invite Jesus to give you courage to trust Him as you advance.*

SATURDAY, OCTOBER 5

"What then shall we do?" Luke 3:10 (ESV)

THE APPLES ON THE TREES lining our south yard were small. Even from a distance, my husband, Bill, and I could see that many on the middle tree were worm-eaten or scar-skinned, unlikely to produce food for those of us who care about fresh fruit and applesauce.

We looked at each other and asked, "What should we do?"

Three groups of people asked the same question of Jesus when He taught about the importance of producing good fruit—fruit that shows changed hearts and lives. Jesus told them that if a tree doesn't produce good fruit, it would be chopped down and tossed into the fire. It wasn't an outrageous pronouncement. That's what my husband seriously considered doing with our row of unproductive apple trees.

The people listening to Jesus asked, "What should we do?"

"And he answered them, 'Whoever has two tunics is to share with him who has none, and whoever has food is to do likewise'" (Luke 3:11). Jesus expected good fruit and generosity to follow.

"Tax collectors also came to be baptized and said to him, 'Teacher, what shall we do?' And he said to them, 'Collect no more than you are authorized to do'" (vv. 12 and 13). Jesus expected fairness and integrity.

"Soldiers also asked him, 'And we, what shall we do?' And he said to them, 'Do not extort money from anyone by threats or by false accusation, and be content with your wages'" (v. 14). Jesus said that a sign of good fruit is to be content with our pay.

Specific and practical advice. If we expect something loftier, we miss what good fruit looks like. —CYNTHIA RUCHTI

FAITH STEP: *If a piece of fruit is part of your nutrition plan today, pause a moment before eating it and consider the fruit of your life.*

SUNDAY, OCTOBER 6

Blessed are those who mourn, For they shall be comforted. Matthew 5:4 (NKJV)

WHEN I GOT DIVORCED, I mourned the demise of my marriage—something that was once very much alive had died. At the time, I was in need of peace and comfort. Throughout the New Testament, Jesus was often summoned to comfort those in need. Unlike the haughty religious leaders of the time, Jesus was hands-on. His time was relatively short on earth, so He made every effort to touch as many people as possible. Many of them needed comfort and restoration.

In Luke 8:41, we see Jairus, a rich Jewish ruler who threw himself at Jesus's feet, seeking His help. Jairus's daughter lay near death, and he'd heard about Jesus and the miracles He performed. Not only did Jesus bring this father's sick child back to life; He even healed another desperate woman of her long-term illness along the way (v. 48)! He also brought emotional comfort to this heartbroken father and physical comfort and relief to this woman, whose pain and suffering had been a constant burden for twelve long years. Both had been in mourning in some way when they'd met Jesus. The father was deeply grieved at the loss of his child's health and the woman the health of her body. The experience goes beyond how we understand the word in the traditional sense. That's something I've come to understand during trials in my own life, especially at the end of my marriage.

The good news is, Jesus was there to comfort me and see me through the death of my "happily ever after." And He is there to offer comfort to everyone who mourns their individual shortcomings, heartbreaks, and disappointments. —CAROL MACKEY

FAITH STEP: *Are you in mourning over a relationship, financial loss, or health diagnosis? Whatever it is, the Lord is waiting to comfort you and breathe new life into that which you thought was "dead" in your life.*

MONDAY, OCTOBER 7

Heaven and earth will pass away, but my words will never pass away.
Matthew 24:35 (NIV)

LAST NIGHT, I HAD A terrible nightmare—a night terror, really. Lying awake in the darkness like a frightened toddler, I reached for my husband, David, and softly hugged his warm, slumbering body. Just touching my hand to his chest helped settle my mind. Moments later, roused from sleep, he spoke gentle words that calmed my frayed nerves. "Shh. You had a bad dream. You're safe, honey." I fell back to sleep, safe and secure in his arms.

This morning, I battled several anxiety-triggering situations. Stressors requiring my immediate attention piled up as fast as dirty laundry, until the tiniest irritation threatened an emotional outburst. It was time to pull myself free and race like a child to the Lord.

Occasionally when I'm upset, all I need to do is rest my hands on the Bible. Knowing the love, strength, and wisdom it holds is sufficient for me. Sometimes that's all I can do, as tears blind my eyes and make reading impossible. The peace held between its covers seeps through and makes things easier.

His words are here for all of us, ever-ready to draw us close, quiet our fears, and empower us. They are wise, comforting, and eternal, just like His love. —HEIDI GAUL

FAITH STEP: *Sit, simply holding the Bible, and recognize the might and magnificence within your grasp. Read and then post these verses on your refrigerator for when you need His comforting touch: Revelation 21:24, John 16:33, and Isaiah 41:10.*

TUESDAY, OCTOBER 8

For many were giving false testimony against Him, but their testimony was not consistent. Mark 14:56 (NASB)

MANY YEARS AGO, I HAD a surprise visit from two of the dads in our subdivision. They informed me that my older teenage son, Eric, and his friend had engaged in filthy, offensive talk on the school bus in front of their younger sons. When they said it had happened the previous afternoon, I told them that Eric hadn't ridden the bus then because of track practice. Then they said it occurred on the morning ride.

I knew this did not sound like my son, but I called the moms of the "bullied" kids. They were shocked at my questions and said that the other student was the one who had talked inappropriately on the *afternoon* bus ride. One mom told me that yes, her sons had been picked on—but not by Eric.

Jesus knew how it felt to endure slander. In some ways, people still bear false witness about Him today. People often label Him a famous rabbi, a prophet, or simply "a good man." Surveys show that even some who identify as Christ followers don't believe He lived a sinless life, even though 2 Corinthians 5:21, Hebrews 4:15, and other verses make that truth clear.

If we follow Jesus, it's crucial that we know what the Bible teaches about His identity, His character, and the purpose of His earthly ministry: He is the sinless Son of God who willingly offered His life for us. We have plenty of written testimony to help us portray Him accurately to the world around us. —DIANNE NEAL MATTHEWS

FAITH STEP: *If you haven't studied the Gospels lately, consider reading through the book of John, taking notes on what Jesus said about Himself.*

WEDNESDAY, OCTOBER 9

*Jesus called out to them, "Come, follow me, and I will show you
how to fish for people!" And they left their nets at once and followed him.
Matthew 4:19–20 (NLT)*

I AM CONSTANTLY STICKING MY head out the back door or down the hallway and calling to my boys. "Jack! Will! Addison! Come here, please!" I have things I want to tell them. Like how they need to finish doing their dishes. Or that their monthly letter from their Grandma Foth has arrived. Or that I love them the most. I have so many things to share with them. Whenever I call them, I am looking for a response. *Have they heard me? Are they ready to do what I have asked? Why aren't they coming?*

I want them to come so that I can look into their eyes and see their faces. Our conversations are important to me. It does neither of us any good if they just keep doing what they are doing and ignore my calls.

We often forget that our relationship with Jesus is a call-and-response relationship. He is calling out to us to follow Him. Just like the disciples, we should drop everything we are doing and come to Him. He has called us to Himself. *How are we responding? With silence and indifference? With a quick thought of "I'll talk to Him later"?* Or do we run and fling ourselves into His arms and say, "I want to hear everything you have to say. It is the most important thing in the world to me"?

His Word is life. It breathes hope and renewal into our weary bones. His Word gives us a path to follow and leads in the way everlasting. I think we should come when He calls. —SUSANNA FOTH AUGHTMON

FAITH STEP: *Read Matthew 4:18–25. The disciples' lives changed radically when they followed Jesus. How has yours changed since you began following Jesus?*

THURSDAY, OCTOBER 10

With every sun's rising, surprise **us** *with Your love, satisfy us with Your kindness. Then we will sing with joy and celebrate every day we are alive.*
Psalm 90:14 *(VOICE)*

"JESUS HAS MORE IMPORTANT MATTERS to deal with than my small problems!" Those words from an acquaintance surprised me, then made me wonder. How did I really feel about that statement?

I think I've always believed that Jesus cares about the details of our lives. I remember one day years ago, the temperature reached three-digit heat. Our dog had destroyed our small, above ground swimming pool, and we asked Jesus to provide another pool for our daughters. Three days later, a friend called: "Could your girls use a swimming pool? My kids have outgrown theirs." We included Jesus in so many details that our grown children joke about the times we hesitated over buying pizza after church.

But as the years pass, it's easy to slip unconsciously into a "Don't bother God with little things" mentality. So before my husband and I planned three fishing trips recently, we asked Jesus for a relatively small thing: in the middle of rising summer temperatures, could He send cooler weather and productive fishing? Each time, clouds hovered, cool winds blew, and we kept snagging big fish.

Does Jesus always say yes to our small requests? No, but He does care about them. Most important, He cares about me—and you—and everything that affects us. Why? I suspect because we are His children. And because He loves to surprise and give good gifts to His kids (Matthew 7:11). —REBECCA BARLOW JORDAN

FAITH STEP: *Ask Jesus to help you with the small matters in your life today. Then thank Him for His answers.*

FRIDAY, OCTOBER 11

You are the salt of the earth. Matthew 5:13 (NIV)

THIS YEAR FOR PROFESSIONAL DEVELOPMENT, we teachers got to hear a speaker named Manny Scott. He is one of the original *Freedom Writers* from the movie by that name. It stars Hilary Swank as the teacher who helped a class full of disadvantaged students change their lives through writing.

Manny shared a lot of ideas and techniques for how we might reach students and help them succeed. His emphasis was on the least of these—students from marginalized communities. He seemed to understand the desperation we teachers feel sometimes. There are times these children seem unreachable.

He said, "I know a lot of you are thinking, Manny, you can lead a horse to water, but you can't make him drink."

Yep. That's exactly what I was thinking.

"And that's true. You can't make him drink. But you can make him thirsty."

Manny went on to encourage us to be the salt of the earth—just by living our lives and offering our students hope—so that we could make them thirsty for education.

I thought about this in terms of the Christian life. So often, I feel I don't have the right words to say or don't know what to do to get people interested in Jesus. And yet I know if they could only taste, they'd see He's good. They'd want more.

Maybe it's not always about having the perfect words or even doing the perfect thing. But if others see Jesus in our lives, it will make them thirsty for Him. —GWEN FORD FAULKENBERRY

FAITH STEP: *Pass the salt to someone today by inviting them into your life in some aspect. Let them see the way Jesus's love plays out.*

SATURDAY, OCTOBER 12

Don't collect for yourselves treasures on earth, where moth and rust destroy and where thieves break in and steal. But collect for yourselves treasures in heaven, where neither moth nor rust destroys, and where thieves don't break in and steal. Matthew 6:19–20 (HCSB)

I RAN THROUGH A CEMETERY this morning, Christian rap blasting incompatibly in my headphones. A running buddy told me about a nice route, three miles door to door. The tree-lined run meanders through a large cemetery. I turned under the somber brick arches, the scene more haunting as the gray sky yielded rain.

It was soon clear that the cemetery was far more vast than it appeared from the road. The wandering path passed rows of markers, marble monuments, and bench-framed ponds with towering mausoleums and religious statues on the horizon.

I glanced at names and dates as I trotted by. Husbands and wives, children, entire families, young and old—each life important.

What struck me most were the monuments and crypts: majestic and extravagantly elegant structures, statues, and gilt-framed pictures of those in repose. The group Grits' Christian rap message nearly narrates the scene with lyrics that warn against vanity and greed.

I have stored up some treasure this side of heaven—much less than some, yet more than many—all of which won't do me any good when I'm gone. That's because we are but dust, and we'd do well to build monuments that last into eternity. —ISABELLA YOSUICO

FAITH STEP: *Take a stroll through a cemetery and turn your thoughts to eternity.*

SUNDAY, OCTOBER 13

Let them praise the LORD for his great love and for the wonderful things he has done for them. Psalm 107:8 (NLT)

PSALM 107 IS ONE OF my favorites, because hidden within the poetry is a glimpse into an aspect of our Savior that offers profound comfort.

The psalm describes different groups and the specific struggles they faced. Some wandered in the wilderness, facing hunger. Some sat in darkness, imprisoned. Some suffered from sinful choices. Some faced storms on the sea. But God met each group in its place of need and delivered every one. For the hungry and homeless, He led them to a home and provided food. For the imprisoned, He offered light and freedom. For those suffering the results of their sins, He brought healing and redemption. For those in peril due to the weather, He calmed the storm.

The history of God's faithfulness always lifts my heart in this psalm. But these were not only past acts of deliverance for the children of Israel. They also inform us of the nature of Jesus, how He would deliver us one day—and how He continues to do just that.

The parallels give me goose bumps. During His time on earth, Jesus fed the hungry, freed those imprisoned by stigma or illness or poverty, brought forgiveness for sins, and calmed the sea. He was the embodiment of the rescues written about in the psalms.

What a beautiful reminder! No matter the course our lives take, no matter the specific sufferings we may face, Jesus is here to meet our needs. —SHARON HINCK

FAITH STEP: *Read all of Psalm 107. Which of the four groups do you most identify with? Thank Jesus for demonstrating His desire to meet you in that place of need.*

MONDAY, OCTOBER 14

[Jesus said,] And will not God bring about justice for his chosen ones, who cry out to him day and night? Luke 18:7 (NIV)

I'M A BIG FAN OF quiet hotel rooms when I travel. There's no place like home—*Where have I heard that before?*—but I do enjoy a clean, serene hotel room. It always seems to have better pillows than mine at home.

Midevening, during a recent hotel stay, an ear-piercing chirp startled me. The smoke detector. I checked the room for smoke and sniffed near the door to the hallway but couldn't find the source. The chirping proved to be the result of a rebellious detector.

A maintenance man came to my aid. I suggested that the battery needed to be replaced. But when the maintenance crew member removed the cover, he discovered it was hard-wired. No battery. He pushed the reset button. Quiet returned.

Anticipating an early start the next day, I turned out the lights early and was deep in sleep at one o'clock in the morning when the chirping returned. I called the lobby for help and a desk clerk showed up. His only answer was to move me to a different room. Did I mention it was one o'clock in the morning?

After the incessant chirping incident, I better understand Luke 18. Jesus told a parable about a persistent widow whose cries to a stubborn judge for justice must have sounded like a piercing bleat in the middle of the night. Jesus used the story to remind us that He and His Father don't have to be pestered about our needs. Unlike the widow's judge, Jesus cares, and His faithful caring is what moves Him to respond. —CYNTHIA RUCHTI

FAITH STEP: *Which prayer request that you bring before Jesus may have reached the pestering point, the annoyance of middle-of-the-night chirping? Begin today to thank Him for answers on their way. Notice a difference?*

TUESDAY, OCTOBER 15

No one lights a lamp and puts it in a place where it will be hidden, or under a bowl. Instead they put it on its stand, so that those who come in may see the light. Luke 11:33 (NIV)

AS WOMEN, WE CAN BE particularly adept at hiding our lights under a bowl, or a bushel, or under whatever might keep us from shining too brightly. Personally, I know that for every time I've found myself listening to a male coworker, friend, or relative "mansplaining," there has probably also been a time when I've had something to share but chosen not to. If there is a choice between shining our lights and avoiding making waves, sometimes we may choose not to shine.

One time, my theology mentor asked me to teach her class while she was away. The first thing I did to prepare? I invited four colleagues to join me in teaching the class. I think I was afraid they would envy me if I kept the honor for myself. Recently, I heard that when women are invited into a leadership role in a Christian setting, their first response is virtually always no. Women typically need to be asked *three* times before we say yes. Centuries of patriarchy have conditioned us to hesitate before shining too brightly, and— equally tragic—it has also kept us from celebrating the lights shining in other women.

Jesus shows us how preposterous this is. Our light needs to shine! It needs to be placed in a prominent position so that others can see by it. Who lights a lamp and then puts a bowl over it? Everyone benefits when the light of any one of us shines. —ELIZABETH BERNE DEGEAR

FAITH STEP: *Find a prayer partner and take some time naming each other's light. Then think of ways to offer a stand for each other's light so that it may shine more brightly and so that more people may be illuminated by it. How can you help your friend shine, and how can you let him or her help you shine?*

WEDNESDAY, OCTOBER 16

Under his direction, the whole body is fitted together perfectly, and each part in its own special way helps the other parts, so that the whole body is healthy and growing and full of love. Ephesians 4:16 (TLB)

MY DOCTOR OF TWENTY-TWO YEARS retired, so I found a new one whose specialty extended beyond symptomatic pain to include whole-body wellness.

I first visited my new physician because of recurring hip pain. Though I've been fairly healthy, I have dealt with other chronic issues for many years. After a series of tests showed some areas of deficiency, she took time to explain how healing was a chain reaction, involving all the parts of the body, not just one area. I understood enough about the process to follow her directives.

Continual testing revealed other hidden problems, and my doctor addressed those too. One by one, we worked through my weaknesses. Treatment took time and patience, but I made significant progress. The hip pain disappeared, and over time my health and strength have greatly improved.

I understand so much more now about the uniqueness of our bodies and how much one part influences the others. That truth has brought new spiritual clarity to me concerning the metaphor Jesus used about the Church—all of His believers—being the Body of Christ. If even one person fails to use his or her unique gifts to honor Christ, the Head of the Church, it affects the rest of the Body. When we all work together patiently as Jesus intends, we'll fit perfectly as Jesus's healthy Body on earth, growing in a strong love relationship with Him. —REBECCA BARLOW JORDAN

FAITH STEP: *Place a thermometer nearby for a week to remind you how important you are to the Body of Christ.*

THURSDAY, OCTOBER 17

Since God chose you to be the holy people he loves, you must clothe yourselves with tenderhearted mercy, kindness, humility, gentleness, and patience. . . . Above all, clothe yourselves with love, which binds us all together in perfect harmony. Colossians 3:12,14 (NLT)

TOPS AND JACKETS OF VARIOUS colors and designs hang in my clothes closet. Some I rarely wear and should probably give away or take to a thrift store. But the denim jacket I bought at a secondhand store is among my closet favorites. I can wear it with anything—a casual dress, a turtleneck sweater, or a summer blouse—and it looks nice.

I recently forgot that jacket at a beauty salon after having my hair cut. I didn't miss it for several days because the weather was warm. But by week's end, the temperatures dropped. My heart sank when I went to fetch it from its usual place but discovered it missing.

I searched other closets and my car. I mentally retraced my steps. And I prayed, "Jesus, You know where it is. Please help me find it." Imagine my gratitude when He brought the beauty salon to mind. A quick phone call reassured me that it was hanging where I'd left it.

I value my jacket as a part of my physical wardrobe. Of greater importance, though, is my spiritual wardrobe. Do I wear attitudes that would be better discarded, or do I clothe myself in the character qualities that Jesus demonstrated?

I'll admit that temporarily losing my favorite jacket was a bit stressful, but it certainly helped me view today's verse in a new light, and for that I am grateful. —GRACE FOX

FAITH STEP: *Put on a sweater or jacket. As you do, ask Jesus to help you clothe yourself in selfless love. Invite Him to help you sort your spiritual wardrobe and discard attitudes that don't belong.*

FRIDAY, OCTOBER 18

And we know that for those who love God all things work together for good, for those who are called according to his purpose. Romans 8:28 (ESV)

MY FLORIDA TOWN IS VERY artsy. Among the proof is an abundance of visible mosaics. The public library walls boast several colorful compositions. There are several whole houses around town encrusted to the shingles with odds and ends. Wild compositions of repurposed crockery, toys, bowling balls (yes, you read correctly), and, well, junk—interspersed with the tidy, more familiar glass and pottery tiles.

Together with the tropical waterside setting, the overall effect is dazzlingly vibrant, colorful, and striking in a distinctive way. People travel from all over to visit our town, home to many arts and music festivals. The town also attracts an eclectic mix of permanent transplants, including many artists, musicians, and writers inspired by both the natural and creative beauty of the place. The combination of lush nature and funky art feels magical and inspiring.

A year into living here myself, I'm still excited and awed to stroll the streets of my town, energized by the creativity.

It's a lot like life.

Jesus takes the simmering shards and broken, mismatched bits of our lives, along with the "normal," even squares and natural elements, to create something better. When these are placed in His hands, Jesus composes beautiful and enduring masterpieces that bless us and others. —ISABELLA YOSUICO

FAITH STEP: *Buy a simple mosaic stepping-stone kit. Use a permanent marker to write a word or two to represent aspects of your life on each tile or element before embedding it. Ambitious? Hunt for symbolic objects to add to your creation.*

SATURDAY, OCTOBER 19

Set a guard over my mouth, O LORD; keep watch over the door of my lips. Psalm 141:3 (NRSV)

EVER LEFT A CONVERSATION FEELING cheated because it was so one-way that you might as well have not been present? Maybe you know someone who has a habit of cutting people off midsentence so they can offer their own opinions on a subject. Or someone who rattles on with one personal story after another, without giving anyone else a chance to share. Whew! Some conversations can leave us feeling exhausted after trying so hard to jump in.

We have good reasons to ask the Lord to guard our mouths. We also have to control our mouths if we want to develop good listening skills. When we listen well to others, it communicates respect and shows them we care. Jesus demonstrated the power of being an effective listener. People felt comfortable sharing their needs and sorrows with Him: Martha and Mary after their brother, Lazarus, died and the woman cured of a long-term bleeding illness. People also felt emboldened to ask Him questions: the Samaritan woman at the well, a Jewish ruler named Nicodemus, His disciples.

Our failure to listen patiently to others can make us miss out on so much: the chance to make a new friend or deepen an existing relationship, the opportunity to encourage a fellow believer, or the chance to share Jesus with someone who needs to hear about Him. Even worse, if this inability carries over to our prayer lives, we may miss out on hearing that still, small voice. Yes, a guard over my mouth is something I need for sure. —DIANNE NEAL MATTHEWS

FAITH STEP: *How can you improve your listening skills? Ask Jesus to help you imitate Him in this area.*

SUNDAY, OCTOBER 20

Finally, all of you, be like-minded, be sympathetic, love one another, be compassionate and humble. 1 Peter 3:8 (NIV)

MY HUSBAND, DAVID, AND I are very close with an older couple in town. What started out years ago as yard work has developed into an intimate friendship, close as family. With our parents gone, I think Jesus sensed a void in our lives that needed filling. Walking their dog, watering plants, and getting together for meals has provided precious times for all of us.

Physical limitations keep them from visiting our house. Our home's entry involves a staircase, which our "adopted mom" can't maneuver. Instead, we spend hours on the phone, baring or sharing our hearts. Sometimes, conversations mimic the gripes of teenage girls; other days, the talk takes on the characteristics of a mother-daughter heart-to-heart. Either way, I'm blessed. We both are.

I bake a lot, so I'll often send cookies along when David heads over there. "Mom" always reciprocates. It's the way her generation worked. Yesterday, my husband returned home with a bag of candy. Hidden inside was something I almost didn't notice: a candy dish. White porcelain with light blue and red accents—it matched my kitchen perfectly. But "Mom" has never been in my home. When I told her how well the piece fit my décor, silence followed. For she and me, that's rare. I know we both recognized the Lord's hand in the gift.

Through this journey with them, I've come to realize that whenever relationships blossom, we delight Him. Whenever He takes an active part in deepening our friendships, He delights us. —HEIDI GAUL

FAITH STEP: *When has Jesus stepped in to enrich one or more of your friendships? Make a list including the inexplicable ways He's enhanced your relationships. Count your blessings!*

MONDAY, OCTOBER 21

Then shall the King say unto them on his right hand, Come, ye blessed of my Father, inherit the kingdom prepared for you from the foundation of the world: For I was an hungred, and ye gave me meat: I was thirsty, and ye gave me drink: I was a stranger, and ye took me in: Naked, and ye clothed me: I was sick, and ye visited me: I was in prison, and ye came unto me.
Matthew 25:34–36 (KJV)

I TEACH A LOT OF literature from the Victorian period, when the world was reeling from the publication of Darwin's theory of natural selection. People were losing their faith en masse because they could not reconcile this new science with their version of Christianity. People still struggle with a choice between science and religion, but for me that's a false choice.

I appreciate the discoveries of that time and the descriptions of what happens in the natural world. But it's a dark truth, for sure. The theory highlights the cruelty of the natural world, which is bad news for the poor, sick, very young, or elderly. Still, this truth only propels me toward God. It highlights our need to transcend natural instincts by taking a higher way.

Following Jesus means we take seriously our responsibility to eradicate suffering in the world. That's what distinguishes it from many other belief systems. Jesus inverts the idea of natural selection, calling us to deny ourselves, pick up our cross, and follow Him into soup kitchens, hospitals, prisons, and homeless shelters. Wherever people suffer—that's where Jesus leads us. And as we participate in building His kingdom, we become supernatural agents, taking on divine love that overcomes the natural way of things. —GWEN FORD FAULKENBERRY

FAITH STEP: *Where might you follow Jesus today in order to alleviate suffering? Visit your local nursing home. That's a great place to start.*

TUESDAY, OCTOBER 22

And He said to me, "My grace is sufficient for you, for My strength is made perfect in weakness." Therefore most gladly I will rather boast in my infirmities, that the power of Christ may rest upon me. 2 Corinthians 12:9 (NKJV)

I WAS RUNNING LATE ONE day for an appointment in Manhattan. After I got off the commuter train from Long Island, I hurried to the entrance of the subways and pulled out my MetroCard so I could get on the express uptown. But as I swiped my card and tried to press my way through the turnstile, it wouldn't budge. "Insufficient Funds," the screen blinked. I'd forgotten to refill my card with enough money. The folks behind me were instantly annoyed because I was holding up the line.

I eventually got to my appointment, but the whole situation made me think: what if Jesus had "insufficient" grace? We'd be in big trouble. The good news is, that will never happen. His love for us is eternal and so is His grace. As the hymn goes, "Jesus paid it all." There is no shortage of blessings, no shortage of resources, no shortage of anything. God looks at our spiritual bank accounts and they are always full, overflowing with grace—thanks to Jesus and His finished work on Calvary. Wherever we are lacking, He supplies. He fills in the gaps. —CAROL MACKEY

FAITH STEP: *What area of your life do you need Christ to fill? Ask Him to replenish it now. He has more than enough of whatever you need!*

WEDNESDAY, OCTOBER 23

Jesus said, "Father, forgive them, for they do not know what they are doing."
Luke 23:34a (NIV)

I COULD TELL FROM HIS tone that the cashier was annoyed when I set my basket in the wrong place. I apologized and moved it. When I leaned in close to read the buttons on the debit card machine, I felt him staring at me.

"It bugs me when people do that to you," my friend Julie said on the way out. "I saw a woman give you a dirty look when you accidently cut in front of her to check a price. I wanted to say, 'Can't you tell that my friend is struggling to see?'"

"Welcome to the world of the visually impaired," I said to Julie.

At first glance, people have no idea that I can't see well. I've been mistaken for aloof, unintelligent, and rude. Even people who know me have a hard time figuring out how challenged my vision is. Those who really know me are kind and supportive; the best thing I can do is forgive those who aren't and move on. Jesus has helped me realize that some strangers simply don't understand, and others simply don't want to. Still, I'm guilty of judging others superficially.

Jesus endured the ultimate cruel misunderstanding. Yet He forgave, because "they do not know what they are doing." He recognized that He'd been condemned by ignorant human beings, many of whom would later repent. When His unfathomable capacity for forgiveness sinks in, we begin to see those who've wounded us differently—as imperfect humans who just don't know. —JEANETTE HANSCOME

FAITH STEP: *When have you felt misunderstood? When have you misunderstood someone else? Ask Jesus to deepen your sensitivity for those who are different.*

THURSDAY, OCTOBER 24

Do not conform to the pattern of this world, but be transformed by the renewing of your mind. Then you will be able to test and approve what God's will is—his good, pleasing and perfect will. Romans 12:2 (NIV)

WE HAVE TWO CARS. OUR old car and our good car. Our old car is a minivan that looks like we have driven it through a war zone, and the inside smells like old cheese. Our good car is an SUV that we bought used a few years ago. It looks nice and still has a faint odor of new-care smell. Up until recently, our good car has been good. Then it wasn't.

The steering started to go all wonky. (*Wonky* is clearly a technical term.) When turning to the right, the entire car would shudder and groan. We took it to our mechanic. The suspension had to be replaced along with the wheel bearings. And yet without them, our good car wasn't any good. It couldn't function the way it was meant to function. It couldn't fulfill its purpose. Brand-new parts were in order. A full-blown auto renewal.

Likewise, we regularly need new parts on our journey of following Jesus. We may not have a steering system, so to speak. But our thoughts, our dreams, and our desires, which direct us in life, need renewing on a regular basis. Our minds need to be revamped by the power of Jesus. Without His renewal, without His truth shaping our thinking, we can't function properly. We begin to break down. We can't go where He wants us to go or be who He wants us to be without His constant care and input in our lives. We need His wisdom to show us where to go and how to live. —SUSANNA FOTH AUGHTMON

FAITH STEP: *Meditate on this verse today. What does it mean to be transformed by the renewing of your mind? Ask Jesus to renew your thinking and bring it into alignment with His good, pleasing, and perfect will.*

FRIDAY, OCTOBER 25

*It is not what goes into the mouth of a man that defiles **and** dishonors him, but what comes out of the mouth. . . . Matthew 15:11 (AMP)*

I'VE HEARD THE WARNING SEVERAL times. No smoking is allowed in the lavatories on planes. But on a recent flight, my fellow travelers and I were subjected to secondhand smoke of the *language* variety.

In that confined space of the plane's interior, we couldn't escape the foul words that lingered in the air. A plane is noisy enough in flight to cover most conversations. But the man in 11B somehow made himself heard many rows in front of and behind him.

What came out of his mouth contaminated him . . . and all those on whom his words fell. He illustrated what Jesus said in Matthew 15:11.

The verse that follows verse 11 is a curiosity to me: "Then the disciples came and said to him, 'Do you know that the Pharisees were offended when they heard this?'" (Matthew 15:12 NIV).

I can picture Jesus raising His eyebrows at that. Pharisees had a reputation for being offended by truth. In this case, it wasn't secondhand truth either. It came straight from the mouth of Jesus.

Jesus couldn't afford to worry about who He offended when He told the truth (Matthew 15:14). He was making a larger point to those who were nitpicking about eating a meal without ceremonial purification. They were focused on what they put into their mouths and unconcerned about their hearts. But their hearts were spewing foul-smelling, dangerous, soul-polluting distortions.

May what comes out of our mouths always edify and uplift others while it exalts the source of truth: Jesus. —CYNTHIA RUCHTI

FAITH STEP: *Breathe in fresh air. Now ask yourself, "Am I contributing to the sweetness of the air around me or polluting it with my words?"*

SATURDAY, OCTOBER 26

And we know that in all things God works for the good of those who love him,
who have been called according to his purpose. Romans 8:28 (NIV)

OVER MY CHRISTIAN LIFETIME, I'VE had two life verses—Bible passages I believe Jesus gave me as rudders for my spiritual journey. The first one, Proverbs 3:5–6, which tells me to "trust in the LORD" and "lean not on [my] own understanding," has guided me for a long time. An intellectual at my core, this verse reminds me there is Someone far wiser than I.

Then, when I discovered that becoming a Christian was not going to make me or my life perfect, I found the words of Romans 8:28 most comforting. Becoming a Christian didn't erase the effects of a difficult childhood either. Raised as I was in a family marred by addiction, mental illness, poverty, and isolation, Romans 8:28 has proven abundantly true. Over time, I've seen God use the very experiences that might have crushed me for my good and the good of others—including these devotionals that tap my experience to hopefully minister to someone else.

Romans 8:28 says, "*All* things God works for the good of those who love him (emphasis mine)." I've been blessed to experience this. Many times, I've glimpsed that God has even used my mistakes to bless me and others in the family of Christ. I've seen it often enough that I can entrust the murkier circumstances to Him too.

The transcendent and omnipotent God of the universe can and does use all our collective experience, and broken selves to accomplish His good purposes. As one preacher says, "God uses broken people, because broken people is all there are." —ISABELLA YOSUICO

FAITH STEP: *Troubled by a mistake you've made? Repent, if it's necessary, then entrust it to Jesus, who tells you He can use it.*

SUNDAY, OCTOBER 27

May my prayer be like special perfume before You. Psalm 141:2 (NLV)

THROUGH THE YEARS, MY UNDERSTANDING of prayer has deepened beyond my childish cries for Jesus to help me pass a test in school or convince my parents to let me date. Rather than using prayer only as a way to receive—though God's Word tells us to ask (Matthew 7:7)—I began seeing it as a gift I can give to others, but especially to Jesus.

One woman demonstrated that gift beautifully in Luke 7:38. Eager to express her love to Him, the sinful woman approached Jesus, who was eating at a table. She stooped before Him. Her prayerful tears mixed with an expensive jar of perfume that she used to wash Jesus's feet. Then she dried them with her long hair and added kisses of gratitude. Jesus immediately read the judgmental thoughts of Simon the Pharisee, his host. He rebuked Simon, but applauded the woman for her great love.

I grew excited one day when I read in Revelation 5:8 about bowls of incense holding the prayers of God's people. The sinful woman's tears mingled with her bottled perfume, a pleasing "incense" or sacrifice to Jesus. Does Jesus actually "bottle" our prayers like perfume?

Both joy and tears have accompanied my prayers: sometimes weeping over others, sometimes crying in grateful praise for Jesus's faithfulness. I've been imagining that when I enter heaven, Jesus will hand me a bottle labeled "Rebecca's perfume." If He does, I can hardly wait to kneel and pour that sweet fragrance over His feet in loving gratitude. —REBECCA BARLOW JORDAN

FAITH STEP: *Imagine your prayers are like perfume to Jesus. Give Him a gift of that "perfume" as you spend time in prayer with Him today.*

MONDAY, OCTOBER 28

Some people have gotten out of the habit of meeting for worship, but we must not do that. We should keep on encouraging each other, especially since you know that the day of the Lord's coming is getting closer. Hebrews 10:25 (CEV)

MY SISTER-IN-LAW HAS BEEN VOLUNTEERING with a Christian ministry that helps convicts transition into life outside prison. One day, as she met with inmates to help them put together résumés and ideas for future employment, one of the men looked at the name of their organization. He said, "Oh, this is the one where you have to go to church to participate, isn't it?"

My sister-in-law smiled. "No. This is the program where you *get* to go to church…a place where you meet others, find support, and can network about jobs and housing leads. And more important, this is the place where you get to hear about your Savior who loves you."

What a wonderful description! Attending church services isn't an odious requirement; it's a tremendous gift made available to us by the Body of Christ.

Fellowship can be fraught with challenges. As we gather, we find others who prefer different music or have different worship styles, and we sit with folks who have annoying coughs or screaming babies. We encounter disagreements and contrasting opinions.

Yet it's in that messy place of community that Jesus teaches us about His love and how to love others. As our voices unite in worship, He renews our strength to face our burdens, and He reminds us we aren't alone. —SHARON HINCK

FAITH STEP: *Attend church this week with the joyful anticipation of drawing closer to Jesus. As you look at the congregation, ask Him to reveal His love for each person.*

TUESDAY, OCTOBER 29

I no longer call you slaves, because a master doesn't confide in his slaves. Now you are my friends, since I have told you everything the Father told me.
John 15:15 (NLT)

"ARE YOU READY?" MY HUSBAND, Gene, asked. His folks had invited us to their home along with the rest of the immediate family, and the time had come to head their direction.

"Ready," I replied. *Ready to make a good impression, that is.*

I'd married into the family four years prior and had always felt inferior to my mother-in-law and four sisters-in-law. They held university degrees, but I held only a Bible college diploma. They had pursued careers, but I was only a stay-at-home mom. They exuded confidence, but I wrestled with insecurity.

I wanted to prove myself to them, so I'd offered to bring a homemade treat to the gathering—cinnamon buns baked in an angel food tin. Monkey bread, some folks call it.

The moment I stepped outside with my gooey masterpiece, it inexplicably rolled off its plate and under the deck. Dirt and pine needles coated it. My only recourse was to throw it in the trash.

I arrived at the party empty-handed and apologetic for not bringing the treat I'd promised, but everyone welcomed me nonetheless. Their response helped me understand that they loved me for who I was, not for what I could do.

That's a hallmark of true friendship. And it's what makes our relationship with Jesus so special. We don't need to try to impress Him with what we do. He loves us for who we are. —GRACE FOX

FAITH STEP: *Take a few moments to write either a note or an email or to phone a friend. Express your appreciation for who she or he is.*

WEDNESDAY, OCTOBER 30

O my people, trust in him at all times. Pour out your heart to him,
for God is our refuge. Psalm 62:8 (NLT)

MY TWO-YEAR-OLD GRANDDAUGHTER, LILAH, CIRCLED the living room, showing her finger to each one of us in turn. Beginning with her mommy and daddy, Lilah had six people look at her "owie." We each reacted by saying something like "Oh no!" or "I'm sorry" and maybe offering a gentle kiss. It didn't matter that there was barely anything to see on the injured finger. She had bumped it, and we were all ready to express sympathy—just as we had done the other times she exhibited an owie during our visit.

As I watched Lilah go around the room, a thought came to me: She shares her hurts so freely because she knows she is loved. And then a second thought struck me: *Am I that open with Jesus?* I know without a shadow of a doubt that He loves me—He demonstrated that when He died on the cross. But do I believe that He is concerned about every single thing that concerns me? I have to admit that sometimes I hesitate to pray about something that hurts me because it seems trivial in light of others' more urgent needs. Or maybe it's an old wound that I feel like I should have "gotten over" by now.

Life gives each one of us plenty of owies; some of the most painful ones are not seen with human eyes. Hurtful words, unfair treatment, broken relationships, disappointment over the way our lives have turned out, grief caused by the loss of a loved one. Jesus wants us to freely come to Him with all our bumps, scrapes, and bruises, regardless of whether we think they're worthy of His attention. Because to Him, they all are. —DIANNE NEAL MATTHEWS

FAITH STEP: *What's causing you pain right now? Whether it's an old or new owie, take it to Jesus and let Him express His love and concern for you.*

THURSDAY, OCTOBER 31

Not only that, but we rejoice in our sufferings, knowing that suffering produces endurance, and endurance produces character, and character produces hope. Romans 5:3–4 (ESV)

WE AMERICANS LOVE, LOVE, LOVE superheroes. Check out your local marquee any time of year and you're sure to find one or more Marvel or DC blockbusters. Kids and adults both clamor for heroics, and caped costumes sell out everywhere for Halloween. I'm a big fan too!

But most superheroes start with tragedy, disadvantage, underachievement, cowardice, or outright terror. Almost always, superheroes are broken people called to something greater than themselves. Often, we glimpse a tiny spark of greatness that will enable them to forge ahead.

I'm remembering high school lit class. In some stories, the hero's journey takes him through various difficult and often dangerous stages before he attains the prize or saves the world.

I understand that there is loving camaraderie forged in shared trials. In real life, we long for the mentor's wisdom, protection, and encouragement. We applaud the brave and noble choices. We cheer the wins along the way and the ultimate conquest.

And while we may weep at the hard circumstances that formed the hero, in real life, we want to skip that part altogether. We want to avoid the painful mess of becoming a man or woman of steel. Worse yet, we often want to avoid people in those messy stages of life.

But it's really in the mess where the hero develops his or her character, his perseverance, his hope. It doesn't always seem heroic or promising, but in Christ, it is. —ISABELLA YOSUICO

FAITH STEP: *In light of this reflection, journal your journey. Imagine you're a superhero. What's your mission? Draw or collage a picture.*

Friday, November 1

[I]f you have anything against anyone, forgive him [drop the issue, let it go], so that your Father who is in heaven will also forgive you.
Mark 11:25 (AMP)

ONE OF THE HARDEST COMMANDMENTS of Jesus, for me, is the order to forgive. Anything. Anyone. Seventy times seven. But how do we do this when whatever wrong we've suffered is raw—and our feelings still fresh? Worse yet, probably, when the other person isn't sorry?

Corrie ten Boom helped me with this when she wrote, "Forgiveness is an act of the will, and the will can function regardless of the temperature of the heart." I think the idea here is that we can separate our feelings from our wills—and sometimes we must. I tend to want to feel whatever I'm doing. To feel love when I'm supposed to be loving. To feel compassion when I'm supposed to be kind. To feel bold when I need to be brave. And it's nice when our feelings match up with our will. But it's not always going to be that way. One time, in the midst of postpartum, I didn't feel loving when my baby wanted to eat. I felt like staying in bed and sleeping. Another time, I almost threw up when I cleaned a cancer wound on my aunt's leg. I almost never feel bold when it's time to be brave. I just make myself do it anyway. Forgiveness can be like this—only harder. We feel like we cannot forgive someone who has broken our hearts. Even if they are sorry, but especially when they're not. But Jesus is greater than our feelings. He provides us the power for any commandment He gives. And often, it's the power of the will. Do what's right in your will, and eventually your feelings will follow. —GWEN FORD FAULKENBERRY

FAITH STEP: *What name comes immediately to mind when you think of forgiving? Will yourself to drop the issue you have with that person, even if the person is you. Don't worry about how you feel. For today, just forgive.*

SATURDAY, NOVEMBER 2

I thank my God upon every remembrance of you. Philippians 1:3 (NKJV)

YEARS BEFORE SHE DIED, I noticed my mom was more forgetful than normal. I'd ask her about common things, and she'd struggle to give me an answer. Or, when she did, her answers were obtuse, loopy, or just plain wrong. Then I found out the truth. What I had feared was now confirmed: Mom had dementia.

Some days, she was clear as a bell, talking, laughing, and joking just as she always did. Then other days she became combative, accusatory, and cursed up a storm. It was tough to witness. I prayed. I became sad. *Where is my mother? This woman can't be her.*

Over time, I saw her get increasingly worse, just as the doctors had predicted. My brother John turned down work to be with her because he knew her days were numbered. I lost my job seven months before Mom died, giving me more time to spend with her. But even though I knew she needed my support, I really needed hers too. I was going through a divorce, and she'd been through a divorce too. I needed her guidance. But through her illness, Jesus somehow brought us together as a family, ex-spouses included. That gave me peace. Satan is a formidable foe, and we should keep our guard up, but God has the last word, and Jesus will have the last laugh (John 12:31). I lost my mother, but was restored by the loving memories of our family reconnecting with her during that time of need. So I know that whatever the devil has stolen will be fully restored by God—possessions, health, peace, everything! He gave Job a double portion of blessings after all his losses (Job 42:10), and He's able to do the same for us all. —CAROL MACKEY

FAITH STEP: *Memories are all we have in the end. Write out some cherished ones you have with the people you love most. Save them in a special memory box.*

SUNDAY, NOVEMBER 3

It was by faith that the people of Israel marched around Jericho for seven days, and the walls came crashing down. Hebrews 11:30 (NLT)

MY HUSBAND, LARRY, AND I consider praying together for our children and grandchildren as one of our most important ministries. Every morning, we lift their names to Jesus.

One morning we used Joshua 6 and the destruction of Jericho as a prayer principle. After crossing over the Jordan River, Joshua and the Israelites faced the city of Jericho. This large city, fortified with high walls, formed a huge barrier to conquering the land God had promised them. But Joshua obeyed the Lord's instructions. The army marched around the city once a day for six days. On the seventh day, they circled seven times. On the last round, as the priests blasted their trumpets, all shouted simultaneously. At that moment, the walls collapsed.

Our grandkids were entering adolescence, so they would face walls as they tried to be faithful to Jesus. We began praying for Jesus to tear down any obstacles to their stability: insecurity, emotional imbalance, or wrong friendships. Adding another principle, from 2 Corinthians 10:4–5, we rejected our own weapon of offering unsolicited advice. Instead, we used the spiritual ammunition of faith-filled prayer, asking Jesus to destroy any "Jericho" walls or strongholds that might try to hinder our children's or our grand-children's future lives—just as He's done for us through the years.

Some barriers may require more time and patience. But in Jesus's perfect timing, what a joy it will be to see His faithfulness at work as walls come crashing down! —REBECCA BARLOW JORDAN

FAITH STEP: *Walk around your house seven times this week, as a symbolic way of asking Jesus to tear down any walls or barriers in your life—or in others' lives.*

MONDAY, NOVEMBER 4

Therefore, if anyone is in Christ, he is a new creation; old things have passed away, and look, new things have come. 2 Corinthians 5:17 (HCSB)

MY SON PIERCE'S FIRST FLORIDA basketball season was wonderful. The coach was a longtime resident and former local star, a seasoned pro who skillfully affirmed the kids, bringing out their best. He and Pierce built a nice rapport, and we looked forward to having the same coach next season.

But when the draft came around, Pierce was picked by another coach, who was just plain different than his beloved first coach. Seeing Pierce's disappointment, I tried hard to conceal my own, urging him to keep an open mind and reminding him that he'd have a lot of different coaches over time. Still, Pierce was sad and anxious about the change.

As the season went on, I made a point to avoid the subject, not wanting to pick a scab. Finally, a few weeks into the season, I asked Pierce how the new coach was working out.

"Oh, he is so great," he said with sincere enthusiasm. "He's just really nice and has taught me so much." He went on and on about his new coach's outstanding qualities and impact. Indeed, the team gelled and made it to the championship game, losing only by a few points to the reigning champions. As awesome as his former coach was, Pierce's new coach was an even better fit.

Kids deliver so many lessons! How often have I dreaded a "last season" loss and dreaded the "new season" only to find the new season was better than ever? Can I trust that Jesus knows best with matters of greater importance? Yes! —ISABELLA YOSUICO

FAITH STEP: *Are you facing a disappointing change to the unfamiliar and unexpected? Thank God for last season and trust God with your new season. In Christ, the new has come!*

TUESDAY, NOVEMBER 5

Then Jesus said, "Whoever has ears to hear, let them hear." Mark 4:9 (NIV)

YEARS AGO, WHEN I LIVED in Alaska, I knew a man named Joel. Joel was a funny, smart young man in his early twenties with Down syndrome. Joel was the kind of person you could talk to about a wide range of subjects. We loved playing cards together and laughing. He had a strong sense of right and wrong, but was also open-hearted and nonjudgmental. If a friend was crying, he would put an arm around his buddy and have him laughing soon enough.

One time, we were at an event and a local politician gave the kind of speech we've all heard before. He was saying all the right things, thanking all the right people, and making all the right promises. Joel got anxious and said loudly to me, "I don't understand what he's saying! What is he saying? I don't understand!"

I don't think Joel's lack of understanding had anything to do with his ability to interpret the words used by the politician. It's that the politician was speaking to us as constituents, not as human beings. I know Joel's heart. It doesn't know the language of agenda and insincerity. Since that day, I can distinguish between someone speaking from the heart and someone trying to manipulate me. When they do the latter, my heart says, "I don't understand!"

Joel's ears, I believe, are just the sort of ears that could really have heard and understood Jesus when He spoke. What's more, I believe that when Jesus is listening to us now, He hears like Joel. We can't glad-hand Jesus; we just have to open ourselves up to authentic connection with Him. —ELIZABETH BERNE DeGEAR

FAITH STEP: *This morning, speak to Jesus in your most authentic, honest way. Don't worry about how it sounds. Let Him hear you as you are.*

WEDNESDAY, NOVEMBER 6

In these last days he has spoken to us by his Son, whom he appointed the heir of all things, through whom also he created the world. Hebrews 1:2 (ESV)

MY HUSBAND, BILL, AND I took a spontaneous day off to visit an art museum about an hour from home. He's not the art lover in the family, but it was a togetherness opportunity, and the art museum is known for its nature/outdoors gallery displays.

Part of the traveling display section of the museum included Japanese pottery. I'm glad I wasn't the person tasked with writing descriptions of the beautiful works of art. Indescribable beauty. We marveled over the artists' skill in shaping and sculpting, and the unique glazing techniques, one glaze resembling pools of turquoise water.

One art piece caught and held my attention. The artist must have needed more than two hands to accomplish the unique shaping and overlay. Cooperative creation. What must it have been like to work that closely with a master artist to create something so beautiful?

I don't often think about the presence of Jesus at the creation of the world. But the Bible clearly tells us He was not only there but involved.

The biblical writer John says, "All things were made through [Jesus], and without [Jesus] was not any thing made that was made" (John 1:3 ESV). The Apostle Paul says, "There is but one God, the Father, from whom all things came and for whom we live; and there is but one Lord, Jesus Christ, through whom all things came and through whom we live" (1 Corinthians 8:6 NIV).

The faithfulness of God to provide a Savior-Redeemer for us through Jesus began in eternity's past and included cooperative creation of biblical proportions. Imagine! —CYNTHIA RUCHTI

FAITH STEP: *Whether it's winter or summer where you live, find something from nature today that will remind you to thank Jesus for His role in creation.*

THURSDAY, NOVEMBER 7

Dear brothers and sisters, when troubles of any kind come your way, consider it an opportunity for great joy. For you know that when your faith is tested, your endurance has a chance to grow. So let it grow, for when your endurance is fully developed, you will be perfect and complete, needing nothing.
James 1:2–4 (NLT)

JUST THIS WEEK, I FOUND out that a dear friend of mine has cancer. Another friend's child is facing a series of medical tests. And still another friend is facing great financial difficulty. These are all people who love Jesus and are doing their best to follow Him. I find myself wanting there to be some kind of immunity to life's pain for those of us who are journeying with Jesus. Instead, it seems like there are troubles at every turn. And, honestly, I am never filled with joy at the thought of myself or my friends facing trouble or suffering. I am filled with angst and worry and fear. Un-joy.

When I read in James 1 that I should consider troubles an opportunity for joy, I think, *What in the world? That makes no sense.* But lately, I have been looking at this verse differently. Life for Jesus's followers was rarely easy. There was persecution and hardship at every turn. But each trial was an opportunity to see Jesus at work. Every roadblock was a chance to see Jesus overcome and move on their behalves. Every painful experience was an invitation for Jesus to bring comfort and wholeness and healing. The joy in the midst of suffering comes because Jesus is so close to the hurting. His presence and power alone grow our faith and endurance, letting us know that we are not alone. He will never leave us or forsake us. —SUSANNA FOTH AUGHTMON

FAITH STEP: *Turn on your favorite worship music. Let it fill your spirit with the knowledge that you are not alone. Jesus can bring joy with His presence in the middle of your struggles.*

FRIDAY, NOVEMBER 8

Oh, that I had wings like a dove; then I would fly away and rest!
I would fly far away to the quiet of the wilderness. Psalm 55:6–7 (NLT)

A GIRLFRIEND RECENTLY TOLD ME about several personal storms she was experiencing: Her husband had been laid off, her daughter's marriage was about to end, a grandchild had suffered injuries in a car accident, and her sister needed help after having surgery.

"I feel like I'm in a storm with gale-force winds and mile-high waves," she said. "I wish I could just get on a plane and escape for a little while."

David felt the same way after running from Saul and his henchmen. Today's verse gives us a peek at how he wished he could escape the melee and find a sanctuary for his soul.

I identify with the longing for calm and silence, and I suspect you can too. Sometimes life gets crazy. Too many voices shout for our attention. We lack adequate sleep. We feel the weight of our burdens and the burdens that others carry too. Most of us don't have the luxury of flying away to escape the pressure. But we can all escape the stress for a few minutes each day by sitting in quietness, alone with Jesus.

When I feel battle-weary, I retreat to a black leather love seat in my family room. I invite Jesus's presence into that place. Then I open my Bible and ask Him to speak the words He knows I need to hear. Meeting with Jesus in the quiet of that place refreshes me and restores my soul. —GRACE FOX

FAITH STEP: *Do you have a special place where you can retreat for spiritual renewal? If not, prepare an inviting space that offers an atmosphere of peace.*

SATURDAY, NOVEMBER 9

And when you pray, do not keep on babbling like pagans, for they think they will be heard because of their many words. Do not be like them, for your Father knows what you need before you ask him. Matthew 6:7–8 (NIV)

I WAS EXHAUSTED AFTER I finished an editing job for a client who was also a friend. Because of my health issues, the project had taken a lot out of me. Still, I savored doing meaningful work and earning a bit of money. As I prepared to email her my notes and invoice, I realized it was her birthday. I felt a quiet nudge from Jesus to offer the work as a gift. So I did. However, I admit that, afterward, I had a grumpy conversation with Jesus, reminding Him that I don't have many opportunities for a paycheck.

A few days later, a different friend stopped by my house. She'd asked to pick up a set of my novels to give as a gift. While I signed the books for her son, she opened her purse. I started to tell her the cost of the books, but she handed me a check. "I filled this out before I came. I gave you a little extra as a present."

My mouth gaped, and then tears filled my eyes. Her check covered the cost of the books plus almost the full amount of the edit job I'd given away. I hugged her and explained my emotional reaction.

Through her gift, Jesus reassured me that He can provide in unexpected ways. He knew my need for income, but He also knew that I needed to practice my generosity. He knew that my first friend needed a birthday gift and that my second friend enjoyed the blessing of giving. He worked His purposes for all three of us in a beautiful circle of provision. —SHARON HINCK

FAITH STEP: *Dare to give a generous gift today, and thank Jesus for all His gifts.*

SUNDAY, NOVEMBER 10

*When you search for me, you will find me; if you seek me with all your heart,
I will let you find me, says the LORD. Jeremiah 29:13–14 (NRSV)*

I ONCE HEARD A MAN say that his faith would be much stronger if he had lived during the time Jesus walked the earth and had seen Him in the flesh. The Bible talks about many people whose lives were transformed after seeing Jesus face-to-face. A short tax collector named Zacchaeus climbed a sycamore to get a look at Jesus and became a changed man. When Thomas saw the resurrected Jesus, he was awestruck with the understanding that Jesus was his Lord and Messiah.

On the other hand, most of the people who were acquainted with Jesus on earth misunderstood Him because they looked at Him from a human perspective. And the Pharisees and religious leaders, in particular, usually failed to see Who Jesus was; even when He stood in front of them, speaking God's truth and trying to open their eyes.

Today, we have advantages that people living in biblical times lacked, including the entire Bible to show us Jesus. He's pictured in the Old Testament sacrifices and festivals, as well as in the symbolism behind every object in the Tabernacle and, later, the Temple. Not to mention the Gospel accounts of His years of public ministry and teaching.

We know Jesus is all around us. We see Him in the life of someone whose demeanor and lifestyle He has transformed. Or in the godly actions of individuals wholeheartedly serving Him or accomplishing things they could do only through His supernatural power. If we want to see Jesus more clearly, all we have to do is look for where He is working and join in. Then others will see Jesus in us. —DIANNE NEAL MATTHEWS

FAITH STEP: *How will you look for Jesus today?*

MONDAY, NOVEMBER 11

But rejoice insofar as you share Christ's sufferings, that you may also rejoice and be glad when his glory is revealed. 1 Peter 4:13 (ESV)

I GET PUMPED BY MILITARY recruiting commercials that show the buff and burly soldiers pushing through the pain to save a beachhead, dodging bullets to rescue a fellow soldier, or leaping from helicopters into churning dark waters at night. And I did like to see G.I. Jane defy the odds with mental toughness.

Many of us are inspired by such campaigns. Even bookish, artsy types like me might be tempted to sign on for a tour of duty.

Countless movies testify to the idea that overcoming pain for glory is intoxicating and appealing to the sleeping hero inside us.

But what about spiritual heroism? What if the cost of God using us mightily is pain?

I mean, really. Who *wants* to share in Christ's sufferings?

Here, Paul puts it bluntly, there's no room for misunderstanding. The apostles' stories bear this out: they all died for their faith. Pain is the price of admission.

The great assurance we enjoy is eternal glory and a life full of impact and purpose.

Suffering isn't always heroic, but suffering for Christ can bear fruit that lasts a lifetime this side of heaven and for eternity and beyond.
—ISABELLA YOSUICO

FAITH STEP: *Can you think of a situation in which someone you know revealed God's glory through their suffering? How about you?*

TUESDAY, NOVEMBER 12

When Joshua was near Jericho, he looked up and saw a man standing in front of him with a drawn sword in His hand. Joshua approached Him and asked, "Are You for us or for our enemies?" "Neither," He replied. "I have now come as commander of the LORD's army." Joshua 5:13–14 (HCSB)

MY FRIEND CORRIE RADKE HAS a blog called *Choosing Colorful*. There's an entry there with the title "God Is Not on My Side." In it, Corrie writes, "When we claim to be on God's side, we're announcing that we've arrived at the spot where we are no longer in need of revelation and that means we're attempting to be like God."

I agree with this. Corrie references the story of Jonah to illustrate her point, but I kept thinking of Joshua and his meeting with the man we understand to be Jesus. Joshua's first question when he met Him was, "Whose side are you on?" And, essentially, Jesus told him, "I'm on my own side." This is the point of Corrie's essay—that God is on His own side. Never ours. If we happen to get it right, we may find ourselves on His side and, of course, that's great. But we should never assume He's on ours.

There's great freedom in this, I believe, because it takes the focus off ourselves and turns it to Jesus. I find when I come back to Him and try to align my views with Him, I end up on the side of love every time. And it makes sense if you think about it. God is love.

—GWEN FORD FAULKENBERRY

FAITH STEP: *The next time you find yourself defending a position you believe is right, ask yourself, is it more important for me to be right or to love?*

WEDNESDAY, NOVEMBER 13

Then the master said to the servant, "Go out into the highways and hedges, and compel them to come in, that my house may be filled." Luke 14:23 (NKJV)

WHEN I FIRST BECAME A Christian, I could barely contain my excitement about my newfound faith. I read my Bible every day without fail, prayed fervently, and was in church almost every time the doors were open. I was on fire for the Lord. I loved Him and wanted others to love Him too. At the time, I worked at a major newspaper where I found other Christians to fellowship with; we even had a weekly Bible study during lunchtime. But one of the most fulfilling experiences early in my faith was sharing Jesus with nonbelievers. Most of these folks were not hostile toward the Gospel; they had just never heard it. They had no idea who Jesus was beyond the baby in the manger.

My job was my mission field, and there were plenty of souls ripe for the harvest. But I really invested my time and effort in the single mothers. I had been an unmarried mother myself, and I had a heart for them. Although my son's father was in his life and we later married, I understood the challenges they faced. My story and my walk with Jesus, I liked to think, helped those ladies, and that means something to me. Jesus wants us to share the Good News with everyone in our circle. He has many children, but He wants them all to know how much He loves them! So He's counting on us to fulfill the Great Commission (Matthew 28:19–20).
—CAROL MACKEY

FAITH STEP: *Is there someone in your everyday life who doesn't know Jesus's love? Invite them to church. Some people may feel uneasy at first about being in a formal congregation. If that's the case, invite them to an informal church event—a picnic, potluck, or retreat.*

THURSDAY, NOVEMBER 14

And what pity he felt for the crowds that came, because their problems were so great and they didn't know what to do or where to go for help.
Matthew 9:36 (TLB)

As I LOADED MY GROCERIES on the conveyor belt and then prepared to pay, the employee bagging my groceries started what soon become a study in patience. Mine.

The employee pitched nonstop questions, each one punctuated by a high-pitched giggle. "Do you want the carton of eggs bagged separately?" "Is it okay if I put both packages of hamburger in one bag?" "Where do you want me to put your canned goods?" *In a bag.*

The checkout clerk had obviously worked with this employee before. The clerk sighed. Loudly. The others in line behind me did too. The process was taking four times longer than it should have.

Normally, my nature would have been to join the sighers, but something about the look in the bagger's face made me rein in my irritation.

What was the response Jesus had to people like the store employee who was so unsure of herself?

He had pity. Compassion. As the Living Bible expresses in Matthew 9:36, He was moved over their plight, "because their problems were so great and they didn't know what to do or where to go for help."

Nothing in my life was more important in that grocery store moment than showing compassion like Jesus would. Now to work on making that my default response. —CYNTHIA RUCHTI

FAITH STEP: *Will your path cross a store employee's or coworker's today? If so, in honor of the compassion Jesus shows, watch for a way you can reflect His nature in your interactions. You may never know the difference you can make.*

FRIDAY, NOVEMBER 15

"Father, if you are willing, please take this cup of suffering away from me. Yet I want your will to be done, not mine." Luke 22:42 (NLT)

THE SUBJECT LINE OF THE email grabbed my attention. "How do we pray about our chronic illness?" A reader had reached out to me for guidance.

I know how to pray when there is a short-term need, and Jesus either provides the answer, guides in a tangible way, or makes clear His answer is no. Then I trust and let go. But what about long-term issues? Chronic illness, estranged family members, injustices, financial struggles that endure year after year. How do I continue in prayer?

As I answered the email, I thought about ways Jesus has guided my prayers in recent years. We know that He invites us to pray persistently. He gives us the example of the widow pestering the unjust judge in Luke 18. But there are many ways He may steer our prayers.

When a struggle continues, we can ask for grace to endure the next day, or hour, or minute. We can also invite His glorious presence into our painful midst. As we focus beyond our personal needs, we can support others in similar struggles by interceding and praying beyond ourselves. And we can pray with thanksgiving.

No matter how difficult the ongoing trial, I can give thanks for little blessings all around. A soft pillow, the view of swaying tree branches through my window, and meaningful emails from readers. And after giving thanks, I can offer the powerful prayer Jesus modeled in Gethsemane.

Like Jesus, we can surrender our longings to the Father and pray, "Not my will, but Thine be done." —SHARON HINCK

FAITH STEP: *Think about an ongoing need. Pray about it persistently, ask for grace to endure until the answer comes, ask that Jesus will be glorified in the situation, intercede for others, and pray with thanksgiving.*

SATURDAY, NOVEMBER 16

Therefore, if anyone is in Christ, the new creation has come:
The old has gone, the new is here! 2 Corinthians 5:17 (NIV)

THIS WEEKEND MY HUSBAND, DAVID, and I took a drive to the coast. As the day wore on, the weather grew chilly, so after lunch we searched for indoor pastimes. Cruising along a winding tree-lined lane, we spotted a glass-art gallery. The wooden building itself was whimsical, with oddly shaped windows and painted like a gingerbread house. David and I exchanged glances, parked the car, and entered.

The artist, an older man with a relaxed manner, stood in the center of a popular shop, surrounded by a large group of people. All of us listened, rapt, as he walked us through the many steps required to make a blown-glass orb. His work was obviously that of a master. The globes were beautiful, their colors bright and well formed. Vases, trays, jewelry, and bowls also filled the shop.

One image stayed with me for the rest of the day. The glassblower shared a curious fact for the children watching: he said that all glass pieces start out as sand.

As we traveled home, I reflected on how the artist's words rang true for believers. Before I knew Jesus, I was nothing more than dust. But through His love, He changed me. Much like the artist with the beautiful orbs, our Lord stayed with me as I endured the fires of life, and when I was refined enough to bend to His will, He molded my spirit into someone new. I am one of Christ's masterpieces, a reflection of the love and patience He's shown all of us. May I reflect His light well. —HEIDI GAUL

FAIT STEP: *Look at different glass items you have in your home, each one different yet special to you. Think of their humble starts—and yours—and give thanks for the changes Jesus has made in you.*

Sunday, November 17

But to you who are willing to listen, I say, love your enemies! Do good to those who hate you. Bless those who curse you. Pray for those who hurt you.
Luke 6:27–28 *(NLT)*

WHEN MY SISTER AND DAD heard the same radio sermon separately and felt prompted to pray for my former husband, I knew I should do the same. I confess that I fought the side of me that felt justified in leaving him off my prayer list. He'd abandoned me and our sons and caused a lot of pain. But in my sister's recap of the sermon, she'd reminded me that he'd made choices that would reap consequences and that he needed Jesus's help. So I prayed.

Several months later, someone's comments left me wounded.

You need to pray for her, I sensed Jesus telling me.

But she was horrible to me!

"Pray for those who hurt you," remember?

Again, I fought. *This is not the first time she has been mean.*

I began to pray for some areas of her life that I knew were difficult, and my heart began to soften.

It's easy to pray for those we love, but Jesus asked His followers to pray for those who've abused, betrayed, or been unkind to us or to others. It's hard to understand, but He was willing to do it, so why not us? As a dear friend reminded me, "It's hard to hate someone when you're praying for them." Praying for difficult people reminds me that they are humans with needs, who act the way they do for reasons that only Jesus fully understands. —JEANETTE HANSCOME

FAITH STEP: *Who would you consider your enemy? Take a moment to pray for this person. If you find it difficult, ask Jesus to bring a specific need to mind.*

MONDAY, NOVEMBER 18

Before the mountains were born, before you gave birth to the earth and the world, from beginning to end, you are God. Psalm 90:2 (NLT)

MY SON MATTHEW AND HIS wife dropped in one morning while running errands. Over homemade muffins and freshly brewed coffee, they told me and my husband, Gene, about visiting Victoria, British Columbia, for their tenth wedding anniversary two weeks prior. Then came the news we expected—someday—but hoped we'd never hear.

"We've always talked about moving to Vancouver Island, and we've decided that now's the time," said Matthew. "We've looked at houses with a real estate agent and found one we like. If my boss will allow me to work remotely from home, then we'll sell our house and go."

I genuinely felt happy for them as they pursued their dream. At the same time, I felt like crying. His boss eventually said yes, which means my seven grandchildren no longer live within a distance that allows us to babysit and attend ball games, ballet recitals, and birthday parties. Now, they live a five-hour drive and a two-hundred-dollar ferry ride away.

This recent change has been difficult, but Jesus has grown more precious to me through it. Each time my heart misses this family, I call on Him and He reassures me of His sovereignty in both their lives and mine. He's even given me peace on those special occasions we can no longer celebrate with them.

Change happens, but Jesus remains the same from beginning to end. He's sovereign and faithful no matter what changes we encounter. Remembering that He remains constant even though our lives feel disrupted makes the experience easier to accept. —GRACE FOX

FAITH STEP: *Memorize Hebrews 13:8—"Jesus is the same yesterday, today, and forever." Thank Him for being your solid Rock, unchanging and immovable.*

TUESDAY, NOVEMBER 19

He decreed statutes for Jacob and established the law in Israel, which he commanded our ancestors to teach their children, so the next generation would know them, even the children yet to be born, and they in turn would tell their children. Then they would put their trust in God and would not forget his deeds but would keep his commands. Psalm 78:5–7 (NIV)

MY HUSBAND SCOTT'S FAMILY TREE can be traced back three generations to Southampton, England. His mom's cousin sent him a newspaper clipping telling him about how his family members had paid for the stained glass windows in a chapel there. He has since learned that another relative was an Anglican priest. He had no idea that he had come from a long line of pastors. He'd thought he was the first. I am a third-generation pastor's wife. I didn't set out to be one. I just really liked Scott a lot, and he happened to be a youth pastor at the time.

How is it that these generational patterns repeat themselves? How does that work?

It's not a coincidence that tendencies are passed down from one generation to the next. I know that Scott's ancestors and my ancestors prayed on our behalves. Their choices affected our lives before we were born. They lived their lives in a way that honored Jesus and, in turn, laid the foundation for us to build a relationship with Him.

I didn't know my great-grandparents, but I have heard stories of their faith. Just like their genes have shaped me, so have the stories of their belief in Jesus. When we decide to follow Jesus, we are shaping not only our future, but future generations. *Isn't that amazing?* Our prayers for them will echo throughout history and link them to Jesus, the One Who loves them most of all. —SUSANNA FOTH AUGHTMON

FAITH STEP: *Write out a prayer of blessing for your future descendants. Ask Jesus to lay the foundation for a strong faith in Him in their lives.*

WEDNESDAY, NOVEMBER 20

For God has not given us a spirit of fear, but of power and of love and of a sound mind. 2 Timothy 1:7 (NKJV)

MY MOM TOLD ME I had the ability to talk using somewhat proper sentence structure when I was only eighteen months of age. To this day, I credit her for my expansive vocabulary and love of reading. But walking was another thing. "She just won't let go," my mom would say, shaking her head, when her friends asked why I couldn't walk without clutching the furniture or holding tightly on to someone's hand. My fear of falling was greater than the joy of independence. Eventually, I did let go and experienced the freedom that comes with independent mobility.

Years later, I thought about my challenge as a toddler, and the disciple Peter immediately came to mind. When Jesus summoned him to join Him on the dark, murky waters, Peter didn't hesitate. He had no fear. "So He said, 'Come.' And when Peter had come down out of the boat, he walked on the water to go to Jesus" (Matthew 14:29). Peter didn't question Jesus or waffle about whether the water was too deep, too cold, or just plain scary. He took a leap of faith. And whatever fears he had disappeared when he saw the Lord's outstretched hand.

Jesus is calling us to do things we could never imagine ourselves doing—if only we conquer our fears. I know the spirit of fear is not by His design. We overcome through His love. What are your fears? Starting a business? Flying in an airplane? Writing a book? Whatever they are, know that Jesus is at the end of it, saying "Come" with outstretched arms. —CAROL MACKEY

FAITH STEP: *Admit your fear to a prayer partner and ask him or her to pray that Jesus help you conquer it. It may take time, but remember He is with you every step of the way.*

THURSDAY, NOVEMBER 21

If we live, we live for the Lord; and if we die, we die for the Lord. So, whether we live or die, we belong to the Lord. Romans 14:8 (NIV)

I RECENTLY VISITED AN OLD friend, a former professor of mine who just turned ninety. A classmate alerted me that he was very sick. She knew I would want to say good-bye.

My teacher hugged me when I stepped through the door. I could feel his bones. His hands shook while we sat across from each other in his living room visiting. One of the things we talked about is how strange it is to interface with death for a long period of time and what it does to your psyche. "I never planned for this," he said of hospital visits, loss of appetite, and loss of strength. "It's like my body betrays me."

On the drive home, I thought about how hard that must be—dying—and how I haven't planned for it either. I'm focused on living life to the fullest, on all the things I want to accomplish and do and be. The visit with my teacher made me think about how I want to die well whenever that time comes.

We make our plans, but Paul said that, in a sense, it's all the same. If we live, we live for Jesus, and if we die, we die for Him—it all belongs to Him. That's a comfort if I let it be. All that my life is, all I accomplish or don't, belongs to Him. It is Jesus Who infuses it with meaning. Not the doing or the being. And death also finds meaning in Him. Whatever happens, He is with me. I belong to Him. —GWEN FORD FAULKENBERRY

FAITH STEP: *What does it mean to you to belong to Jesus? Do a word study on* belong. *Write down any new insights that come to you.*

FRIDAY, NOVEMBER 22

"I am the bread of life," Jesus told them. "No one who comes to Me will ever be hungry, and no one who believes in Me will ever be thirsty again."
John 6:35 *(HCSB)*

MY TEN-YEAR-OLD SON IS A serious fan of Stephen Curry, the basketball star. As far as sports heroes go, "Steph," as he is widely known, is a fine choice. He's a Christian from a strong family, so I don't really object to my son's starry-eyed obsession.

Steph is often shown chewing on his mouthguard, worn by players to protect their teeth. My son *had* to have one. After hearing him out, I encouraged him to use some birthday money to buy it.

We went to a sporting goods store and stood before rows of mouthguard, dumbfounded by the assortment. It took him nearly twenty minutes to choose one. Then I had to hold him back from tearing it open before leaving the store.

Once it was out of the package, my son proudly placed it in his mouth, faking a few shots for effect. After a minute, he spat it out. "It's kind of hard to breathe," he remarked.

He carefully read the molding instructions, then set it down. I offered to help him, but he wandered off. "Maybe later."

A week later, and the must-have mouthguard was still on my kitchen counter, unused.

I've traveled the same road myself. A better job, a new house, that special vacation...all seemed to promise fulfillment, but never did.

Jesus tells us He is the only One Who can truly satisfy. When I bring my worldly wants to Him, I find the hunger and thirst are less urgent. —ISABELLA YOSUICO

FAITH STEP: *Is there a nonessential item you're longing for? Pray for guidance to jot down three words the item really represents.*

SATURDAY, NOVEMBER 23

And he said to them, "O foolish ones, and slow of heart to believe all that the prophets have spoken! Was it not necessary that the Christ should suffer these things and enter into his glory?" And beginning with Moses and all the Prophets, he interpreted to them in all the Scriptures the things concerning himself. Luke 24:25–27 (ESV)

WITH THE GRANDCHILDREN LIVING IN our home this year, I often fight back giggles when bizarre issues trigger a meltdown. At dinnertime, my granddaughter has been driven to tears when the zucchini touches the mushrooms or when she's given the Cinderella spoon instead of the Minnie Mouse spoon. My grandson may scream because the toast on Mommy's plate is better than the toast on his.

My son and daughter-in-law are endlessly patient. They respond with compassion, even as they offer the children a new perspective.

The men on the road to Emmaus suffered from a limited perspective as well. Jesus may well have hidden a rueful smile as they moaned about everything that had gone wrong. He had every reason to tell them they were being foolish and slow to believe. Yet, after that gentle rebuke, He went on to explain why the situation the men believed was intolerable was instead part of His plan.

I'm sure there are times I seem like a pouty toddler to Jesus. I'm unreasonable about things that don't go my way. I'm frustrated by limitations. I'm fearful or angry when my little world feels out of control. But if parents can be patient with their child's immature reactions, I know He can be even more patient with me. When I'm in despair and missing the big picture, I ask Jesus to open my eyes to His presence, just as He did for the men on the Emmaus road. —SHARON HINCK

FAITH STEP: *Next time you see a toddler having a meltdown, thank Jesus for His endless patience with our own immature and foolish moments.*

SUNDAY, NOVEMBER 24

The third time he said to him, "Simon son of John, do you love me?"
Peter was hurt because Jesus asked him the third time, "Do you love me?"
He said, "Lord, you know all things; you know that I love you." Jesus
said, "Feed my sheep." John 21:17 (NIV)

THE STORY OF JESUS ASKING Peter to feed His sheep makes me think. I understand this disciple's trials and the failures that darken his testimony. Despite my usual boldness, there have been times I've also denied my faith. And the shame hurts.

As an inspirational writer, I depend on God to provide me with words for my craft, thoughts that encourage other Christians and bring them closer to Jesus. Sometimes sentences flow easily; other times, I need to yank them from thin air.

This week, I received a rejection on a project dear to my heart. The hurt caused me to question if Jesus wanted me in this field—otherwise, why wasn't it easier? Like Peter abandoning his calling to return to fishing, I considered going back to optometry.

But just as the other disciples rallied around Peter, so did my friends cheer me forward. Through loved ones, Jesus told me to try one more time.

I'm learning that when I cast my nets where the Lord wants them, they come back full. And that when Jesus asks if I love Him, He already knows the answer. He's only reminding me that if I love Him, my focus should be on others, not myself. I like to think that, through my writing, I am feeding His sheep.

Whatever title He's given me, I'm honored. Because Jesus trusts me with His work. —HEIDI GAUL

FAITH STEP: *Participate in a mission you've felt drawn to, but hesitated over. Cast your nets in a new direction and watch Jesus fill them. Feed His sheep!*

MONDAY, NOVEMBER 25

Yes, the LORD pours down his blessings. Psalm 85:12 (NLT)

WHEN I VISITED MY DAUGHTER's family for the Thanksgiving holiday just before Lilah's second birthday, I enjoyed seeing her progress in language. The first morning, Lilah woke up around five and I sat in the kitchen as Holly gave her a prebreakfast ahead of the big family one. When Holly set a plastic bowl on the table, Lilah turned to me with her fine, blonde, bedhead hair sticking out and her big, brown eyes shining. "Bowl!" she shouted. Her mom poured the Rice Krispies. Lilah raised her little arms and shouted to me, "Ceeweal!" Followed by "Moolk!" and "Poon!"

Even as I laughed at Lilah's excitement, which seemed out of proportion to me, my heart felt full. Such purity in her expression of joy. Such simple gratitude. I thought about how my thanksgiving often includes qualifiers: *Lord, thank You for my family, but I wish we weren't so scattered.... Thank You for this house we found in our new location, but now we could really use some new furniture.... I praise You for the job my son found, but at his age he needs benefits....*

I wondered if it would be possible to regain that childlike attitude of simple joy, enthusiasm, and gratitude that Lilah displayed. To smile at Jesus and acknowledge His blessings as I see evidences of His goodness. Friendship! Protection! Forgiveness! Love!

One morning, I found the experiment easy to do. I was exhausted after waking up at 3:00 a.m. because of a sleep disorder, and my brain seemed able to think only one-word thoughts. *Robe! Coffee! Sunrise!...Nap?* I discovered that even one word is still enough to acknowledge blessings from above. —DIANNE NEAL MATTHEWS

FAITH STEP: *Stop periodically throughout your day and offer a one-word exclamation of praise to Jesus for His blessings and what He means to you.*

TUESDAY, NOVEMBER 26

Once Jesus was in a certain place praying. As he finished, one of his disciples came to him and said, "Lord, teach us to pray, just as John taught his disciples." Luke 11:1 (NLT)

A FAMILY PHOTOGRAPH PRINTED ON canvas rests on the mantel in our family room. Each time I look at it, I whisper a prayer for my kids' and grandchildren's well-being. I long for loving and healthy relationships for all my relatives—parents to grown children and their spouses, sibling to sibling, aunts and uncles to nieces and nephews, and grandparents to grandchildren.

One day, I gazed upon that photograph, appreciating its artistic presentation as well as the people in it, and said, "Jesus, teach me how to pray for my family." Instantly this came to me: *Father, paint what You want our relationships to look like on the canvas of their hearts.* Several insights followed.

First, Jesus is the Master Artist, and I am not. He doesn't need me to tell Him what to do. He does, however, want me to surrender my brush and let Him do His job.

Second, the finished product—and perhaps even the process—will no doubt look different than what I think it should. That's okay because the Master Artist is much more skilled than I am.

Third, a masterpiece takes time.

Finally, if the Master Artist gazes at the canvas of my family's hearts and smiles at the finished product, that's enough for me.

The disciples got it right when they asked Jesus to teach them to pray. He did the same for me, and my prayer life will never be the same. —GRACE FOX

FAITH STEP: *Are you unsure about how to pray for loved ones? Ask Jesus to teach you. Listen for His response and write it down.*

WEDNESDAY, NOVEMBER 27

How could we sing a song about the Eternal in a land so foreign, while still tormented, brokenhearted, homesick? *Psalm 137:4 (VOICE)*

BELIEVING THAT OUR JOY IS connected to our circumstances can cause serious discouragement and wrong perspectives. Some of the Jews experienced that during their seventy years in Babylonian captivity. Psalm 137 records their memories of that time as they gathered by the river as prisoners. They had hung their harps on the willow trees, convinced they had no song to sing. Looking back, they lamented the painful events, times when their captors would mock them, calling for happy songs. But their music was lost in their depression and sorrow. What could they possibly sing about during this dark time of their history?

Fast-forward a few centuries later to the Apostle Paul in prison. His circumstances were anything but perfect. Like the Jewish captives, he too felt tormented, brokenhearted, and homesick at times. Yet nothing could silence the music of his heart that had begun the moment he said yes to Jesus. In fact, as he sang one night, Jesus sent an earthquake, shaking the prison doors open (Acts 16:25–28).

Perhaps, Paul had learned a lesson long forgotten by the Jews in captivity. Joy has more to do with our heart beliefs than our outer circumstances. I've uttered many complaints myself. No matter where I am or whatever difficulties I experience, I want to keep on singing the song Jesus has planted in my heart. —REBECCA BARLOW JORDAN

FAITH STEP: *Draw a smiley face and place it where you'll see it often. Thank Jesus that nothing can silence His song in your heart.*

THURSDAY, NOVEMBER 28

God sets the lonely in families, he leads out the prisoners with singing.
Psalm 68:6 *(NIV)*

I KNEW MY FRIEND SUSAN'S family loved food, but when I arrived at their home and looked at the spread, I understood how deep their love of cooking and eating truly went. Several hours later, we sat around the table playing their favorite game, Mexican Train Dominoes. I'd never felt so stuffed in my life.

It was my first Thanksgiving as a single mom, and the first that my sons would spend without their dad. I could easily remember the 2011 holiday as sad, but whenever I think about that particular Thanksgiving, I remember it as a day when I felt as filled up with love as by delicious food. It was one of many reminders that, though my family would never be the same again, we still had many reasons to be grateful. We had friends, who in so many ways reflected the love of Jesus. They welcomed us, filled us up, and showed us that we weren't alone. No matter what happened, we would always have a family.

Susan's family was one of several in our church who had embraced me and my boys that year and filled our lives with blessings at a time when, on the surface, our world looked far from blessed. Through them, we learned that family has more to do with love and the bond we share through Jesus than bloodlines and last names.

I remain thankful for that time spent with those who reminded me that, in Jesus, we are always welcome and loved. —JEANETTE HANSCOME

FAITH STEP: *Do you know anyone who doesn't have a family to celebrate Thanksgiving with? Invite them to join your celebration. If you don't have anyone local to invite, send cards to faraway friends who are having a difficult time this holiday season.*

Friday, November 29

He gave. 1 Timothy 2:6 (NLT)

Overheard at a local store:

> Woman: "We're not going to give our grandson a gaming system for his birthday without games to play on it."
> Man: "You did look at the price tag of this thing, didn't you?"
> Woman: "No one's saying they're not expensive. But if he has the system and no games..."
> Man: "Well, maybe he'll have to wait until Christmas for a game."

I walked away before I heard the conclusion of their discussion. But I didn't go away empty. My heart was full of gratitude for the generosity of Jesus, so unlike the grandfather who would have been content to give a partial gift because of the cost.

Jesus gave beyond what was expected. And He still does.

In 1 Timothy 2:6, we read that Jesus gave Himself as a ransom for all. He gave himself as Living Water so the thirsty would never thirst again. He gave Himself as Living Bread so the hungry would never hunger again. He gave previously skunked fishermen so many fish that their nets bulged and broke with the weight of their haul. He gave enough food to the crowd listening to Him that all were satisfied and the scraps left over filled not a dustpan but twelve overflowing baskets.

He gave the blind man his sight...and a mission in life.

Jesus gave us the promise of eternal life, but even more than that, He opened the "wallet" of heaven's treasures and offered us abundant life for here and now.

Jesus-generosity. Unequaled. —Cynthia Ruchti

Faith Step: *In what area of your life have you been giving barely enough? Tips? Service? Caregiving? Consider today your first day of living Jesus-generous.*

SATURDAY, NOVEMBER 30

*The eternal God is your refuge, And underneath **are** the everlasting arms. Deuteronomy 33:27 (NKJV)*

THREE YEARS AGO, MY DEAR friend Janelle's son had a freak accident on his all-terrain vehicle that crushed his leg. He spent much of fifth grade in a wheelchair, enduring multiple surgeries and undergoing therapy to get him back on his feet. Finally he healed, and he had seemed well until an infection manifested in the leg this year. Eighth grade for him meant he had to wear a PICC line everywhere he went—a special catheter that infused antibiotics directly to his heart.

Now lab work shows the infection is gone. God only knows whether there might be microbes hiding down in the tissue; no one else can know for sure. It's up to Janelle and her husband to choose whether to remove the PICC line now or wait—basically a leap of faith.

I asked her how she was doing, and I wanted to say Jesus would make it all better. *Just pray, and you will know the answer and everything will be great because Jesus loves you.* But those clichés we pass around are really half-truths at best, aren't they? I believe with all my heart that Jesus loves us. The rest? Anybody's guess.

Here's what I said instead: *I can't tell you or myself that leaping in faith means we'll never fall. I hope every last bacterium has breathed its last, but the truth we both know is that we don't know. What I do know from experience is that underneath us are the everlasting arms. Jesus helps us face whatever comes. He gives us grace for the moment we're in.*

This is not all we'd ask for if we're honest. But it's enough. Jesus is enough, come what may. His grace is sufficient for us.
—GWEN FORD FAULKENBERRY

FAITH STEP: *Write down Deuteronomy 33:27—the part of it quoted above—and commit it to memory. Let it help you rest your heart in His faithful love.*

SUNDAY, DECEMBER 1

The people who walked in darkness have seen a great light; those who dwelt in a land of deep darkness, on them has light shone. Isaiah 9:2 (ESV)

I LOVE THE SYMBOLS WE use during Advent and Christmas. Each year, our family sets up an Advent wreath. The circle shape represents the gift of eternity that is given to us because of Jesus. The evergreen boughs remind us that the love of Jesus is constant, endures, and is for all seasons. And each candle represents a specific part of the blessing of the Incarnation.

When we light the first candle, on the first Sunday in Advent, we call it the prophecy or "hope" candle. Everything recorded in the Old Testament prophesied the coming of Emmanuel, who would bring light into our darkness.

The flickering glow of that first candle stirs our hope. The Light has come, dwells with us, and will come again.

Advent is an interesting time of waiting for something that we already know has happened: Jesus's birth. We also look ahead to His return. As we find the prophecies that pointed to His birth, we also find Scripture that hints at the end of the story. Just as Israel eagerly waited for their Messiah, we eagerly wait for Christ's return at the end of time. While we wait, we are comforted by the light He brings into our daily lives. His presence with us casts aside the shadows of sin, fear, and doubt. His example kindles the flame of faith in our hearts. His grace warms and changes our hearts so that we can offer love to others in His name. —SHARON HINCK

FAITH STEP: *Create an Advent wreath—a drawing on a paper placemat, or a ring of small candles in holders, or a traditional one from a store—embellished with pine boughs. Light (or color in) the first candle and thank Jesus for being the promised Light.*

MONDAY, DECEMBER 2

And having come in, the angel said to her, "Rejoice, highly favored one, the Lord is with you; blessed are you among women!" Luke 1:28 (NKJV)

HAVING CHILDREN IS A BLESSING. There is also no greater responsibility, but there's no greater joy. Although my two sons are grown men in their thirties, I still worry if they're eating properly, if they put their seat belts on, and if the women they are dating are good people. At times they resent my intrusion, but I don't care. You never stop being a mom, no matter how old they are.

In my heart, I feel that I was chosen to be mother to my sons and that we were meant to be a family. When God chose Mary as mother of the Savior of the world, He didn't just choose any woman. He chose a godly young woman, a virgin, due to wed an upstanding man named Joseph. I've imagined how Mary felt when the angel of the Lord appeared to her saying, "Rejoice, highly favored *one*, the Lord *is* with you; blessed *are* you among women!" I think I would have fainted! But it was an honor that would be bestowed upon only one woman: Mary. The New Testament doesn't speak much about Mary, but we know one thing. Jesus loved Mary. As He lay dying on the cross, He turned to the disciple John and said, "'Behold your mother!' And from that hour that disciple took her to his own *home*" (John 19:27).

She was a precious part of His family. And the good news is we all are. —CAROL MACKEY

FAITH STEP: *You don't have to have children to be a loving and guiding force in someone's life. Find ways you can volunteer at a group home, women's shelter, or halfway house in need of nurturing.*

TUESDAY, DECEMBER 3

Therefore God has highly exalted him and bestowed on him the name that is above every name. Philippians 2:9 (ESV)

WHEN MY THREE BROTHERS AND I were babies, our dad settled on a nickname for each of us. The names didn't have any reasoning behind them, and a couple of my brothers' nicknames were downright odd. As we grew older, Dad stopped using the boys' nicknames on a regular basis, but he kept on calling me "Lulu" or "Lu." As an adult, I found it a little annoying, until I read this Chinese proverb: "The child with many names is much loved."

Maybe that's one reason I love how the Bible is filled with names for Jesus, each one revealing a specific aspect of His character or role. Just a single verse in Isaiah labels Jesus "Wonderful Counselor, Mighty God, Everlasting Father, Prince of Peace" (9:6). And one of my favorites is found in Matthew 1:23, "Immanuel, which means God with us."

God knew that specific names for Jesus would comfort and sustain us during different seasons of our lives. When we're hungry for something more, we can find nourishment from the Bread of Life (John 6:35). When we need guidance, we can talk to the Good Shepherd (John 10:11). When we go through dark days, the Light of the World is there for us (John 8:12). When we're missing a loved one, we can find comfort from the Resurrection and the Life (John 11:25).

Yes, God gave Jesus the "name that is above every name." He also gave Him every name that we will ever need to know Him by.
—DIANNE NEAL MATTHEWS

FAITH STEP: *Which name for Jesus do you most need to meditate on today?*

WEDNESDAY, DECEMBER 4

You say, "I am allowed to do anything"—but not everything is good for you.
You say, "I am allowed to do anything"—but not everything is beneficial.
1 Corinthians 10:23 (NLT)

SOMETIMES I'VE FELT LIKE GOD is holding out on me.

After the liberating Good News of the Gospel, somehow, it seemed like many things were suddenly off-limits to me, even though they aren't plainly addressed in the Bible.

Why can't I dress a certain way or watch a certain movie? Am I really free or not? Well, strictly speaking, those things are totally permissible, but are they beneficial?

In this verse, Paul is talking about meats offered to idols. But the passage hints at a broader context for matters of Christian living not plainly addressed in Scripture. Technically, Jesus's blood covers it, but is it beneficial to me or to anyone? I can binge-watch any number of raunchy Netflix hits, but is it doing me any good? Am I a better person as a result? Am I happier? More effective?

I like to read the occasional hairdresser gossip magazine telling myself I'm checking out the fashions. And while that's largely true, I admit I sometimes come away feeling envious or disappointed at my discount store wardrobe or ordinary life. Other times, I feel titillated to an uncomfortable degree.

Paul suggests simple questions to determine the benefit of available options, if it's not immediately obvious. Does it glorify God? Does it draw people to Jesus? —ISABELLA YOSUICO

FAITH STEP: *Do you have any habits the Holy Spirit seems to be nudging you about? Do you see any correlation between some of those habits and your mood? Ask God to help you let them go and note the difference in how you feel.*

THURSDAY, DECEMBER 5

Then the father said to him, "Son, you are always with me, and all that is mine is yours. But we had to celebrate and rejoice, because this brother of yours was dead and has come to life; he was lost and has been found."
Luke 15:31–32 (NRSV)

BEFORE MY CONVERSION, I WAS terrified of flying. And then Jesus took all my fears away in one miraculous sweep, and for the first time in my adult life, I enjoyed flying.

My religious conversion has lasted and grown deeper over the decades. But the fear of flying has slowly crept back in. That joyful zest for air travel that I experienced in the first blush of my Christian faith is now more of a wistful memory.

When my jitters first returned, I wondered if I had a lack of faith. I so strongly associated my faith in Christ with the release from this phobia. But Jesus assured me that my nervousness was not punishment for lack of faith. As the parable of the prodigal son teaches us, the heavens celebrate when we go from "lost" to "found." My conversion was like a huge intake of air after holding my breath my whole life. So much joy and courage and peace filled me, there was no room for fear. But we can't breathe like that all the time. These days, the Spirit moves through me in less dramatic ways.

As my spiritual life found its natural rhythm, I learned to accept myself as Jesus does—with all my very human fears and faults. Instead of wishing He could remove my fear of flying for good, I sought out a therapist who has helped me manage it. These days, I accept the wonders of air travel and the butterflies that come as the gifts of a blessed life. —ELIZABETH BERNE DEGEAR

FAITH STEP: *Dramatic stories of conversion can be inspiring, but, today, can you find the presence of God in some seemingly mundane aspect of your daily life?*

FRIDAY, DECEMBER 6

In his great mercy he has given us new birth into a living hope through the resurrection of Jesus Christ from the dead. 1 Peter 1:3 (NIV)

"WHAT IS IT ABOUT THIS family and hope?" my youngest grandson asked. "We have a cousin named Hope, and there's hope everywhere in this house!"

I love his exuberance on the subject. Ours *is* a house filled with hope. It shows up in books on the bookshelves, mugs, pictures… it's everywhere. I may have mentioned before that a young visitor came to our home and counted the items in our house bearing the word *hope*. She stopped counting at forty-seven.

It is a house filled with Jesus, our Living Hope.

When the FedEx delivery guy steps into the family room with a box, I pray he says, "What is it about this family and hope?" When our hope-filled friends bring their hope-deprived friends with them for a group outing or a meal, may that question be on their minds too. When neighbors bring a jar of honey from their beehives or a small neighborly remembrance at Christmas, may they also leave saying, "What is it about this family and hope?"

What is it? We have devoted ourselves to our Living Hope—Jesus. He infuses every moment with a new, eternal perspective. In troubled times, we cling to Him. In victorious times, we thank Him for the gift. He is the source of our hope. Though some may consider our house a hope museum, because of the presence of Jesus, it is instead a *living* tribute. —CYNTHIA RUCHTI

FAITH STEP: *What in your home communicates a message of hope? Your welcome mat? The Bible on your coffee table? How will you enhance the hope theme?*

SATURDAY, DECEMBER 7

For this reason we also, since the day we heard it, do not cease to pray for you, and to ask that you may be filled with the knowledge of His will in all wisdom and spiritual understanding; that you may walk worthy of the Lord, fully pleasing Him, being fruitful in every good work and increasing in the knowledge of God. Colossians 1:9–10 (NKJV)

I LOVE GOOD FOOD. WHEN I was growing up, meals weren't just for filling an empty stomach. Food represented love, especially during the Christmas season.

As I've grown in faith, my focus has shifted from the season's overindulgence toward understanding the gift of Jesus's birth. Yet I struggle with holiday weight gain. Every year, the challenge increases. Though I eat less, the scale remains frozen at the dreaded number.

Last January, my church introduced a new ministry that helped me address my holiday weight and that nourished my faith simultaneously. It's called prayer walking, and the concept is simple. I need only take a daily walk, spending the time in prayer with the Lord.

Paul writes that we're to pray continually. But before I started in this ministry, I doubted I could find enough to pray about to fill the time. I was amazed to discover the more I prayed, the more ideas came to my mind. Walking with friends broadens my perspective, providing fresh concerns and blessings.

My daily walk gave me many benefits, weight loss being only one. I feel closer to Jesus and more confident of the choices I make in my life. I also feel fit both physically and spiritually, knowing I never walk alone. —HEIDI GAUL

FAITH STEP: *Take a walk through your neighborhood. Offer Jesus your concerns, thank Him for His blessings, and pray over each home you pass.*

SUNDAY, DECEMBER 8

But you, Bethlehem Ephrathah, though you are small among the clans of Judah, out of you will come for me one who will be ruler over Israel, whose origins are from of old, from ancient times. Micah 5:2 (NIV)

IN OUR HOME, BY THE second Sunday in Advent, we usually have our decorations up, and the excitement for Christmas is building. We gather around the Advent wreath and light the "Bethlehem Candle." The light grows as Christ's birth draws nearer.

This candle reminds us of Mary and Joseph's obedient response to God, as well as their trip to Bethlehem. I hated to travel when I was pregnant, so I always pause to admire Mary's journey.

The city of Bethlehem also challenges my thinking. The King of Kings, who has always been, didn't arrive in a capital city with a powerful army. He chose a humble young woman to give Him human birth, in a small town of a small clan in a rough-hewn shelter.

I draw great comfort from this glimpse of our Savior. When I think of the great men and women of the Bible and throughout history, I feel like the least significant among His people. I'm daunted by stories of brave missionaries or the huge accomplishments of leaders of various ministries. He offers to live in our hearts and our lives, but I struggle with doubt. Could Jesus—the Lion of Judah who comes to rule over all—really make His home within me?

Long before His birth, He made clear that His dwelling is with the small and humble and the rough-hewn.

Do you ever feel insignificant? As we light the Bethlehem candle for the second Sunday in Advent, we can take heart. This same Jesus who chose Bethlehem for His arrival chooses us for His own. —SHARON HINCK

FAITH STEP: *Light the first Advent candle and remember the promises it represents. Then light the second candle and rejoice that Jesus dwells with us.*

MONDAY, DECEMBER 9

What I'm trying to do here is to get you to relax, to not be so preoccupied
with getting, so you can respond to God's giving.... Steep your life in
God-reality, God-initiative, God-provisions. Don't worry about
missing out. You'll find all your everyday human concerns will be met.
Matthew 6:31–33 (MSG)

AS MY PARENTS GREW OLDER, every Christmas I would struggle with what to give them. If I offered to update their wardrobe with a new shirt or blouse, they'd insist they didn't need clothes. What about a more personal item? Something for the house, then? No matter what I suggested, the reply was the same: "No real needs."

My parents adopted the same philosophy. An inspection of their closets one day revealed that they rarely, if ever, bought any new clothing. Instead, my mom delighted in giving things to us—her children. And after my father's death, I read his old letters and I discovered how much he enjoyed giving to others as well—especially to those in need.

Maybe that thinking was their way of embracing Jesus's teaching in Matthew 6. He encouraged His listeners not to worry about clothing and other items. Life consisted of more important matters.

Some of those "more important matters" may involve making our own needs and wants secondary to others and allowing Jesus to use us to help supply others' needs. This Christmas, I may respond to my own kids' gift-giving questions as my parents did: "No real needs."

Except the need to relax, steep my life in Jesus—and maybe give away more clothing from my amply supplied closet.
—REBECCA BARLOW JORDAN

FAITH STEP: *Sort through your closet. What do you need to keep? What can you give away? Renew your commitment today to put Jesus first in your life.*

TUESDAY, DECEMBER 10

Understand, therefore, that the LORD your God is indeed God.
He is the faithful God who keeps his covenant for a thousand generations and
lavishes his unfailing love on those who love him and obey his commands.
Deuteronomy 7:9 (NLT)

I VISITED A NEW FRIEND's home shortly before Christmas. "Come, see our tree," she said as she led me into the living room.

Twinkly lights, red baubles, and yards of curly white ribbon bedecked the tree. It resembled something from the pages of a home decorating magazine. But it was the stash of gifts that left me speechless. Presents of every size and shape sat in piles beneath its limbs and spilled several feet beyond.

Each time I recall that scene, the word *lavish* comes to mind. The dictionary defines it as "bestowing something in generous or extravagant quantities." It describes my friend's Christmas giving, but it also describes Christ's love for those who obey Him.

What does Christ's lavish love look like? It looks like selflessness. He gave up all personal rights and assumed human form to dwell among mankind (Philippians 2). He died a criminal's death so that we might experience forgiveness, freedom, and abundant life (John 3:16). Now He sits at God's right hand and prays for us (Romans 8:34), and He is present with us at all times (Matthew 28:20).

It's impossible to describe Christ's lavish love in a few sentences. Someday, when we meet Him face-to-face, our understanding will be complete. Until then, we should continue to walk in obedience to His commands. That's the best way we can show our love for Him. —GRACE FOX

FAITH STEP: *Take a few moments to ponder the depth of Christ's love for you.*

WEDNESDAY, DECEMBER 11

But clothe yourselves with the Lord Jesus Christ and forget about satisfying your sinful self. Romans 13:14 (NCV)

I GUESS YOU COULD SAY that my dad was not into clothes. For sixty-nine years, my mom made the decisions on clothes purchases, and each day she laid out what he would wear. When he died, Mom encouraged family members to take the items they could wear or wanted to have as keepsakes. My niece Kelli was thrilled to choose a few of her beloved grandpa's shirts. Several months later, Kelli arrived in the red-and-green plaid flannel shirt that Daddy always wore during our Christmas gathering. What a sweet reminder that although our loved one was not with us physically, his spirit remained in our hearts and our memories.

I've never wanted anyone to choose my clothes for me in the morning, but I will admit to sometimes needing help with how to "dress up" my spirit. That's why the Bible reminds me to clothe myself with Christ each day. To deliberately model His character traits of kindness, forgiveness, gentleness, mercy, and sacrificial love. To choose to imitate Him instead of wearing my sinful tendencies like pride, resentment, and self-centeredness.

If I want to model Jesus, I need to spend time with Him every day—staying in close personal fellowship through prayer and the Word, studying what the Bible says about Him, meditating on His teachings, and observing how He treated people. Then I'll be more careful to "dress" in a way that reflects the One Whose Spirit lives in me (Romans 8:9). —DIANNE NEAL MATTHEWS

FAITH STEP: *Thinking about your day ahead, focus on one character trait of Jesus that you need to imitate in your activities and interactions with others. Then consider what you need to take off in order to live that out.*

THURSDAY, DECEMBER 12

I know how to live on almost nothing or with everything. I have learned the secret of living in every situation, whether it is with a full stomach or empty, with plenty or little. Philippians 4:12 (NLT)

I FOUND A SCENTED CANDLE for our living room in a home store the other day. I got in line behind a mom and her little girl. The line to the register wound its way through a maze of goodies displayed on either side. The girl asked, "Mom, can I have these fruit chews?"

"No, we are not getting any candy."

Moments later she asked, "Mom, can I get nail polish?"

"No."

"How about this pillow with an *E* for Emma?"

"No, we aren't buying anything else."

This little girl wanted something more. She kept asking. With each step, I grew more impressed with her mom. Finally, when we got to the register, I leaned forward and said, "Good job! I also want to buy everything that I see here."

The lady laughed. She said, "It is hard to say no!"

We never like to hear no in life. We want so much. It is easy to grow discontented. We want more talent or a better career or a different relationship. We find ourselves asking Jesus, "Can I have this? What about this? Or this?" Sometimes, Jesus says no. But He promises to give us all that we need for life in this moment. He can grant us grace to be content right where we are. It is not wrong to ask Jesus for more, but peace pours in when we are able to look at the life we have been given with contentedness and gratitude. —SUSANNA FOTH AUGHTMON

FAITH STEP: *In what area of your life do you struggle to be content? Ask Jesus to show you how to be grateful in this season of your life, knowing that He will provide for your every need.*

FRIDAY, DECEMBER 13

Open my eyes that I may see wonderful things in your law. Psalm 119:18 (NIV)

My LOVE OF LETTERING BEGAN with my writers' group's Christmas gift exchange, when I went home with a set of calligraphy markers and a notepad. I'd dabbled in calligraphy before, but this time I was ready to get serious. I couldn't wait to write some pretty words.

I decided to make calligraphy a part of my quiet time for a while. If a Bible verse or a line in my devotional touched me in a special way, I wrote it out. The benefits went beyond improved handwriting. It forced me to slow down as I read and focused on each word, one letter at a time, as I copied the verse and gained confidence, first with the markers and later with a fountain pen. When I graduated to a dip pen, I moved calligraphy to the dining room table after dinner. If a verse turned out especially nice, I shared it on Facebook or with a friend—my way of encouraging others with what had encouraged me that day.

In the process, I made a wonderful discovery: this allowed me to connect with Jesus in a hands-on way and see new meaning in familiar Scriptures. I no longer wanted to rush through Bible reading and miss the richness of that one verse that felt like a direct message from Him.

How often do we race through our time with Jesus, like one more obligation or chore? When we slow our pace, even if that means reading three verses instead of three pages, His Word has a chance to sink in and become personal and stick with us through whatever we are facing that day. —JEANETTE HANSCOME

FAITH STEP: *This week, slow down as you read your Bible and ask Jesus to help you find that one verse you need. Try a creative way to record that special verse, or share it with someone.*

SATURDAY, DECEMBER 14

Freely you have received, freely give. Matthew 10:8 (NKJV)

HAVE YOU EVER ENCOUNTERED A Scrooge or a stingy person? You know, the ones who never offer to pick up the tab at lunch even though they are financially stable? Or the person who claims she wants to volunteer a couple of hours at the soup kitchen but finds other ways to occupy her time? Whenever I've encountered people like that, I'm not only put off but also reminded that that's not how God wants us to be.

God blesses us abundantly, offering us all every good and perfect gift (James 1:7). But His greatest gift to us was Jesus, Who is the gift of salvation. That's why we must continue the cycle of giving and generosity.

Scripture is clear: when it comes to being generous, we should just do it. God loves a cheerful giver (2 Corinthians 9:7). And Jesus didn't give to receive. He had no ulterior motives or tricks up His sleeve. He gave out of love, expecting nothing in return, and we should too. Whether it's money, time, resources, advice, or even love, Jesus is our example of generosity. He gave and continues to give us all things for life and godliness (2 Peter 1:3). He gives His all. We will never lack! —CAROL MACKEY

FAITH STEP: *Pray and ask the Lord whom you can bless today. It doesn't have to be money; it can be time, groceries, babysitting, or simply a hug.*

SUNDAY, DECEMBER 15

So they hurried off and found Mary and Joseph, and the baby, who was lying in the manger. When they had seen him, they spread the word concerning what had been told them about this child. . . . The shepherds returned, glorifying and praising God for all the things they had heard and seen.
Luke 2:16–17, 20 (NIV)

ON THE THIRD SUNDAY IN Advent, we light the shepherd candle. Although the other candles on the wreath are usually purple or dark blue, the shepherd candle is traditionally pink—a reflection of the joy the shepherds experienced at hearing the Good News.

Just as the Bethlehem candle reminded us that Christ comes to humble places, now we consider the humble shepherds.

Their initial reaction to the angel's proclamation was fear. I have to admit, if I saw a night sky lit with an angel choir, I'm sure I'd tremble. But after they were given the news, they hurried to find the babe—a Good Shepherd come to save these shepherds and all of humanity. They saw Him, and it forever changed them. They spread the word, excited to share the joy. And as they returned to their ordinary lives, they gave glory to God. I'm sure after that night, their daily tasks glowed with a new sense of wonder and hope.

Jesus does more than act in our lives. He invites us to respond. During this Advent season, we can take a cue from the shepherds. We can hear the story with awe. We can draw close to Jesus and look deeply into His life as we read the Scripture and pray. We can share the wonderful news of His coming with others. And as we leave our devotional encounters with our Good Shepherd, we can return to our day glorifying and praising God. —SHARON HINCK

FAITH STEP: *Underline all the verbs in Luke 2:16–20. Think about seeing, spreading the word, glorifying, and praising. Look for ways to carry out the same responses today.*

MONDAY, DECEMBER 16

And we all, who with unveiled faces contemplate the Lord's glory, are being transformed into his image with ever-increasing glory, which comes from the Lord, who is the Spirit. 2 Corinthians 3:18 (NIV)

As I WRITE, AN UNRULY pile of loose yarn covers the table beside me, waiting to be rewound. I avoid glancing over, knowing what lies ahead.

Last autumn, I had knitted a shawl for my daughter. The pattern seemed simple enough. I followed the directions carefully, racing to finish the project in time for Christmas.

Christmas morning, she opened the box and pulled out the shawl, her joy obvious. Wearing it for a meal out, she received compliments. But the next morning, she called me to her room. Seeing the item spread across her bed, I felt my spirits falling. Three holes glared at me where I'd dropped the stitch variation. Repair, if not impossible, would be ugly. I'd have to redo the entire thing.

I put off doing the job for as long as possible. Yesterday, I finally began the tedious chore of unraveling the piece. In a couple of hours, I'll rewind the strands and start again.

Seeing the mess lying there next to me reminds me of the chaos that was my life before I met Jesus.

I promised myself that whenever I pick up my needles, I'll pray. I'll ask Jesus for the patience to transform this mass of fuzz, once again, into a glorious shawl. Then I'll thank Him for the changes He's making in me. —HEIDI GAUL

FAITH STEP: *Pick up a craft project you've set aside because of a mistake. As you rework the piece, recognize the patience shown by Jesus as He transforms you. Give thanks!*

TUESDAY, DECEMBER 17

Glory to God in the highest, and on earth peace, good will toward men.
Luke 2:14 (KJV)

THE ANGELS COULD HAVE SAID anything. There was no protocol to follow that night, no script. In fact, if you think about the story of Jesus's birth, there's nothing conventional about it. Two teenagers, unwed, make this rigorous trip to Bethlehem, as the law dictates, and have a baby in a barn. Shepherds sleeping out in the field to protect their sheep are roused by a bunch of angels. There are so many, they light up the night sky. And even though all the carols claim they were singing, the Bible says the angels were praising God and *saying*, "Glory to God in the highest, and on earth peace, good will toward men."

Think about it. This was the first thing anyone else besides Mary and Joseph had said about Jesus. *Glory to God.* This seems obvious. But the next part is what I find interesting. *And on earth peace and good will toward men.*

This is what the angels celebrated, what they understood as the purpose of Jesus. What His birth did on high was bring glory to God. And for earth? The birth of Jesus meant peace. Good will toward men.

Frederick Douglass said, "I know there is a hope in religion; I know there is faith and I know there is prayer about religion and necessary to it, but God is most glorified when there is peace on earth and good will toward [all people]." I think he was right. If we pay attention to the angels, we'll be about the things Jesus came here for: peace and good will toward all. —GWEN FORD FAULKENBERRY

FAITH STEP: *Make a list of the things you do with Jesus as your motivation. Cross off anything that doesn't promote peace and good will toward all people. Then add things that do as He brings them to mind.*

WEDNESDAY, DECEMBER 18

Carry one another's burdens; in this way you will fulfill the law of Christ.
Galatians 6:2 (HCSB)

MOST BIBLE SCHOLARS AGREE THAT the law of Christ is to simply love (Mark 12:28–31), so the meaning of Paul's assertion in Galatians is clear.

During my recent visit with a newer girlfriend, she shared a few challenges from the previous few days. A fresh transplant like me, she'd been reluctant to reach out to new friends, wary of sharing her troubles with people who still felt unknown. I told her to reach out next time she hit a snag and promised to pray. Soon after, I got a text from her, apologizing for her "drama." Here's how I replied:

"It didn't feel like drama. It's life! Sometimes a little messy or complex. In this season of my life, I most value authenticity and candor in my friendships. Please don't airbrush with me."

I meant it. Having just celebrated a half century on the planet, I am more interested in the quality of my intimate friendships. I find quality relationships are grounded in honesty, reality, and messy openness. I am also more willing than ever to be available to others in the messiness of life, even strangers or new friends. I believe that's what Christian community aspires to be.

Extending a loving hand and a caring ear to someone else who is suffering gets me out of my own head and usually involves affirming the very truths I need to hear (Proverbs 11:25).

Thank You, Jesus, for the reminder that carrying each other's burdens is a loving privilege and necessity. —ISABELLA YOSUICO

FAITH STEP: *Is there someone in your life who needs help carrying a burden? Pick up the phone and offer love.*

Thursday, December 19

Blessed are the peacemakers, For they shall be called sons of God.
Matthew 5:9 (NKJV)

A FRIEND COMPLAINED TO ME that her husband always leaves the kitchen cabinets open after he retrieves something from them. Every time, she tells him, "You forgot to close the cabinets," and he immediately closes them but will forget the next time. Finally, one day, she said to me, "Carol, I give up. Now when I see the cabinets open, I just close them." She ultimately chose to keep the peace. Smart cookie.

If you're a wife or have been, you know what I'm talking about. Even the most loving spouses can push each other's buttons by doing (or not doing) something the other spouse asks. It can be a small thing that builds over time. Then, eventually, tempers may flare, unkind words can be exchanged, and more love is needed. Marriages have broken up over much less than what my friend experienced, but she decided it just wasn't a big enough deal to fight over. She made peace by simply completing the task herself. Granted, not every instance of conflict is as easy to solve as this one. Some issues are truly painful and need a third-party resolution. Jesus has experience with conflicts, small and otherwise. And His Gospel is peace. He is always there to help us bring peace where there is confusion. —CAROL MACKEY

FAITH STEP: *Are you unsettled about a particular issue? Jesus has given us His peace (John 14:27), so there's no need to worry or fret. You can rest easy in His peace and love.*

FRIDAY, DECEMBER 20

Let perseverance finish its work so that you may be mature and complete, not lacking anything. James 1:4 (NIV)

I LOVE MAKING HOMEMADE ROOM sprays and body products out of essential oils. This year, I started making body butter. When I made some for my sister Sherry, she requested a jar to give to a friend. Instead of using the same recipe that I'd used in the past, I decided to try something original. Halfway through the process, I regretted trying to be creative with someone else's gift. It smelled too sweet, and the mixture wouldn't stay firm. I tossed and turned half the night, trying to figure out a solution. I wanted to throw the whole batch away and start over. The idea of wasting ingredients motivated me to make what I had work. I looked up troubleshooting methods, prayed, and tweaked the scent. It didn't turn out exactly as I'd hoped, but Sherry assured me that her friend would love it. I decided the next time someone hired me to make *anything,* I would stick to what has worked in the past. But that day, I had the satisfaction of overcoming a hurdle and gaining valuable tools for the future.

Whether we choose to take on a challenge or it takes us on, there is usually a moment when we're tempted to give up. We lose sleep, feel inadequate, beat ourselves up for mistakes made along the way, and wonder how quickly the world would end if we said, "Forget it." When we refuse to quit and cry out to Jesus for direction, we get to experience the relief of finishing the work, and we treasure what we've gained for the next thing that feels too big for us. —JEANETTE HANSCOME

FAITH STEP: *What is your biggest challenge today? Ask Jesus to help you persevere and to point you toward resources you need along the way. Refuse to give up!*

SATURDAY, DECEMBER 21

He will cover you with his feathers, and under his wings you will find refuge; his faithfulness will be your shield and rampart. You will not fear the terror of night, nor the arrow that flies by day, nor the pestilence that stalks in the darkness, nor the plague that destroys at midday. Psalm 91:4–6 (NIV)

As a child, I was afraid of the dark. At bedtime, I couldn't sleep for fear that a bogeyman lay in wait, hidden under the bed or in my closet. I knew if I let down my guard for even a second, he would get me. Thankfully, I outgrew that terror.

Now that I'm an adult, there are still times I lie awake at night. But the monsters I now face are more subtle. Devious in their attacks, they plague me with anxieties over things both known and unknown. In the darkness, I hear them telling me I'm worthless, unloved, stupid. Or that my income is too small and my bills too large. And that there is nothing I can do about it.

Last evening turned into one of those nights. I tossed and turned, searching for an escape, my pillowcase wet with tears. Then I remembered I don't need to run or hide. I can stand up to the enemy. Because deep inside, I have the Word reminding me "the one who is in you is greater than the one who is in the world" (1 John 4:4). Jesus is always with me, protecting me from any and all my enemies. When I feel threatened, scared, or hurt, I can run to Him for refuge. He understands my deepest fears and, with Him, I can overcome them. —Heidi Gaul

Faith Step: *Write down every one of your fears. Pray for Jesus's protection, strength, and guidance as you face each of them together. Then rip up the list and toss your fears into the trash where they belong.*

SUNDAY, DECEMBER 22

Do you think that I cannot appeal to my Father, and he will at once send me more than twelve legions of angels? Matthew 26:53 (ESV)

ON THE SUNDAY BEFORE CHRISTMAS, our family hurries home from church, excited to light the "Angel Candle." The circle of light was finally complete on our Advent wreath, and our celebration of Christmas was just around the corner.

It's no wonder so many ornaments feature angels. They played a huge role in Jesus's arrival on earth. Gabriel appeared to Mary to prepare her for the role she would fill. Then an angel came to Joseph in a dream to encourage him to take Mary as his wife. The night Jesus was born, a whole host of angels filled the skies over the Bethlehem fields to sing with joy. Later, an angel warned Joseph of Herod's plot to kill Jesus, so they could escape to Egypt; and later still, an angel told Joseph when it was time to return to Israel.

The intersection of the heavenly realm with the experience of humans on earth is especially vibrant during the wonder of the incarnation, but there are other glimpses of angels throughout Jesus's life. After the temptation in the wilderness, angels came and ministered to Him. And as He prayed in the garden on the eve of His death, an angel came to strengthen Him.

All of this interaction with angels makes Jesus's words in Matthew 26 especially powerful. The Lord of heaven and earth, who was comforted by angels, chooses the road of suffering to reveal His glory.

As we prepare our hearts for our celebration of Christmas, we are reminded of the reason for His birth. He loves us enough to take on the burden of humanity, to die, and to rise again. Glory to God in the highest! —SHARON HINCK

FAITH STEP: *Take a cue from the angelic choir and sing praise to Jesus today.*

MONDAY, DECEMBER 23

He pays even greater attention to you, down to the last detail—even numbering the hairs on your head! Matthew 10:30 (MSG)

LAST CHRISTMAS, MY YOUNGER SON, Kevin, gave me a gift bag that included a cute blue tunic (I had previously mentioned my new collection of stretchy pants that needed longer tops), a big scented candle in greenhouse lilac (heavenly!), a high-quality journal in sea-foam green, and my favorite kind of pen with a soft, flexible grip. I also seem to remember a box of fine Swiss chocolates, although they disappeared quickly. What really made this gift bag special was that it proved how well Kevin knows me. He had taken the time to notice what I like and enjoy.

It's nice to be understood by our friends and family, but Jesus's knowledge of us goes much deeper than our likes and dislikes, habits, and personality quirks. He knows us down to the tiniest detail, inside and out. The unspoken needs and longings that we never express aloud. The past hurts and the long-cherished dreams we secretly harbor in our hearts. The good intentions we wake up with each morning. To know that our Creator understands us so well is a comforting thought. Or is it?

He also knows all our weaknesses and hidden faults. Those moments that we've stumbled in our walk of faith. Every single thought that's passed through our minds that would shame us if exposed. And that's frightening—or it would be, except for one truth: Jesus knew all those unpleasant details about us when He chose to die for us. He really, really knows us, inside and out. And loves us in spite of it all. Now, *that's* comforting. —DIANNE NEAL MATTHEWS

FAITH STEP: *Can you think of something that would embarrass you if others knew about it? Thank Jesus for loving you in spite of it.*

TUESDAY, DECEMBER 24

"Glory to God in highest heaven, and peace on earth to those with whom God is pleased." Luke 2:14 (NLT)

DURING THE CHRISTMAS SEASON, I usually hang a simple marquee sign that lights up the word *PEACE* across our carport. Until this year. When I turned it on, it read *ACE*. I have another marquee sign for the bookcase next to our fireplace that reads *JOY*. It was also losing bulbs. I thought I could change some out and have either *PEACE* or *JOY* instead of *ACE* and *OY*. I switched out the bulbs, but now, neither of them lights up. So I decided that I would buy some new marquee lighting spelling *HOPE*. The letters arrived yesterday. No *H*. Just *OPE*.

This seems to be a reflection of my life. Searching for complete *peace, joy,* and *hope,* but not quite there yet. I think that is where Jesus comes in. Into my brokenness. Our brokenness. With the brightness of His love. The One Who was born in a stable, amid the muck and bellow of animal cries, is used to bringing peace, joy, and hope into our messy lives. He does it with angel choirs and brilliant stars and extravagant gifts. Loving us right where we are. Bringing His glory and holiness when we have none of our own, so that we can stand together, loved and restored. Holding out our hands to the heavens, we can shout, "It's so good that You came!" and "What in the world would we do without You?"

It is because of Jesus and His presence in our lives that, on this cold December morning, we can have truckloads of *OY*, an overwhelming sense of *OPE*, and an all-encompassing blanket of *ACE* on earth, good will toward men. —SUSANNA FOTH AUGHTMON

FAITH STEP: *Step outside into the cold, raise your hands in the air, and thank Jesus for the peace, joy, and hope that He has showered down on your life.*

WEDNESDAY, DECEMBER 25

He took with him Mary, his fiancée, who was obviously pregnant by this time. And while they were there, the time came for her baby to be born; and she gave birth to her first child, a son. She wrapped him in a blanket and laid him in a manger, because there was no room for them in the village inn.
Luke 2:5–7 *(TLB)*

AS A CHILD, I WAS always fascinated by the Christmas story: the animals, the shepherds and wise men, and, of course, the baby Jesus. I loved the baby Jesus. Something about a God Who came into the world as a baby was so relatable. It was a beautiful way to be introduced.

As an adult, I still love the baby Jesus, of course. But I am increasingly drawn to the weirdness, the messiness, of the story. *His fiancée, who was obviously pregnant.* Think about that a moment. This is the way God chose to bring His son—Himself—into the physical world. We really need not read on from there to the fact that she laid Him in a feed box, which to this farm girl conjures slobbery hay and grain at best, cow poop at worst. *Because there was no room.*

Somehow, this wider angle seems a fitting introduction to today's world—to my world. Here I sit with laundry up to my ears. A television warning of war. A calendar stuffed full. Kids going four different directions, friends and family sick. Food addiction, bills, and a new semester of classes bear down on me. No room. Messy. Scary. Even embarrassing. And into this chaos comes Jesus, Emmanuel, to be with us. —GWEN FORD FAULKENBERRY

FAITH STEP: *In the moment during your Christmas holiday that seems the messiest, the weirdest, the loneliest, or the most chaotic, pause and say this prayer: "Come, Lord Jesus. Thank You for entering into this place with me."*

THURSDAY, DECEMBER 26

I'll never quit telling the story of your love. Psalm 89:1 (MSG)

EDITING IS A NECESSARY PART of a writer's job. Most authors love to craft their initial stories, but rewriting takes a backseat. Some spell-check and revise as they go, while others wait until completing their first drafts. If we're wise, we writers try to leave ample time for edits before our deadlines.

But I remember one time when I thought my manuscript was finished, and I was ready to hit the Send button. Around midnight, as I was proofing for the last time, I discovered a major error. I was two chapters short! So, for the next six hours, I spent my first all-nighter writing the last pages of that book, grateful that I still met the deadline.

Unfortunately, we don't always catch everything. What a blessing to know that even when we authors do our best editing, our editors usually spot and correct the mistakes we miss. With their professional expertise, they can polish and shine a manuscript to make it the best possible publication.

Our spiritual lives include a similar principle. Jesus's Spirit is always at work in us, helping us to do what some have called "minding the checks"—obeying Jesus's convicting Spirit prompts daily. But because we are human, our life stories include chapters we'd like to edit or chop. Fortunately, His love and grace will do that for us. For believers, when we sin, He is our Advocate with our holy, heavenly Father. When Jesus shows us our sin error, and we confess it, He is always faithful to forgive us and restore our fellowship with Him (1 John 1:9).

Jesus is always polishing us to make our unique stories of His love the best it can be. —REBECCA BARLOW JORDAN

FAITH STEP: *Are there portions of your life you'd like Jesus to edit? Thank Him today for His love and grace.*

FRIDAY, DECEMBER 27

And just as you want men to do to you, you also do to them likewise.
Luke 6:31 (NKJV)

A YOUNG MAN I RECENTLY had a conversation with commented on a lyric he claimed was written by his favorite pop singer. "I love that!" he said. "Isn't it, like, *deep?*"

"You do know that's from the Bible, don't you?" I hoped he caught the importance of recognizing that the wisdom the pop singer spouted originally came from Jesus.

"I don't remember where I heard this, but…" begins many sentences in modern conversations. My stomach clenches when the "somewhere" from which the uninformed person quotes is the Bible.

Imagine how Jesus feels about it! He has His ways of letting people know it's His original work. One of those ways is *us* and our efforts to encourage biblical literacy within our circles of influence. In text images, on social media, in conversations with our children, grandchildren, or friends, and in the appropriate situations.

"Listen to this. Some guy said on a television commercial, 'Do to others what you'd want them to do to you.' Brilliant, right?" a member of a support group might interject.

"It sure is. And it was when Jesus first said it."

When Jesus walked the earth, He knew the Scriptures available to the people at that time—the Old Testament. He often quoted from it. He also encouraged His followers to study, listen, and learn from Him as He had learned from His Father. Jesus is the Living Word.

But we can only know what He said and effectively communicate it to others if we study His teachings. —CYNTHIA RUCHTI

FAITH STEP: *Do you have access to a red-letter Bible? If so, take time this week to read only those Jesus words. And celebrate what He said.*

SATURDAY, DECEMBER 28

And the Word became flesh and dwelt among us, and we have seen his glory, glory as of the only Son from the Father, full of grace and truth. John 1:14 (ESV)

MY SON ISAAC HAS DOWN syndrome. For the longest time, Isaac didn't speak much at all and what he did say was largely unintelligible. Since the development of kids with Down syndrome can vary dramatically and they are unpredictable in their level of function, there was no telling if and when Isaac would speak.

The possibility of not being able to understand Isaac was painful to me. Apart from the practical frustration of not being able to understand his wants and needs, I longed to know what he was thinking and feeling. I wanted to *know* him.

Over time, Isaac did learn to speak more intelligibly, and in the last year, has progressed dramatically. It brings our family so much joy to be able to better understand him. We finally have a window into his very precious soul.

I am reminded that my longing to connect with Isaac must mirror God's longing to connect with me. Communication. Relationship. Intimacy. And just as I can know Isaac better through his words, I can know God better through His Word, Jesus. —ISABELLA YOSUICO

FAITH STEP: *Read John 1:1–18 and reflect on the Word made flesh. Write down all the words that describe the Word Who was from the beginning.*

SUNDAY, DECEMBER 29

But the time is coming—indeed it's here now—when true worshipers will worship the Father in spirit and in truth. The Father is looking for those who will worship him that way. John 4:23 (NLT)

ON EITHER SIDE OF OUR church stage sits a container holding a dozen worship flags. Everyone's welcome to use them during the music portion of the Sunday service. More often than not, however, the majority remain untouched.

I've never walked to the front of the sanctuary during the song service and waved a worship flag. Why not? I'm embarrassed to admit it, but I'm afraid of making a mistake. What if I do it wrong? What if my attempts aren't good enough and, heaven forbid, people think less of me?

Fear isn't a problem for the children in our congregation. They boldly march to the front, choose their favorite flags, and twirl them in the air. Lost in the wonder of the moment, they're oblivious to the congregation and musicians. They don't sing, dance, twirl, and spin because they hope to appear superspiritual or to impress God or the members of our congregation. Their motives are pure: They sing and dance because they love Jesus and they know He loves them. That simple yet profound truth stirs their emotions, and they respond with an outpouring of praise.

I watch the children and smile at the freedom they enjoy. Fear doesn't hinder them from showing their love for Jesus. They celebrate Him in spirit and in truth. I could learn a lot from them. —GRACE FOX

FAITH STEP: *Think of an action you can take to bring variety to your worship, either in private or in a group. Ask Jesus for courage if you're hesitant to incorporate it for fear of others' opinions.*

MONDAY, DECEMBER 30

Now if we are children, then we are heirs—heirs of God and co-heirs with Christ, if indeed we share in his sufferings in order that we may also share in his glory. Romans 8:17 (NIV)

MY FAMILY IS SPREAD OUT across the western states of Oregon, California, and Colorado. We try to stay informed with what is going on in each other's lives by phone and text. But once a year, after Christmas, my parents bring us all home. They fly all twenty-two of us, aunts, uncles, and cousins, to their house for a week of fun. We chat and drink coffee, play games, have fun in the snow, and take naps. We love being in each other's company. We love laughing and catching up.

During the week, the adults take time to pray for each other. We share the highs and lows of the past year and our hopes for the coming year. We cheer on the victories and empathize with the struggles. If someone is going through a particularly rough season, we all feel it. We care about each other. If one person is hurting, we are all hurting. This is our family. We hold each other in our hearts. We share the good stuff and the bad stuff.

Being a part of Jesus's family is the same. We hold each other in our hearts. What He cares about, we care about. We share in the good stuff that He is doing. But we also share in His suffering. When part of His family hurts, we all hurt. And the beauty is that we can hold each other up in prayer. We can cry together and rejoice together. We can encourage each other and know that Jesus is knitting our hearts together with love. And there is nothing more beautiful in this life. —SUSANNA FOTH AUGHTMON

FAITH STEP: *Jesus's family is your family. Reach out and encourage someone today who needs to know His love and care.*

TUESDAY, DECEMBER 31

My God is changeless in his love for me. Psalm 59:10 *(TLB)*

THROUGHOUT THE YEAR I HAVE invited the Lord to point out anything wrong in my heart (Psalm 139:24). That's a good thing. Jesus accepts our confessions and loves a pure heart. Unconfessed sin blocks our fellowship with Him and makes us vulnerable.

On the other hand, my relationship with Jesus doesn't change when I sin. Jesus is faithful to forgive (1 John 1:9). Sometimes, after offering that prayer for cleansing, I've parked temporarily on my weaknesses and failures instead of seeing myself as Jesus does: as His beloved, forgiven child. That has created a pause in my ability to move forward. I know the error of asking Jesus to show me what's right in my heart or to boast of any good points. Jesus wouldn't even call Himself good, claiming that none are good—except God (Mark 10:18).

One popular Pinterest meme I posted, which describes us in Scripture as *loved, redeemed, victorious, transformed,* and *favored,* has been reposted numerous times, suggesting that many others may need the same reminder about their worth in Christ. I understand that Jesus values us. I know that just as we are saved by grace, Jesus also wants us to live by His grace.

But like other believers', I allow my fluctuating emotions to affect my perspective. After confessing the wrong things in my heart, what do I pray next? Surprisingly, when I ask that question, I hear Jesus's sweet whispers reaffirming what I know: I belong to Him, He accepts me as I am, and His love for me is changeless. I can rest in the knowledge that I am His and He is mine—forever.
—REBECCA BARLOW JORDAN

FAITH STEP: *This coming year, as you confess any wrong things in your heart to Jesus, remember to thank Him for His changeless love and acceptance.*

ABOUT THE AUTHORS

 SUSANNA FOTH AUGHTMON is an author and humor writer in California. She is the mother of seventeen-year-old Jack, fifteen-year-old Will, and twelve-year-old Addison. Susanna is also wife to Scott, who is lead pastor of Pathway Church in Redwood City. Susanna's books include *Hope Sings* and *Queen of the Universe*. She loves to use Scripture and personal stories as a way of embracing God's grace and truth every day. Susanna often connects with her fellow readers through her blog, newsletter, Facebook page, and speaking engagements. Find out more about Susanna on her website TiredSuperGirl.com.

 DR. ELIZABETH (LIZZIE) BERNE DEGEAR, BCC, is a chaplain and Bible scholar. As a chaplain, Lizzie offers pastoral care to people in church and hospital settings, leading spirituality groups with those facing addiction and those in psychiatric units. She also provides memorial services for people who have known homelessness during their lives. She has been teaching Bible study at her local church for many years and is the author of *For She Has Heard,* about the standing stone in the book of Joshua. She has lived in Rhode Island, New Mexico, Alaska, and France, and now makes her home in New York City with her husband and two children.

 GWEN FORD FAULKENBERRY lives and writes on her family's ranch in her hometown of Ozark, Arkansas. She is wife to Stone; mother to Grace, Harper, Adelaide, and Stella; and a professor of English at her local university. Gwen has written more than a dozen books and finds writing to be a practice in good mental health. She also enjoys playing the piano, singing at her church, cooking, and going on long walks with her two Boston

Terriers, Patch and Mocha. Oh, and coffee. Gwen enjoys coffee. Probably a little too much.

 GRACE FOX and her husband Gene are career missionaries, directing International Messengers Canada. They train and lead short-term volunteers to assist their organization's missionaries in twenty-five countries, including Nepal, Lebanon, Peru, Uganda, and in Eastern Europe. Grace made a massive transition last year when she and Gene moved onto a forty-eight-foot sailboat. She now writes from a marina near the Vancouver International Airport. The author of nine books, she recently wrote a Bible study titled *Forever Changed*. She enjoys the travels her ministry requires, but she's always grateful for time at home with her three married kids and seven grandkids, ages one to eleven years. Connect with her at www.gracefox.com and www.Facebook.com/gracefox.author.

 When HEIDI GAUL is not busy leading her Bible Study Fellowship group, she enjoys needlecraft, hiking, and travel, be it around the block or the world. She's also an award-winning writer who took home the 2015 Cascade Award for devotionals. Her pieces can be found in several issues of *The Upper Room* and in two Guideposts devotionals, *Every Day with Jesus* and *Mornings with Jesus 2019*. Her stories are included in ten *Chicken Soup for the Soul* anthologies, and she's a staff writer for The Great Commission Project. Her current project is a devotional/craft book to be titled *Redeemed and Restored*. Heidi and her husband live in Oregon's Willamette Valley.

 JEANETTE HANSCOME is a writer and author from the San Francisco Bay Area in California. She's written five books, including *Suddenly Single Mom: 52 Messages of Hope, Grace, and Promise*. Jeanette serves on the West Coast Christian Writers Conference Board and is also a speaker, workshop leader, and proud mom of two sons, one grown and another almost. She had the honor of receiving the True Grit Award at the 2017 Mount Hermon Christian Writers Conference and recently joined her first community chorus. You can read her weekly blog posts at JeanetteHanscome.com.

Mom of four and grandmother of three, SHARON HINCK and her hubby recently enjoyed a special adventure with her son, daughter-in-law, three grandchildren, and their dog: they all shared a home for a year while her son finished seminary. The close promixity made for wonderful memories and plenty of writing material! Sharon is delighted to be a contributing writer for *Mornings with Jesus* and is also working on a new series of novels scheduled to release this year. When she's not writing, editing, or staying connected with family, she and her husband love hiking along the shore of Lake Superior, practicing organic gardening, and attending their small-group Bible study.

REBECCA BARLOW JORDAN is a best-selling author and contributing writer of more than twenty books, including *Mornings with Jesus,* the *Daily in Your Presence* series and the *Day-votions*® three-book series for women. As a "day-voted" follower of Jesus, she loves helping others find a deeper intimacy with God. When she's not writing, you might find Rebecca spreading mulch in her Northeast Texas perennial gardens or trying to snag another bass on the lake with her high school sweetheart—her retired minister husband—with whom she's still madly in love. She loves curling up with her Bible, coffee, and the Love of her life, Jesus. Rebecca also enjoys reading Christian fiction and spending time with her family, including her four grandchildren. Read her weekly blogs at RebeccaBarlowJordan.com.

CAROL MACKEY is the author of *Sistergirl Devotions: Keeping Jesus in the Mix on the Job*. For this devotional, Carol was voted the 2010 Breakout Author of the Year by the African American Literary Award Show, and Ebony

Magazine named it "Best Book to Take to Work." Her latest book, *Faces of Praise!: Photos and Gospel Inspirations to Encourage and Uplift*, was published in October 2017. Carol was also editor-in-chief of Black Expressions Book Club, which was voted the best book club by the African American Literary Awards several times. She lives in New York.

 DIANNE NEAL MATTHEWS has enjoyed sharing her everyday life and faith journey with *Mornings with Jesus* readers since the 2013 edition. She is the author of four daily devotional books, including *The One Year Women of the Bible*, and recently collaborated on *Daily Encouragement for the Smart Stepfamily*. Dianne has also published hundreds of articles, guest blog posts, and stories for compilation books. She and her husband of forty-four years currently live in southwest Louisiana and have two children and three grandchildren. You can visit her Facebook author page or website (DianneNealMatthews.com).

 CYNTHIA RUCHTI started her career in the chemistry lab but took a Jesus-detour into writing. That was more than thirty years ago. Since that time, she's written and produced a scripted radio broadcast about practical concerns from a biblical perspective and published more than twenty novels, nonfiction books, and inspired stories hemmed in hope. Cynthia has recently stepped into position as an agent for Books & Such Literary Agency. She also teaches at writers' conferences and speaks at women's events as well as serving on her church's worship team. She and her grade-school-sweetheart husband live in the heart of Wisconsin. Connect with her at CynthiaRuchti.com or Hemmedinhope.com.

 ISABELLA YOSUICO longs to live authentically, abiding in God's love. She enjoys frolicking with her family, reading, running, random adventures, having deep conversation, going the beach, music, and singing. *Mornings with*

Jesus 2019 is Isabella's third *Guideposts* book, along with *Embracing Life: Letting God Determine Your Destiny*, a Bible study for women navigating challenging life events. Isabella is also founding president of MightyTykes, a special-needs product company inspired by her youngest son, who has Down syndrome. Isabella, her husband Ray (an artist and addictions counselor), and their two sons Pierce (the athlete) and Isaac (the minister/ musician), live life fully on Florida's Suncoast. Connect with Isabella at IsabellaYosuico.com or MightyTykes.com or on Facebook or Twitter.

Scripture Reference Index

TOPICAL INDEX

A NOTE FROM THE EDITORS

WE HOPE YOU ENJOYED *Mornings with Jesus 2019*, published by the Books and Inspirational Media Division of Guideposts, a nonprofit organization that touches millions of lives every day through products and services that inspire, encourage, help you grow in your faith, and celebrate God's love.

Thank you for making a difference with your purchase of this book, which helps fund our many outreach programs to military personnel, prisons, hospitals, nursing homes, and educational institutions.

We also create many useful and uplifting online resources. Visit Guideposts.org to read true stories of hope and inspiration, access OurPrayer network, sign up for free newsletters, download free e-books, join our Facebook community, and follow our stimulating blogs. To delve more deeply into *Mornings with Jesus,* visit MorningswithJesus.org.

You may purchase the 2019 edition of *Mornings with Jesus* anytime after July 2018. To order, visit Guideposts.org/MorningswithJesus, call (1-800) 932-2145, or write to Guideposts, PO Box 5815, Harlan, Iowa 51593.